IT ALL BEGAN WITH A SCREAM

IT ALL BEGAN WITH A SCREAM

By Padraic Maroney

BearManor Media

2021

It All Began With A Scream

© 2021 by Padraic Maroney

Copyright registration number: TXu 2-244-810

Published in the United States of America by:

BearManor Media
1317 Edgewater Dr #110
Orlando FL 32804

bearmanormedia.com

Printed in the United States.

Typesetting and layout by John Teehan

ISBN—978-1-62933-780-7

CONTENTS

ACKNOWLEDGEMENTS

ON DECEMBER 20, 1996 my brother took a group of my friends and me to see a little horror movie called *Scream* on opening night. While watching it, something awoke in me and over the last 25 years my career path has kept coming back to that movie. The first movie I ever professionally reviewed was Wes Craven's *Music of the Heart*. But with the publication of this book, I can finally take the mantle away from Gale Weathers to say that I have written THE book on Woodsboro.

Along with thanking my publisher, Ben Ohmart, publishing this book wouldn't have been possible without the following people who have helped and encouraged me along the way.

First, to everyone who was so generous with their time to participate with this book. So many took time out of their busy schedules to talk with me about their place in *Scream* history. It's apparent from speaking with everyone how special their experience was and how much Wes meant to all of them. I would be remiss to not acknowledge the help of Claire Raskind, who is not quoted in the book, but behind-the-scenes was sweet enough to help connect me with some of the filmmakers.

I also couldn't have achieved this without Marilyn Castro, who endured many of my meltdowns and freak outs—sometimes concurrently. Lynn Masino for helping me to sound literate and educated. Denise Keegan Goldfield, who has been a mentor and friend to me for 20 years, was always willing to help and offer support through the research and proposal process. Tara Bennett, who helped guide me through the book publishing world.

Lastly, none of this would be possible without Kevin Williamson having written the script for *Scream*. Many times over the last two decades I've gotten close to meeting or interviewing Mr. Williamson but have yet to connect. I hope that he appreciates the care and affection that has gone into writing this book to tell the story of the saga that he created all those years ago.

SECTION 1

WHAT'S YOUR FAVORITE SCARY MOVIE?

Actor David Arquette, assistant director Nick Mastandrea, and director Wes Craven. (Photo courtesy of Nick Mastandrea)

RE-INVENTING
A GENRE

BY THE MID-1990S, horror movies had fallen out of favor. The genre that had flourished for decades was going through an identity crisis as it struggled to find what the audience yearned to see. Historically, the horror genre's popularity has been cyclical. It ebbs and flows every so often, as the types of horror that people are thirsty for changes.

In the 1930s, Universal Movie Monsters were the rage. Dracula, Frankenstein, and The Mummy all terrorized cinemas throughout the decade. In the 1950s and 1960s creature features like *Tarantula!* (1955) and *The Blob* (1958) took over, mixing horror with science-fiction as a reflection of the political themes of the time and fears of nuclear weapons.

In 1978, a movie came along that helped popularize a relatively new subgenre—the slasher film. Slasher films are generally defined by a killer (usually hidden by a mask) who murders a group of people (usually with sharp, pointy objects). Many of the films revolve more around the villains than the protagonists, with the villains gaining as many fans as the movies themselves. The first slasher films, *Psycho* (1960) and *Peeping Tom* (1960), came out the decade prior, but it was *Halloween* (1978) that created the craze that would carry through the next decade. It launched Jamie Lee Curtis' reign as the scream queen, a title she seemed destined to obtain as the daughter of *Psycho* star Janet Leigh, and was the beginning of a successful franchise that includes almost a dozen sequels and a pair of rebooted films centered on serial killer Michael Myers. Curtis earned the crown by starring in a string of classic horror movies between 1978-1981.

Despite a dedicated and ravenous fan base, horror movies are rarely respected. Instead, they are often viewed as disposable entertainment that doesn't always involve quality in front of or behind the camera. However, Hollywood loves that horror films can be produced for a relatively small budget without casting well-known actors, and therefore have much better odds of generating a tidy little profit for their producers regardless of quality. In fact, *Halloween* held the distinction of being one of the most profitable independent films for decades.

After the success of *Halloween*, another horror icon in-the-making arrived with Jason Voorhees in *Friday the 13th* (1980). The 1980s also gave birth to Freddy Krueger in *A Nightmare on Elm Street* (1984), with Krueger, Voorhees, and Michael Myers reigning throughout the decade and becoming the modern-day version of the Universal Movie Monsters. They were joined by second-tier horror icons Pinhead, from the *Hellraiser* (1987) movies, and Chucky, from *Child's Play* (1988).

Eventually, audiences grew tired of the seemingly unkillable villains in 1980s' slasher films. Seeing the same boogeymen get killed and then easily resurrected in the sequel became redundant. Instead, audiences turned to thrillers like *The Hand That Rocks the Cradle* (1992) and *Basic Instinct* (1992) to get their scares, albeit with much less gore. In an effort to squeeze any last possible money from the franchises, the movie studios plotted Jason and Freddy's cinematic demise as the 1990s began.

A Palm Springs Horror Story

In 1994, *A Nightmare on Elm Street* director Wes Craven returned to the franchise he created to offer a meta take on the slasher film with *Wes Craven's New Nightmare* (1994). Many of the actors from the original film returned to play fictional versions of themselves, albeit still battling Freddy Krueger. Ironically, it was well received by critics, but audiences did not turn up. The film grossed only $18 million at the box office which was almost half of the domestic gross made by its predecessor *Freddy's Dead: The Final Nightmare* (1991) just three years earlier.

While that transpired, a young unknown writer, Kevin Williamson, was working on a screenplay that would ultimately help revitalize the genre and bring it to new heights. The origins of *Scream* (1996) began when Williamson wrote a one-act play in college about a girl being taunted on the phone by unknown caller.

Williamson grew up in North Carolina idolizing Steven Spielberg. He wrote and filmed his own movies at a young age but took a break from writing when he got a scholarship for acting to attend East Carolina University. After college he moved to Los Angeles, enrolled in a screenwriting course at UCLA and began writing again. His first script, *Killing Mrs. Tingle*, inspired by one of his real-life high school teachers who told him he would never make it as a writer, sold to Focus Features but ended up languishing in development.

Williamson was watching a 1994 episode of the television newsmagazine *Turning Point* on ABC. The episode profiled serial killer Daniel Rolling, who was given the moniker The Gainesville Ripper after killing five college students over the course of four days in the northern Florida city.

The story goes that Williamson was down to his last few dollars when he wrote the original *Scream* script while staying at a friend's house in Palm Springs. He got so freaked out by the television show that he called a friend and they started quizzing each other about classic horror movies while the writer checked the house for a possible intruder.

"I was getting so spooked. I was being scared out of my mind. During the commercial break, I heard a noise. And I had to go search the house. And I went into the living room and a window was open," Williamson told CNN in 1998. "I'd been in this house for two days. I'd never noticed the window open. So, I got really scared. So, I went to the kitchen, got a butcher knife, got the mobile phone."

Still spooked and suffering nightmares when he went to bed, Williamson woke up early in the morning and began writing the opening using that that one-act play he wrote in college as the basis for a scary movie that would feature a cast of characters who had seen all the same horror movies the audience had seen. These characters were savvy enough to know many of the horror genre's trappings and would have to use that knowledge to outwit the killer stalking them. Williamson wrote a horror movie that he would want to watch. The script took him just that one weekend to write. He titled it *Scary Movie*.

"Kevin is clearly a student of horror movies, a fan of horror movies and asks the same questions that he found out that millions of people ask, like, 'Why did you walk in that room?' 'Why did you do this?' 'Why did you do that?'" said Jamie Kennedy, who would play film geek Randy

Meeks in the original trilogy. "I think he's probably a cinephile. Clearly, he knows what he's talking about with horror movies, I bet you [Kevin] can do a lot of movies. But he definitely knows this genre like no one's business."

A BIDDING WAR

The *Scary Movie* script became a hot property in Hollywood. It was considered a spec script, which means that it was written without any kind of deal in place. Thus, when it was discovered, it resulted in a bidding war around town with producers eager to make it.

"That time in Hollywood was kind of a big spec world game. You could read every other week that a script sold for $1,000,000," said producer Cathy Konrad.

The script was also one that everyone in Hollywood was talking about and reading.

"I read the original script long before it went into production. In fact, it was sort of passed around as being one of those scripts that agents and managers and actors had read because it was popular and interesting," explained Matt Keeslar, who starred in *Scream 3* (2000) as Tom Prinze. "The idea being, look at this interesting new take on the genre. So, I was a fan of it. I liked the first script."

"The script was just a total page turner, from the funny perspective, the comedy perspective, but also from the horror perspective," casting director Lisa Beach said, agreeing with the actor about her reaction when she first read the script.

Konrad was working at Woods Entertainment, which had a satellite deal with Miramax films. She began her career on the production side of the industry while living in Washington, D.C. Her first job was as an unpaid production assistant on the film *Suspect* (1987), starring Cher and Dennis Quaid. From there she hustled for work before moving out west the following year and eventually got another break while visiting a friend in the country that used to be known as Yugoslavia. She switched over to the other side of filming, with a job working for producer Kathleen Kennedy at Amblin. She continued to work her way up before being hired by Cary Woods to run Woods Entertainment.

Konrad received the script and read it overnight, before calling the Miramax offices in the morning to discuss it.

"Nobody was really looking at these kinds of movies. I mean, the writing was so good, what Kevin had come up with was so unique and so fresh. I wouldn't have said myself, personally, that I was out in the world to make a movie like this. I always advertised as I just want good characters good stories and to be able to put myself in the center of it and really see the world through character ensembles. I mean it's sort of a theme in a lot of my movies. It's a lot of ensemble and just good characters, just good stories. Obviously, *Scream* was a really good, well told story and, you know, one of those rare scripts," said Konrad. "[Kevin's agent at the time] was the king of the concoction of a bidding war. Even though he promised you that you had it exclusively, you pretty much knew that it was out to 10 other people. That's kind of how those games were played back then."

The bidding war came down to two companies, Oliver Stone's production company in conjunction with Paramount Pictures, and Woods Entertainment. Ultimately, Woods Entertainment won, intending for *Scary Movie* to be the first film produced in-house at Dimension Films, the genre offshoot of Miramax. Everything would eventually come full circle when Paramount announced that the studio would be releasing the series' fifth entry in 2022.

Started by brothers Harvey and Bob Weinstein, Miramax had established itself as one of the heavy hitters in the independent film world by releasing the auteur directed films *Sex, Lies, and Videotape* (1989), *The Crying Game* (1992), and *Pulp Fiction* (1994). Bob went on to create Dimension Films as a way to distribute horror and other genre films that didn't fit under the prestigious umbrella that Miramax had established for itself. Weinstein saw *Scream* as an opportunity for Dimension Films to begin producing their own movies rather than just acquiring and distributing films. They had previously released the sequels in the *Hellraiser*, *Children of the Corn*, and *Halloween* franchises.

Bob Weinstein was concerned that the title of the script might confuse audiences. He had a conversation with Williamson to make sure that he understood that the script he bought was a horror movie with humor and not a comedy with horror elements. To help clarify, he thought a new title might help, but it was his brother, Harvey, who came up with the new name. The inspiration hit while Harvey was listening to the song "Scream," by Michael Jackson and his sister Janet.

"I think what Bob did right about this, which again, our little group of creatives, we loved the way that Kevin crafted this and understood why it was called *Scary Movie* and that was part of the fun. It was not a horror movie in our minds, it was kind of puncturing that and turning it inside out and kind of looking at it from another level with humor," Konrad explained.

Konrad explains that changing the title to something that more explicitly let fans know what they were going to see was first and foremost a horror movie helped appeal to the fanbase. Then they could spread the word of mouth if they liked it. "He's like, I can't market a feathered pitch, so to speak, which is, I think, a term that [film producer] Joel Silver coined back in the day, which is, horror and comedy together was not something that you could sell. So, you change the title to *Scream*. He made it what it was to a core audience that would go see it. Then from that base he let everybody kind of advertise and bring the people that wouldn't typically go to a horror movie and say it's not what you think. That was very clever of him to do that for sure."

The name change wasn't made official until midway through production, with the cast and crew having souvenirs donning both the original name and the final name on them, depending on when the item was created. Many of the film's cast and crew still hold a special place in their hearts for the original name.

"I still loved *Scary Movie*, because *Scary Movie* is itself a wink and a nod to it, to what we were doing," said actor W. Earl Brown. "I mean *Scream* has become such the iconic reference. I can't negate that change."

SECURING TOP TALENT

Woods was friends with actress Drew Barrymore's agent at the time and was able to get the actress interested in playing lead character and final girl, Sidney Prescott. This was a huge achievement for the film. Despite horror not being a hot genre at the time, with Barrymore attached the film's profile was increased even higher.

Next, the producers had to find a director who would fit the material. The script was tricky, marrying scares with razor sharp wit, which had been attempted multiple times in the past but had rarely worked. As luck would have it, while all of this was happening, Wes Craven was directing a horror-comedy movie called *Vampire in Brooklyn* (1995) for Paramount. Starring Eddie Murphy and Angela Bassett, the film grossed just $19 million at the box office, but it taught Craven something about mixing the two genres.

"[Wes] said, 'I learned a very valuable lesson when I made *Vampire in Brooklyn*, and it applies directly to this film. We are making a satire of this genre, that's what this is. However, if this movie is not scary, it will not be funny. So, never at any point fall into thinking I am playing comedy here because if you don't play the moment honestly and I don't shoot it honestly; if the horror doesn't work, the comedy's not going to work," Brown recalled Craven telling him prior to the start of filming.

Despite his resume, when Craven's name was brought up in discussions, the team wasn't sure if he was right for the job. They were looking for someone who would match the tone of the material. Among those considered throughout the search were newcomers Bryan Singer, who directed *The Usual Suspects* (1995), and Robert Rodriguez, who directed *Desperado* (1995).

"Our Wild West world over at Miramax was about discovering new talent. I think all of us were really looking under rocks and in corners to find somebody fresh and exciting and new and different that could kind of check those boxes creatively. When Wes's name came into the mix, I think a lot of us initially were like, well, gosh, I mean, you know he's amazing, of course, but I thought the goal was to not make a horror movie," Konrad recalled. "I think we wanted to make, certainly there are those elements to it, but I don't think we wanted to be that literal initially."

Craven fell into directing horror movies almost by accident. He grew up in a poor, strictly religious household, and was only allowed to watch Disney movies. His father died when he was just four years old, leaving his mother and brother, who was 10 years older than Wes, to take care of him. He was awarded a scholarship to Wheaton College and became the first in his family to attend college. It was there that he was able to expand his horizons.

In the 70s, Craven began to make a name for himself with the movies *The Last House on the Left* (1972) and *The Hills Have Eyes* (1977). He further cemented his status in the horror movie hall of fame with the creation of Freddy Krueger in *A Nightmare on Elm Street*. The director had never set out to be a horror director, but found it was easy to get financial backing for horror films. He tried to move away from the genre after his initial success but found it difficult. Despite his success, the direct was never comfortable with being thought of as one of the godfathers of the horror genre.

"He did not like being called horrormeister, or guru of horror," Craven's long-time producing partner Marianne Maddalena explained. "He went with it, but he didn't like it."

His mother never approved of his movies, and only saw one of his films, his lone non-horror movie, *Music of the Heart* (1999). Perhaps because of his strict upbringing, Craven ended up creating a second family for himself with those he collaborated. The director surrounded himself with the same core group over the years and created a family atmosphere on the sets with them. He was loyal to them and in return they were loyal to him.

"Everything else in front of the camera is a variable that I cannot control," explained Mark Irwin, who worked with Craven on four projects. "First A.D. Nicholas Mastandrea worked forever with Wes and you just say, I don't need new variables. I have enough to worry about, I want these guys to help me. So, you establish a unit in terms of security."

One of the longest partnerships that Craven had was with Maddalena. Growing up in Lansing, Michigan, she wanted to become a film producer. She got her foot in the door while working as a stewardess on a yacht in Cannes, France. There she met Harold Robbins, which led to a job back in Los Angeles at his film company.

She became Craven's first assistant on the film *Deadly Friend* (1986) for Warner Bros, starring Kristy Swanson. They hit it off and she first became a producer with the film *Shocker* (1989). Together Maddalena and Craven would work together on nearly two dozen projects during a nearly 30-year partnership until his death in 2015. She credits their success to the fact that they complemented each other.

"We made a great team. Because of his shyness, I could kind of be the upfront person, so he could do his magic. He didn't have to deal with all the politics," Maddalena explained. "He was kind of painfully shy, so meetings were difficult for him. So, I think it was great, as it is usually, to have a partner; always somebody to go in the room with."

Bob Ziembicki, the production designer on *Scream 2* agrees, having witnessed their partnership in person. "[Craven] would defer to Marianne, or on things he might not be as interested in, she definitely would be or then she would confer with Cathy."

Craven was initially approached about being involved in the project by his former assistant, who had been promoted into a development role, while finishing work on *Vampire in Brooklyn*. After reading the script, he agreed to help produce it. But when the question was floated if he would direct it, Craven declined. Before passing, he asked editor Patrick Lussier to read the script, or at least the opening sequence.

"The opening sequence was amazingly well-written and incredibly intense and very brutal. [Wes] had said no, because, I think, at the time he didn't want to do it. He didn't want to make something so extreme," Lussier recalls. After *Vampire in Brooklyn* flopped at the box office, the script eventually came back around. "He decided that, yes, if I'm going to do it, I'm going to lean into it."

Despite the quality of the script, Lussier says they didn't quite realize how special the project was going to be at the time. It was just one of many possible projects for the director to sign on to helm. After Craven declined to direct, the producers sent the script around to some of the big directors at the time.

"I think Wes really considered himself a horror purist and *Scary Movie* had a satirical voice to it. It was very pop culture cheeky. It was sending up the genre and I think he was uncomfortable with the parts of that, that felt like it was making fun of the tropes and of the devices that he himself had created," Julie Plec hypothesizes. "I think he needed to get to the other side of what he considered to be spoof and recognize it as a scary piece in and of itself."

Plec had been hired to replace Craven's previous assistant and was the one who helped Craven change his mind about taking on the project. She reintroduced the project while having lunch at Craven's house, where they had been working while between offices. She let him know that despite talking to different directors they hadn't found anyone yet.

"Julie is so brilliant and so smart and has such a great personality that she got Wes to read it again and maybe look at it in a different light," said production designer Bruce Alan Miller. "There's some humor in it. It's kind of a teen story and it wasn't a horror movie really; it's a murder mystery."

"I said, well, you know they can't find a director for that great script. I think he might have been joking, I don't know. [But] he said, well, tell them to make me an offer I can't refuse,'" Plec remembered. "I went back to Lisa Harrison and told her exactly that. I don't know who she called, but she called somebody... and lo and behold, that's exactly what they did. That's how they got him—money."

Interestingly, it felt almost fated that Craven would take on *Scream* as his previous two projects would act as a primer for the new film. *Vampire in Brooklyn* sought to marry the comedy and horror genres, while *Wes Craven's New Nightmare* was one of the first meta horror movies.

Adds Konrad, "What Wes brings to the table, just that incredible shorthand with the [horror] elements that really work for an audience for that kind of genre. Then we let the script and all of Kevin's work with the humor kind of do its job with the actors."

With Craven onboard to direct and Barrymore to star in the leading role of Sidney Prescott, *Scream* was moving forward. A cast just had to be assembled around Barrymore.

CREATING A KILLER CAST

WITH BARRYMORE ATTACHED, casting director Lisa Beach was hired to fill out the rest of the cast. Beach was hired because she had previously worked with Konrad on director Alexander Payne's breakthrough film, *Citizen Ruth* (1996), and had known Woods from his days as an agent's assistant. It was at the beginning of the casting process for *Scream* that Beach also met Sarah Katzman, who she would hire as her assistant on the film. The two have been working together ever since.

"I saw Sarah Katzman collating at the xerox machine and I thought, that's my girl. I want her for my assistant. So, I went down to Cathy's office and I said, 'Cathy, I would love to hire Sarah as my assistant even though I don't really know her. But I can just tell. The way she was collating was unbelievable,'" Beach recalls.

At the time, Katzman was working as an unpaid intern, having graduated from college in 1994 and had only lived in Los Angeles for a year. Sarah had been working to set up a casting session, something that she hadn't done previously. But Beach liked what she saw.

"Lisa came to the session. That's when we met. Then I was at the xerox machine, copying stuff. She saw me and she was like, 'Do you want to be my assistant?' I was like, my first paying job in Hollywood? Heck yeah! And that was it," Katzman adds about their initial meeting. "Everyone has said, you work for three months as an intern and you'll get a paying job, and it happened."

When starting a new project, the casting directors will first read the film's script and release a character breakdown to the managers and agents in town so that they can submit and pitch clients for the prospective roles. Part of that process includes deciding what they are looking for in the actors they want to cast. They also look at roles that might make sense for a "name" celebrity based on the amount of work it entails.

"There are certain roles that you say, this would be a great cameo, and this role will only work for a week; so, let's get a good, strong name. But then all the others, we knew we wanted new, fun, fresh talent," explained Beach.

Ultimately, it comes down to finding the best actors that are available for each of the roles regardless of how many actors they see.

"The best cast possible; Somebody who would embody whatever in the breakdown. In the breakdown it probably said that Stu was kind of a gawky, awkward goofball, so we saw as many gawky, awkward goofballs as we could," Beach said, describing the casting process.

Casting a wide net, the casting agents said they might initially audition in the range of 100 actors per role, but that gets whittled down to a list of 10 for the producers to see. Those 10 read for the producers in person and talk with them while receiving direction during the audition. Back then the auditioning process was much more intimate, allowing the casting directors to build relationships with the actors and bring them in regularly for roles that they might be a good fit.

BRINGING FAMILIAR FACES TO THE FILM

From the beginning, the *Scream* movies used cameos of beloved actors from the 1970s and 1980s as an additional wink and nod to the audience. In the beginning, these came about through existing relationships Craven had with them. Linda Blair, star of *The Exorcist* (1973), showed up in the original film as a pushy reporter outside of Woodsboro High School. A few years after her breakout role, she starred in the television film *Stranger in Our House* (1978), which Craven directed.

Although his role as Principal Himbry was larger than a few seconds of screen time, Henry Winkler agreed to appear uncredited in the film as a favor to the filmmakers. Winkler's connection to the production ran deeper than just sharing representation with Craven. At the time, Winkler's office at Disney was across the hall from that of Woods Entertainment.

"To have Henry Winkler show up and have this kind of mixed, confused character of a principal; but is he a suspect? That was the nice thing," Irwin said about the cameo.

By the time the third film came around, celebrities had become fans of the franchise and asked to appear in the original trilogy's concluding chapter. This was the case for Carrie Fisher, who made a cameo in *Scream 3* (2000) as Bianca Burnette, the basement dwelling record keeper at Sunrise Studios. Fisher wanted to appear in the film and called the filmmakers to make it happen. Along with appearing in that film, she also did some uncredited work on the script.

It wasn't uncommon to see some of the crew members pop up in the films, either. Beach scored cameos in both the first and third films. She plays a reporter in *Scream* and the tour guide leading a studio tour in the sequel. Tour group members include Craven as well as Jason Mewes and Kevin Smith in character as Jay and Silent Bob, respectively, from Smith's film universe. It was during Beach's cameo in the first film that allowed her to name one of the franchise's characters.

"I can still recite my lines in *Scream* one. 'Local Woodsboro was rocked today by the brutal teenage murders of 18-year-old Casey Becker and her 17-year-old boyfriend Steven Orth.' Steven Orth is actually my cousin, so I made his name up and Wes let me have it," Beach recalled. To this day, she still receives residual checks from her appearances in the franchise.

A TABLOID TWIT

One role that the filmmakers wanted a more established actress for was that of the Pulitzer Prize coveting, tabloid reporter Gale Weathers. They were looking to cast the kids with relatively fresh faces, but since Gale was a little bit older it made sense that an actress with a longer resume might fit the part.

"We went after a few people for Gale Weathers, including Brooke Shields," remembers Maddalena. "That was a lot of Bob and Harvey really pushing names and paying for them."

Shields, along with comedienne Janeane Garofalo, were considered for the role. However, it was *Friends* (1994) star Courteney Cox who auditioned for and was cast in the role. Coincidentally, Garofalo was offered Cox's role as Monica Gellar on *Friends*, but turned it down in favor of joining the cast of *Saturday Night Live* (1975). Cox would famously portray Gellar on the hit sitcom for 10 seasons. Shields would also go on to appear in an episode of the sitcom during its second season. (Austerlitz, 2018)

A Boyfriend to Die For

Not all actors are submitted by their agents, though. In the case of Vince Vaughn, it was the studio that had pushed for him to audition. The actor was about to break out with the film *Swingers* (1996), which Miramax also distributed. Both Beach and Katzman stated that he was too old to be playing a high school student, but the 6-foot 4-inch actor still came in and auditioned for the role of Sidney's boyfriend, Billy Loomis.

"Miramax is like this guy is big, he's going to be a star, you have to read him," recalls Katzman. The only problem? It was the end of the casting process and Vaughn was ill. "He kept saying he was sick, and we kept saying this is your last day. He actually did come in and he *was* sick. He was like, 'I'm not going to go in the waiting room because I'm sick.' He sat in the hallway on the floor."

Vaughn wasn't the only one they had trouble connecting with to audition for Billy Loomis. Already getting noticed in Hollywood, Skeet Ulrich also was elusive at first.

"We kept calling the agent and he never showed up for the auditions. He never came in. He would just cancel, whatnot. It wasn't being difficult, I think he just couldn't get the schedule," Katzman explained.

As luck would have it, Ulrich's girlfriend at the time, Leonora Scelfo, also auditioned for the film. She ended up cast in the small but memorable role of the bitchy cheerleader in the bathroom scene, where she waxes poetically about the therapeutic nature of homicide. During her audition, Scelfo mentioned to Beach that her boyfriend had dropped her off. When Scelfo mentioned her boyfriend's name, the casting director went out to meet him.

"Lisa was like, 'We've been trying to reach this guy.' She went out to his car and talked to him, then he came in [to audition]," Katzman recalled.

Finding A New Final Girl

As the cast was starting to be assembled, the film hit a hiccup when Barrymore decided to switch to the role of opening victim Casey Becker.

Prior to the change, the filmmakers hadn't been looking for a well-known actress for the role. But now that it had fallen into their laps it couldn't have been a better idea.

"We thought Drew was going to play Sidney, right? So, we were really bummed when she changed her mind. But later we realized it was brilliant—but we were still bummed," explains Maddalena. She adds, "It was all her. It was her idea, because she wanted to get out of playing the whole thing and probably didn't want to disappoint Bob and Harvey. So, she came up with that, which is genius."

Adds Konrad, "The idea of it suddenly was, on the one hand, it was not what the studio 100% wanted to hear because we still are in a world of, like, let's get a movie star and do this. Then on the other hand, I think what was so smart [about] it was, you know, she was Drew. She had her draw, but yet she could kind of be a little more invisible in the part and keep people guessing what's going to happen. I think the shock of her death really set the table perfectly for the tone and the rest of the ride."

When the decision was made that Barrymore was going to switch her role from Sidney Prescott to Casey, it led to a search to fill the hole. Beach said that trying to find a replacement for Barrymore was actually the hardest part of the casting process.

"They just couldn't decide. It was the je ne sais quoi," explains Beach about what the producers were looking for in their new leading lady.

Among the actresses being considered were Alicia Witt, Brittany Murphy, and Vinessa Shaw. Contrary to rumors that have persisted over the years, Beach and Katzman said that actress Reese Witherspoon was never seriously considered for the lead role—partly due to her age.

"Everyone who we hired was pretty much in their twenties. [Witherspoon] was definitely a teen and if you got too young and had let's say Skeet," Katzman said, adding that the age difference wouldn't play well on screen with Ulrich six years her senior.

In the end the role came down to three actresses: Neve Campbell, Witt, and Murphy. The actresses ended up doing a screen test with Ulrich before Campbell was officially awarded the role. The two had previously worked on *The Craft* (1996), which was released while *Scream* was filming. Ulrich doesn't know if the familiarity helped with the pairing in the new film.

"We had very little together in *The Craft*. I didn't really spend a whole lot of time with her making that movie," Ulrich said about their previous work together. "[*The Craft*] came out while we were shooting *Scream*, so we got to celebrate together its success and stuff like that. Different parts require different things, so in some ways it could be hindrance to know somebody previously. It worked out [here]."

In hindsight, along with Barrymore's early death catching audiences off guard, it might have also helped viewers to relate to the rest of the mostly newcomers. Barrymore might not have blended into the ensemble as easily as Campbell.

"[Campbell's casting] let an audience be able to identify with each of the members of that ensemble; that friend group and really feel connected to them," Konrad said. "I don't think anybody can say they think they're Drew Barrymore, you know what I'm saying? It was sort of like she would have definitely been great; I don't doubt it. But I don't think it would have had the same kind of fun, which is really a lot of the choices in the script were always about how can we take what Kevin has created here, what he's saying with this, and really punctuate that."

Actress Rose McGowan agrees, "[We] made people care about us and I think that it was kind of like these are your friends. We might be dying, but we're your friends until then and hopefully you'll remember us. People do and that's amazing."

A Bottle of Hair Dye Gets the Job Done

Age was also a factor at play in casting the iconic role of Tatum Riley, Sidney's best friend and the younger sister of Deputy Dewey. Along with McGowan, who ultimately got the role, the casting directors liked actress Natasha Lyonne, who was only 16 years old during the casting process.

"We all loved Natasha Lyonne. Wes really loved Natasha. Natasha was actually young at the time. [She], and also I think Thora Birch came in, and they weren't emancipated," Katzman said about the process. "I do know that Natasha was very much wanted, but I also don't think she was a legal 18, and I don't think she was emancipated."

McGowan's path to getting the role wasn't an easy one, though. She had been offered the part, with a salary of $50,000. Her lawyer at the time countered back with $250,000, upsetting the Miramax executives.

"He went back at like $250,000 and pissed off the executives so much, they made me re-test three times as punishment, and paid me $50,000 and not a penny more; even though everyone else got $100,000," McGowan said. "As if I had done something bad."

The actress, who is naturally dark haired, also thought quick on her feet during one of the auditions. Knowing that Campbell had already been cast and was naturally a brunette, the rules of Hollywood dictate that movies couldn't have more than one brunette. Seeing the blonde-haired Konrad gave her an idea.

"I looked at Cathy and her hair's normal blonde lady [color] and I was, like, 'God, I really want your hair color. I'm going to the hairdresser this afternoon, do you think I could; do you have a good hairdresser to make me blonde," recalled McGowan. "It's like their collective bulbs just went off in their head, right? Oh my God, we can do that with her. It was funny to watch."

While McGowan ended up not being a fan of the blonde hair she had in the film and counted down the minutes until she could return to her natural color, the actress does admit that it was perfect for the character.

"What was good about it was that it was a really kind of mid-Western blonde, almost. It was very 'popular girl blonde' hair color," the actress explained. "It was perfect for Tatum."

Like McGowan, Jamie Kennedy, who shared an agent with the actress at the time, had concerns about how the filmmakers might react to his hair color during an audition call back. At the end of 1995 Kennedy got cast in Baz Luhrmann's adaptation of *Romeo + Juliet* (1996), which starred Leonardo DiCaprio and Claire Danes. Before leaving for the movie, the actor auditioned for the role of Randy, the film nerd who has the infamous speech preaching the rules you need to follow to successfully survive a horror movie. Upon arriving in Mexico to film *Romeo + Juliet* they dyed his hair pink.

"Baz had this tableau, just beautiful pictures on the wall. He had Leo looking all young and sexy and Claire looking all mysterious and sexy. Then the boys were this and that; he had this young energy and wild colors and Hawaiian shirts, and he had like different color hairs," Kennedy explained. "I'm like, you know what, bro. I don't know why I'm thinking this, but I just feel myself with pink hair."

Initially the actor was only supposed to be on location for four weeks, but it ended up being extended to nine. During that time, he had to fly to Los Angeles to audition. The filmmakers were surprised to see his new hair.

"It was a shock when they saw me. But they end up dyeing it, thank God. I just [thought] you could wear wigs and do whatever," Kennedy recalled. "But, yeah, I was actually pretty scared."

Pink hair or not, Beach remembers Kennedy nailing his audition, saying, "He just walked in and he just owned. I can still remember his audition."

The actor, who was competing against actors Breckin Meyer, Seth Green, and Jason Lee, booked the role. Due to the extended time in Mexico, he ended up having less than a week between the time he wrapped on *Romeo + Juliet* and when he had to report to set for *Scream* in early April.

CASTING THROUGH LESS CONVENTIONAL METHODS

Some of the actors didn't go through the typical audition route to gain their roles in the film. Liev Schreiber got his role while meeting with producer Bob Weinstein about another movie. The actor had initially come in to talk to the executive about a role in the Guillermo del Toro creature feature, *Mimic* (1997). However, Schreiber wasn't the right fit for the film. Instead, Weinstein made him an offer to have a seemingly small role in *Scream*.

"[Weinstein] said, look if you want to make some money, I've got this picture and there's this little part where all you have to do is walk down some stairs," recalls the actor. "It was like $20,000 or something. I was like, 'Oh ok, and all I got to do is walk down the stairs?'"

The role that the producer was describing was that of Cotton Weary, the character who is convicted and imprisoned for killing Sidney's mother, Maureen Prescott, during the first film. Up until that point Schreiber had been doing classical theater in New York City and was making $300 per week. Because he had previously done some stunt work, Schreiber thought maybe there was more to the offer than just walking down the stairs; maybe he needed to fall or trip. But the role required him to simply walk down the stairs and be put into a police car.

It wasn't until he got to the set that he even knew his character would be playing a larger role in the grand scheme of the *Scream* universe. Referring to himself as someone who is easily scared, Schreiber wasn't well versed in the horror genre and wasn't familiar with Craven when Weinstein told him he would be Schreiber's director on the film. However, the two quickly bonded.

"If you could make Wes smile, you were having a good day," the actor recalled about the director. "I did it once, and then I couldn't stop trying.

It was something I really enjoyed. He was somebody you wanted to please, somebody you wanted to do well for."

McGowan agrees, adding, "When you got him to laugh, you felt like a million bucks."

The role of Maureen Prescott was another role that needed to be cast but didn't require much screen time as the character only appears in photos during the first film. Due to this, Lynn McRee didn't audition in the traditional sense. Since it was for a role where the character had already passed away, the casting process was more about finding someone with the right look. McRee, who lived locally in Sonoma at the time, showed up to the casting office after receiving a call from her agent, but she wasn't given information about what she was doing there or the project.

"The conversation went something like this, 'Hi Lynn, this is Nancy. I don't have a lot of time, so tomorrow I need you to meet me in Santa Rosa. Here is the address, it will be at this time on this date. I can't answer any questions. I'll see you then.' Click," says the actress. "So, the casting agent calls me directly, not her people, and I get the who, what, where, when, but I don't get the why. What is this about? And I trusted her."

When McRee showed up the next day, she found the casting room filled with other women who looked similar to her. They were brought into a conference room and lined up across from Craven and a group of casting people. The actresses were asked to turn to the left profile, then the right, and then dismissed.

"That was the initial interview that took about two and a half minutes, with lots of lookalikes and that led to me being in the most significant role of my entire career as Neve Campbell's mom," recalls McRee.

The actress spent two hours on set taking pictures with Campbell but left without having been told the backstory about her character. It wasn't until the film was released that she found out more about the character of Maureen Prescott and her tawdry backstory.

W. Earl Brown had worked with Craven on the director's previous two films, *New Nightmare* and *Vampire in Brooklyn*, and the two developed a friendly relationship. Due to that friendship, Craven made a point to save the part of Kenny for the actor. He knew he was too old to play any of the high school characters, but the actor originally had set his sights on playing Deputy Dewey. When he was told that part was already earmarked for David Arquette, the actor looked to Kenny, Gale's cameraman. While Brown didn't have to audition, he did have something else that he needed to do—gain weight for the role. Kenny's weight is specifically referenced in the film when Gale says, "Kenny, I know you are about 50 pounds overweight, but when I say hurry, please interpret that as move your fat tub of lard ass, now!"

"I weighed 230 when I got cast, then like, oh he's supposed to be fat. So, I gained to 250, I've never been back to 230 since," Brown says, before jokingly adding, "Eating ice cream, and pasta and bread. That was sheer terror, sheer horror."

LOCATION, LOCATION, LOCATION...

AND THE CONTROVERSY THAT FOLLOWS IT

WHEN IT CAME TIME to scout locations during pre-production, the filmmakers visited three distinct locales: Napa Valley in Northern California; Wilmington, North Carolina; and Vancouver, British Columbia in Canada. Due to the decidedly different geographical locations and weather patterns, each site had various pros and cons. One of the biggest concerns for the filmmakers was finding a house for the opening sequence. The house had to have a lot of glass, making Casey Becker vulnerable to the killers while also making her think that she was safe within the confines of the house.

"She had to be in a glass box, almost a glass box and was very vulnerable. When you're in a glass house at night, you either have to have curtains or people can see you–she was very vulnerable, even though she thought for a minute that she was safe," Miller explained.

Many of the locations scouted in British Columbia had a woodsier and more outdoor feel to them. "That house was important. Vancouver is in a winter climate; they don't have houses like that. They might have them somewhere, but those are pretty big houses. We didn't see any like that. We saw Pacific Northwest log cabin, wooden houses with little windows because of the winter," Miller recalled about the scouting trip.

Williamson originally envisioned the film being set in Wilmington, but there was another set of problems that made it less than ideal. The primary issue is that it would have been difficult to control traffic. Interestingly, while Wilmington was not well-suited for the original *Scream*, the filmmakers of *Scream* (2022), the fifth film in the series, chose it as the location to film the sequel.

During the visit to Wilmington, the location scout crew, consisting of Craven, Maddalena, producer Stuart Besser, and Miller, got stuck due to an ice storm. Miller recalled a conversation at dinner where Craven expressed his hope that *Scream* would find an audience.

"I remember we were sitting at dinner and Wes said, 'I hope someone sees this movie.' He was so depressed about his career. I guess *Vampire in Brooklyn* was so devastating to him personally," Miller recalled. "If no one had seen *Scream*, I don't know what he would have done."

Indeed, *Vampire in Brooklyn* had some issues behind-the-scenes with constant fights with the studio over the tone of the film, and a tragedy that befell the production. A stunt woman named Sonja Davis died early into filming. In the stunt, Davis, who was doubling for actress Angela Bassett, was supposed to jump 42-feet out of a window backwards and land below on an airbag. She landed incorrectly and was fatally injured.

Besser counters the claim that Craven was feeling depressed about his career. He challenges, "There was a great movie on the page that he wanted to translate to film. I think that he didn't feel any pressure at all about *Vampire*. Listen, we've all made movies that we thought were good and the audience doesn't respond to it. It doesn't mean that you didn't make the best movie possible."

FINDING THE PERFECT LOCATION

It was in Napa Valley, specifically Santa Rosa and Sonoma, that Craven and his team found what they were looking for. However, in order to shoot in California, the production would need an additional two million dollars added to their budget.

"We went to Northern California and Wes just fell in love. He knew he could make it up there and make a good movie," Besser recalled.

The filmmakers went to New York to discuss the film and the need for additional money with the executives at Dimension, but it wasn't an easy sell. While meeting with the Weinstein brothers, they were denied their request for the additional funds. As the meeting ended, they got into the elevator believing that the movie had been called off and that they had been fired. They didn't realize the meeting was still happening upstairs.

"Somebody in Harvey's office said, 'Oh we don't need Wes Craven. We'll just do Joe Blow's *Scary Movie*. That will sell a ticket or two.' And Harvey said, 'Alright, alright, go get them,'" Miller recounted. "Because Wes Craven's *Scary Movie* will sell two million dollars' worth of tickets, I would think. But Joe Blow's *Scary Movie* won't sell a ticket. Somebody ran down and got them out of the taxi and brought them back upstairs."

And with that, they received the money needed to film in California.

A BATTLE OVER CENSORSHIP RAGES

One of the selling points of Northern California was an agreement to film scenes at Santa Rosa high school. The school had the picturesque classic Americana look that Craven wanted for the movie.

The school had a history of being used by Hollywood, previously being featured in the Kathleen Turner-Nicolas Cage comedy, *Peggy Sue Got Married* (1986). In the Fall of 1995, the filmmakers got permission from the school's principal, Mike Panas, to film from April 19 to May 4, 1996, in exchange for a fee of $10,000. During those discussions, there was never a request to see a copy of the script. But when the request eventually came in, the filmmakers found themselves in a battle with the school board that gained national attention. The controversy grew into a case about censorship. It became so big that the California film commission worried it would keep the lucrative industry from continuing to film in their state.

"It's a beautiful high school. It's a fantastic high school. The office, it was great," explained Miller about the attraction to the location. "We weren't going to build anything in the school that I remember, but we did have drawings, floor plans for Wes to work out his directing. So, we had that all drawn, then that town hall meeting. There was this upsurge in 'Oh, don't let those people come into our school,' and I know there was a big meeting. I thought because of money it would probably go away, but it didn't."

"I do remember in the midst of it, we all were quite taken back about it because it was censorship. To me, censorship should be done at the theater. If you don't want to go, don't go. The school was making a thing about the violence and children," said Besser. "I might have, in hindsight, fought harder than I should have. But it was important to Wes, so not fighting hard for it wasn't acceptable to me and my relationship with him."

The ordeal began at the end of March 1996 when one of the school board trustees objected to letting the filmmakers use the school, stating that the film included "scenes showing the evisceration of teenagers." (Anima, 1996) The scenes found most objectionable were the opening sequence and, according to Craven on the *Scream* audio commentary, the scene where Principle Himbry curses at and threatens the students.

"I have a personal problem with participating in something I think there's far too much of in our society," trustee Judith Bauman was quoted saying in *The Santa Rosa Press Democrat.* (Anima, 1996) It was a sentiment that became shared by many on the board, even though the filmmakers had assured the district that there were no murders in the script for the scenes that would be filmed on their campus.

"We're basically condoning it by allowing it to be shot there," fellow board member Jane Zils was quoted as saying in *The Santa Rosa Press Democrat.* "It's gratuitous violence and really demeaning language. It's trash. It's really disgusting. They use the f-word all the time." (Anima, 1996)

"It's been a nightmare. You don't want to think you're in a society that's so reactionary," Craven was quoted as saying to *The Santa Rosa Press Democrat* at the time. "The way this is being depicted, we're some sort of lowlifes who've crawled out of a rock someplace to depict violence." (Anima, 1996)

"Suddenly, we just found ourselves faced with a lot of last-minute people saying we prefer you didn't shoot here," explained Plec. "It had a lot to do with Petaluma had Polly Klaas; I think [the] Polly Klaas kidnapping had just happened in the last couple of years."

In an unfortunate and eerie case of art imitating life the residents of Santa Rosa were still in the process of healing from their own violent past. Just three years prior, a young girl named Polly Klaas was kidnapped from her home in nearby Petaluma. The case garnered national attention over the course of two months in the fall of 1993 until Richard Allen Davis confessed to her murder. In another horrible twist of fate, this battle over the school's use for *Scream* coincided with the start of Davis's trial, ripping open wounds that hadn't yet completely healed.

"It was a time where this young girl has been murdered and it had been a big mistake by the police because they had stopped the guy and she was in the trunk. It was a very sad situation," explained Maddalena.

The debate over using the school for the film grew contentious from both sides. As the school board made verbal attacks about the film, Craven also dug his heels in, threatening to sue if their request was denied.

"We'll do whatever we can to make sure we get some payback to what's been done to us," Craven said. "They led us to believe we could shoot at that school." (Anima, 1996)

The residents of Santa Rosa were divided about how the school board should rule. It led to a heated discussion at a town hall meeting on April 16. Over 800 people attended the meeting, speaking both for and against allowing the production on campus. Students, who believed that having the production at the school could be an educational experience, circulated a petition in support of the film. It received 300 signatures.

"We would laugh because all these parents were, like, we can't let you come into our town and shoot this movie here and in our school. Then you'd go through the town and all the kids were out there like totally Goth and smoking and on skateboards," Plec said. "You were like, I think you already did plenty to mess up the kids in this town by being so protective."

Karin Hoehne had just moved to Santa Rosa, where she and her husband opened a restaurant, prior to the controversy happening. But she said that it was something that was concerning to those involved with the school rather than the entire town.

"We just came from San Francisco. We were not connected to the whole ordeal. I think it was bigger in that school district community rather than the whole city. I did not feel from our customers that we heard anything about it," Hoehne said. "The money would have helped the school. The idea of it was really good. That school had some other movies film [there] already. I think it was just the scary movie thing was the scary part for the parents."

One thing was made clear to the school board members: their lawyer informed them that disagreeing with the content of the script was not legal grounds to deny production. At one point, in an effort to sweeten the offer, the producers offered to increase the fee to use the school from $10,000 to $30,000.

In the end, the school board voted 4-1 against letting the production film on the campus, citing it would disrupt the students' learning process. While no filming would have taken place within the building during school hours, it would have been taking place outside, but still on campus, while school was in session.

"The thing that I think upset all of us more was they were letting *Inventing the Abbotts* shoot at a school, or maybe it was even the same school. There was, I think, teen sex in that," Mastandrea said. "Look, that being said, [*Scream* was a] slasher movie, you could call it that. You can understand some of the parents being upset. But I think, as I recall, that was the thing that kind of weirded us out more than anything; that they let that movie go."

After looking at other locations in the Spring of 1996, Craven and his team went back to the school with revised dates in June for a final attempt at a deal. However, those dates had already been committed to a theater group.

Racing against the clock since the film was already in production, the filmmakers scrambled to find a new location. They found a community center in Sonoma that had previously been an elementary school. The building, however, presented a new set of problems for the producers.

"You wouldn't think that elementary schools would be, but they are small because there are little kids there. The desks are small, the rooms are a little smaller. It still had adults, but it's smaller," explained Miller. "They don't have lockers in elementary schools, so we had to add all of that to make it look like a high school. It was a stretch to believe that was really a high school."

The community center received $27,000 from the production to film over the course of three days in June. To put that into perspective, that amounted to more than the center's entire annual budget for maintenance and improvement.

Looking back at the controversy, Besser believes that some good came out of the ordeal, leading parents and their kids to have discussions together. But in the end, it likely didn't move the needle in changing minds about violence in film. "In hindsight, it didn't matter. The people who felt that way probably still feel that way about art and movies, and those who just thought it was ridiculous and the school could have used the money, still see it that way."

In retrospect, some in the community do think that the situation was overblown. "My daughter went to Santa Rosa high school. The only thing I did hear from some people that were on the PTA then, they said, 'My God, that was so silly. [The district] could have had all this money for laptops and this and this,' which they needed to get for the kids because it's not a very well-funded school," explained Hoehne.

In the end, however, it was Craven who got the last laugh. If you watch the end credits to *Scream*, following the thank you section, you will see that one of the last things to roll on the screen is "No Thanks Whatsoever to The Santa Rosa City School District Governing Board."

A FRAUGHT BEGINNING TO AN ICONIC SCENE

CAMERAS BEGAN ROLLING during the Spring of 1996 in Santa Rosa and the surrounding area. The opening sequence with Drew Barrymore was the first part to be filmed. While the cast and crew were excited about the film, executives at the studio had concerns, especially regarding the mask that would be used for the film. The script didn't explicitly state what Williamson envisioned for the killer's outfit, leading to a point of concern for the filmmakers. This led the production to hire renowned special make-up effects creator Greg Nicotero, now known for his work on *The Walking Dead* (2010) television universe, to create a mask for the villain. However, the producers didn't feel comfortable using any of the masks he presented.

"[Nicotero] had been doing the masks. They were witches, they were goblins with big warty noses, you know that kind of witch look," described Miller of the masks Nicotero initially created.

It wasn't until Miller, Maddalena, and Craven were scouting houses to be used as the Riley household, where Sidney's best friend Tatum and her brother Dewey live, that they found what they were looking for. The house is located on McDonald Avenue in Santa Rosa, a street that had previously been made famous in two classic movies: Disney's *Pollyanna* (1960), starring Hayley Mills, and Alfred Hitchcock's *Shadow of a Doubt* (1943). Each of the houses in those films is on the corner of the same intersection on the street, and only a block away from the one the filmmakers were scouting.

At the time, the Victorian house was owned by a lawyer and his wife who raised their children there. Even though their children had since grown up and moved out to start their own families, the couple kept the bedrooms intact so that when the grandkids came to visit they could sleep in the rooms the way their parents had as children. While looking through one of the sons' bedrooms, Maddalena found a mask reminiscent of Edvard Munch's painting, "The Scream," hanging from one of the bedposts. She instantly knew it was the mask for their film.

"I ran downstairs and said, 'Wes, this is the mask. This is so great,'" Maddalena told her fellow filmmakers.

However, they weren't as easily convinced. The mask was a departure from all of the prototypes that Nicotero had been working on. After a few more weeks passed and still nothing else felt right, Maddalena says that they relented. Miller sent an assistant back to the house to see if they could borrow the mask from the family. The original mask had a white shroud around it which they changed to black. They made a few other changes, too.

"Because of copyright laws, they stretched it a little bit so it's a little bit longer," added Miller about how they altered the mask to change the nose and chin.

The changes were made in tandem with the studio's legal department working out a deal with Funworld, the company that owns the rights to the original mask. Once legal got to use it in the film, the now iconic Ghostface mask was born. Miller opines that the studio might have leased the mask instead of trying to buy the rights based on being unsure how successful the film might end up being.

"The costume designer behind that and creating that character, I think, should go down in history as well because it's such an iconic image in the horror film slasher industry," said Nancy O'Dell, the former anchor of *Access Hollywood* and *Entertainment Tonight* who also appeared in the *Scream* sequels.

Bob Weinstein Wreaks Havoc on Production

Even though the filmmakers were now happy with their mask, Bob Weinstein was not. The producer claimed that he never approved the mask and wanted to send a box of masks to force filmmakers to film footage five different ways, each with a different mask, to find which of the proposed masks would work best.

"I, of course, felt like an idiot because I pushed for it, right," recalled Maddalena.

"It was clear that somebody was asleep at the wheel when all these processes—I mean, we don't just go out and suddenly decide on a hero prop as prominent as a mask and just decide we're going to do it and not check in. So, somehow there was a miscommunication on that side, and they were taking it out on us. What I was mad about was the hoops that they were making us do," Konrad said. "There was a little bit of inside politics of Miramax, I think, going down for Cary [Granat, the head of Production for Dimension Films] where suddenly everybody was on the 911 alert that Bob did not approve any of this stuff and how the fuck can we be shooting if he never approved it."

She adds, "What they were basically doing was just unraveling our morale and really beating up on Wes and that's just, at a certain point, we had wasted so many hours talking about this, it's just stupid. So, I just wasn't going to let the studio bully him like that and it was good. I mean, I'm sure if I did that today, I'd probably been fired myself, but I don't know."

It wasn't just the mask that Weinstein didn't like. They had been filming for a few days and he wasn't happy with the dailies he'd seen. Dailies is a term used in the film industry for the unedited, raw footage collected from each day's shooting that is viewed by producers and select other filmmakers to assess a film's progress. Among the things he didn't like was Barrymore's look.

"Bob and Harvey got all worked up a couple days in, deciding that Drew didn't look sexy enough," Plec said. "[Barrymore] really had a hand in her look and she had chosen that page boy cut. She was really, really happy with the way she looked in the movie and they, of course, I think, had something else in mind."

This led the executives to begin picking apart the footage and calling the set to express their displeasure. "They weren't happy with Wes's direction. They told him, 'oh my God, this is like some TV journeyman did it,'" Lussier recalls. "They were sending in dailies from other movies. Hey, how come you can't direct it more like this? He was incredibly despondent."

All of this led to Konrad battling with the brothers, who were across the country in New York City, over the phone.

"I remember Cathy being on the phone. I remember watching her pacing in the backyard of that house we were shooting at and, you know, Cathy's tough. I love her, but she's tough. She just told him, leave us alone. Wes knows what he's doing and everything with be fine," recalled Mastandrea.

Konrad admits tensions were running high at the time. "What was interesting about that moment—and I'm sure our voices were very heated—which is just that my whole resume was, I grew up working with directors like that. Whether or not you agree 100% with them, the respect for a director is paramount. Obviously, Bob and Harvey stories and how they worked with talent is—they're notorious and they've been well told, and we've heard all the versions of it. I made 11 movies for them. So, I know it very well, and at that point what they were pitching was so audacious to me."

Unsatisfied, Bob Weinstein sent Dimension executives to meet with the filmmakers about his concerns. Granat, and Andrew Rona, Director of Development and Production, visited the set to meet in person regarding the issues that the studio had about what they were seeing. Initially, Granat was going to take Craven, Maddalena, Konrad, and Besser out to dinner to discuss the film, but it was decided he should take just Craven. The producers were left waiting at the hotel to get word on how dinner went.

"I received a phone call. I don't know, it was around 10 o'clock or nine or something, and it was Wes. He said, 'This is your director, do you like scary movies? Come to my room.' I'm like, oh my God, alright. So, we got the funny come to the room [call]," Konrad said.

When she arrived in his hotel room Maddalena and Besser had already arrived. Craven said that he didn't like how the conversation had gone at dinner and that he didn't care about Bob's concerns.

"Cary was saying we have to reshoot stuff and start over in a way and everybody was getting very animated. I kind of stepped in and I said, you know, here's the deal. You guys don't think this mask is scary. You don't think this is this, but you can't keep talking to Wes this way. He's doing a fine job and my suggestion would be that you allow us to cut together the footage that we have to date; we'll screen it for Bob and if you don't like it, you can fucking shut us down. But right now, we have to go and do our job. What you're pitching is silly. It's just silly," Konrad recalled. "So, we sold that idea to Bob and Patrick Lussier went about cutting together the footage that we had to date, which was kind of not the full sequence with Drew, but a good chunk of it."

While filming took place in Northern California, Lussier was "keeping up the camera" back in Los Angeles. This means he received the footage each day after filming and then cut it together within a day or two for the filmmakers to review. This is a helpful process because if anything needs to be re-shot, it can be done before the production leaves a location.

Lussier had been working with Craven since the pilot for the television series, *Nightmare Café* (1992), which was shot in Canada. Canadian rules dictate that any time a foreign editor is brought in for a production, they also need to hire a local Canadian editor as a match to avoid displacing any jobs. Lussier explained that this usually meant the local editor is paid to do nothing, but that was not the case in this circumstance. When the show got picked up, Lussier continued to work on the series and bonded with Craven, leading the director to ask Lussier to edit his next film. He originally planned for that to be a remake of *Village of the Damned* (1995), but he left the project and instead made *Wes Craven's New Nightmare*. The two got along so well that Craven sponsored Lussier and his family when they immigrated to the United States from Canada.

Lussier worked with Craven to finalize the opening sequence and ship a copy to New York. Typically, one of them would have been present for the screening, but the executives didn't want them to come. Because of Konrad's deal with Miramax, she knew many of the people working in the project booth and received a call as the screening was happening in real time.

"The projectionist called me and told me that they were threading the film and everything was set. Then I kind of got a play-by-play. I was outside, they were filming inside, and I was in a parking lot. [The projectionist] was like, okay, it's running, and Harvey just walked in. He's smoking a cigarette. Bob's sitting down, they're now sitting down. They look like they're enjoying it," the producer recalled. "Harvey or Bob like jumped out of their seat at a certain moment. The projectionist hung up the phone and 10 minutes later I got a call from Bob."

After seeing the opening sequence, Weinstein realized he had been wrong.

"Bob apologized, 'What do I know about anything? It's fabulous,'" said Maddalena, adding, "It was really demoralizing. It's no way to treat a director. But that was a trial by fire Wes certainly got."

Konrad adds, "That was the first time and probably the last time Bob ever admitted he was wrong. But, you know, that was big of him and he was like, you guys go ahead."

"Patrick kind of saved the day, where that was concerned, because he just crushed it. He temped it [the music], he had all the sound effects. I mean that's not easy to do in the first 10 days of shooting. He just really delivered," Plec explained.

Along with producers, Granat and Rona were also met with a cast and crew who rallied behind Craven. Many were afraid he might get fired and that the film would get shut down.

"We cared about Kevin. We cared about the script. We cared about Wes. So, when [Granat and Rona] came down to deal with it, basically [we said] if you fire Wes the whole thing shuts down. We are all out, we're not staying," explained Besser. "I remember a conversation with Cary, about him saying, 'Well people need to work.' I go, Cary we're all gone. No one is going to stay because Wes didn't deserve it."

"That was just his process. We had a great team and we rallied," agrees Maddalena. "I think Bob just beats people. No praise, just beat the shit out of you as you go."

Weinstein's tactics would only get worse as the years went on. For composer Marco Beltrami, Craven's go-to composer beginning with *Scream* until his death, working with Weinstein was his first taste of Hollywood. He wasn't aware that the producer's methods were abnormal.

"They would rent a mix stage and want to hear the music—like give me their own notes, independent of the director and I was like, alright. It's sort of weird, like putting me in a little bit of a weird spot with the director. But it was the way they were," said Beltrami. He recalled an even weirder incident. "I was at my brother's wedding in Long Island, at the eastern end of Long Island, and they wanted me to do this movie and they couldn't reach me. I was there at the wedding and I saw four black SUVs pull up and they're waiting for the ceremony to finish. It was like a mafia thing. Then as soon as they were finished, [they were] like Marco, we need to take you back to New York with us."

Besser, for his part, explained that Craven and Weinstein were opposites. "[Wes] is a man of class, intelligence. He always wanted to do the right thing. He really didn't like conflict and he didn't like people that were bullies. Bob came in, in that situation, at that moment in time [as a bully]."

According to the producers, the grandstanding by Weinstein might have also had an ulterior motive—he was trying to get a working edited version of the opening scene out of them to screen at an upcoming film festival.

"They're not allowed to see cut footage for eight weeks after you wrap. He wanted cut footage to take to the Milan Film Festival," said Maddalena.

Besser further explained Weinstein's tactics, "Instead of just coming out and saying something, that was Bob's M.O. Bob comes from a school of bullying, so he always thought that would get it because he [had] always gotten his way when he's done that."

FINDING THE RIGHT VOICE FOR GHOSTFACE

With Weinstein's concerns out of the way, Craven and his team were able to get back to the project at hand. Though she might not have known it at the time, Barrymore helped shape the legacy of the film franchise forever. Switching from playing Sidney to Casey started a trend of having a big opening scene in each of the series' films, something that hadn't been seen since *Psycho*, which also became a staple in horror movies going forward. She also had a hand in the sound of Ghostface.

Initially, the filmmakers were going to have the actress perform the scene with a line reader behind the camera who would feed the lines to her. However, she asked if they could hire a voice actor, allowing her to have someone to play off of in the scene. With that request, they set out to hire someone who could draw out the appropriate reaction from Barrymore in the scene. Enter Roger L. Jackson.

"I heard some other folks who were there to audition say, 'My agent says they are looking for the new Freddy Krueger.' I read the script and I said, 'This isn't Freddy Krueger,'" Jackson recalls. "This is very subtle. This is all cat and mouse. This is really well written. It was all there in the script. I broke down the scene, as you do when you're an actor. It's part of your job. Just figure the elements that were needed."

Realizing that difference helped Jackson to land the job. During his audition, Jackson was given the opening sequence to read. Upon reading it, he realized that the voice needed to be flexible—charming enough to keep the callers on the phone, but also deadly menacing.

"There's some flirtation going on there and since there's only the oral presence—the sound—there's no physical signals you can give, the voice had to be kind of sexy. I know from some experience the sorts of voices that some of the ladies like. It's got to be a little textured, a little colored, have a little interest to it, a little warm, and focus all of the attention on her," Jackson said, describing what goes into the voice he created. "It gets a little darker as the scene progresses. But it's got to stay the same voice, you know? So, I just put on a Barry White there."

He continued, "The charming aspect only comes out a little bit when he's got new victims, somebody new to talk to and he's playing with, or she, since Ghostface can be anybody. That's one of the really interesting aspects of Ghostface, it's not one person. It's not a Michael, a Jason. It could be anybody. Ghostface is really the darker aspects of everyone. You put on the mask, you're capable of doing things you wouldn't do normally. You feel protected and hidden."

They brought the actor to set, though he was only being considered to do the scene live with Barrymore over the phone line. Their initial plan was to have another voice actor, Tom Kane, dub the lines and become the voice of Ghostface afterwards. Jackson hadn't been informed of that plan.

"Well, I didn't know at first it was just to play the scene with Ms. Barrymore. I was there to do my job and I heard on the set that that had been the intention," Jackson explained. The actor heard that they liked what he was doing so much that they planned to keep him, "for which I am very grateful."

Jackson said that he wasn't given much direction from Craven while performing the scene with Barrymore. He was only given notes when he needed to hold back more or push things a little bit further.

In order to create a sense of mystery and elicit a natural reaction from the actress, the director made a conscious decision to keep the voice on the other end of the line a secret. Jackson was on set for his scenes but secluded from the rest of the cast so that they would never meet him or be able to put a face to the ominous voice. That tradition continued not only for the rest of that film, but also all the sequels with Jackson never meeting any of the cast during their shared scenes.

"Except for that first night where I was outside the window of the room that Ms. Barrymore was in, for each subsequent time they put me in a room somewhere and I'm seeing the camera feed so I could see what was going on, but they couldn't see me," Jackson explained. "I was miked for sound, but I was actually talking on a cell phone connected to their phone."

During filming Jackson would be kept on the phone in between takes, staying in character the whole time. This led to some interesting interactions with the cast, who had a variety of reactions to him. Some were scared, some were unnerved, or in the case of Sarah Michelle Gellar, some tried to goad him.

"In *Scream 2*, when they're shooting the *Stab* part of the film; Heather Graham, I was talking to her doing the scenes and between takes I could hear her saying, 'Who is this guy? He's really scary, oh my God, he's creepy.' But Sarah Michelle Gellar, who was in the same film, between takes, she was very Buffy. She was going, 'So scary voice man. You're scary voice man, right? Why are you scaring people with your voice? Why do you like doing that? What's wrong with you?'" Jackson explained. "But I have to keep in character. So, I don't just go, gosh I really like 'Buffy.' I really like your movies, Ms. Graham."

Craven was also able to elicit a reaction from his star by recalling a story that Barrymore, an avid animal lover, had shared with him about a dog being set on fire and abused. While careful to never go too far— Craven was known for being protective of his young actors—he would tell the actress that he was lighting a match to trigger a bigger emotional reaction when necessary.

"[Barrymore] was a delicate soul at that point. So, it wasn't hard to take her someplace more perilous in internal monologue," Irwin explained about the process Craven used to get the actress in the right state of mind. He added, "In order to get her amped up, we'd be rolling, we'd slate it, and he'd be whispering in her ear about how animals are slaughtered for food or vicious, vicious stuff for imagery."

"Wes was so protective, and I know he was with Drew. Drew has said that he was like a father figure to her," Brown adds. "He knew the vulnerability of what they were going through. He knew that instinctively with any actor, but especially in a young woman playing scenes like that."

THE IMPACT OF THOSE 13-MINUTES

Along with the opening sequence's legacy in the horror genre, it had a lasting impact on some of the filmmakers' careers, specifically Lussier and Beltrami.

Beltrami was just out of school at USC when he was hired to work on *Scream*. In school he composed the score for a short film that garnered attention from Sony. His classmates who worked on the film were interviewed on a radio show, after which the host mentioned that Craven was looking for a composer for his next film. They recommended Beltrami.

"The next thing I know, I got a call from Wes's assistant and asked for a demo reel. Remember at the time it was cassette tapes back then, but everyone that I knew [was] trying to imitate John Williams. I didn't have anything like that to put on my reel, so it was more things I'd written that are more electronic type pieces," said the composer. "Wes listened to it, he really liked it. He asked me to come in and meet with him."

He met with Craven, who gave him the opportunity to create a score for the opening sequence on spec, meaning he would create the score in hopes of getting the job but hadn't been officially hired. The catch was that he only had a weekend to complete the assignment.

"This is on a Friday afternoon. [Craven] said, 'Bring it to us on Monday and we'll see how it works.' I was like, oh shit, I don't know how I'm going to do this. I don't even have a studio at home. I had to borrow a friend of mine's studio," recalls the composer.

Nevertheless, he turned in his score and the filmmakers approved it. In fact, they cut it into the film to use for a test screening of the film in Secaucus, New Jersey. The movie itself received an 88 (out of 100) rating from the audience, and the Dimension executives loved the score that Beltrami had created for the opening. They offered him the job to compose the score for the rest of the film.

He was just starting out and had a limited budget from the studio, so Beltrami had to get creative. "One of the things, it became a cool effect looking back at it, but that scene, for instance, with Neve Campbell for her theme. I didn't have enough strings to do what I wanted, so I got all the producers, Wes and Patrick and Marianne Maddalena and Cathy Konrad. I think all the people that were working on the movie. I put them out with the orchestra with the violin section. I was, like, maybe you guys can just whistle, like make it this clustery effect, and they did and that's in the score," said Beltrami. "That's them whistling the sound in that cue, so that was really fun. But back in those days it was fun because you really had a lot of hurdles to figure out and figure out how you're going to get the score done."

That screening helped launch Beltrami's career. He has since been nominated for two Academy Awards for his work on *3:10 To Yuma* (2007), which Konrad and Besser produced, and *The Hurt Locker* (2008).

"I was a little bit undecided whether this is really what I wanted to do. I think just having such a great experience on *Scream*, it really rooted me in this business and knowing that I wanted to do it," said the composer.

Lussier's work on that 13-minute opening sequence also helped launch his directing career a few years later with *Dracula 2000* (2000), produced by Craven and Maddalena. "Cutting that 13 minutes of film, actually, that's what gave me the chance to direct; that's what gave me an opportunity to edit on *Mimic* and all these other films for [Dimension]," Lussier explained.

SUMMER CAMP

AFTER THE ROCKY START to production with the school board and Weinstein's concerns, Craven may have been feeling the pressure to deliver with the film, but he never let it show to his actors. Almost everyone's description of making *Scream* was that it felt like they were at summer camp, and that's not just because the film shot during the Spring and Summer of 1996.

"The amount of stress that was on this man, that we all kind of knew, but we found out much more later; at least I did," noted Kennedy. "I mean that was a lot of pressure. He needed a hit. Kevin was just breaking on the scene. He had a bunch of newbie actors, except Courteney, who's kind of this established thing, but wanted to establish a movie [career]. The brand-new studio wanted a hit. So, there was a lot of pressure and you never felt it."

"We were blissfully unaware as we're hanging out in David's room, smoking weed and singing songs. We didn't know that was going on," agrees Brown.

It helped that everyone was away from home. All of the cast stayed at the DoubleTree hotel in Santa Rosa throughout the production. Craven was one of the few not staying at the hotel; he rented a house in the area. With much of the cast just beginning their careers they were able to bond without having to worry about egos. Plus, neither social media nor paparazzi were a factor yet.

"It was unique," Besser explained. "When they weren't working, they still came to set. That's where they wanted to be. When the weekends came around it was, like, what's the plan? Is everybody going to do this, is everybody doing that?"

A SCREAM LOVE STORY

Prior to converging on the California wine country, Craven hosted a party at his house in Los Angeles for the cast to get to know each other. It was an intimate party, including the actors as well as Beach and Katzman because of the work they had been doing during pre-production.

"Normally when you do a movie, you have a wrap party or something that the studio is paying for. This was purely Wes just saying, hey, before we go up north, I just want to have the people who did pre-production with us and the actors come up and just have a get together. I think he put it all on himself, at his house," explained Katzman, who was touched by the invitation. "It was just a small group of people who had worked on the project and he included me. I couldn't believe it, I'm like I'm just the assistant. It was so nice."

It was during this party that David Arquette and Courteney Cox would first meet, before starting to date and eventually getting married and having a child together. The *Scream* films actually line up with each phase of their relationship. They met during the first film, were dating by the time filming began on the second film, got married just before the third film filmed, and they were in the midst of splitting up while filming *Scream 4* (2011).

While not everyone immediately saw sparks fly between the future couple, it was easy for Brown to see the blossoming romance. Upon arriving in Santa Rosa, he and Arquette had been having dinner together each night. On one occasion, Arquette called Brown and asked if he minded whether Cox joined them for dinner. Brown agreed, as it also gave him a chance to bond with the actress with whom he shared most of his scenes.

"She shows up, the three of us go to dinner and we just had an instant rapport. For three nights in a row, we all three went to dinner and each night I can see their chairs getting closer and closer," Brown remembered.

Director of Photography Mark Irwin believes he may have been the good luck charm on set that helped get them together. He says he has a history of working on films where co-stars end up dating.

"I feel like I am the catalyst when I work on a film; on *Dumb and Dumber*, Jim [Carrey] and Lauren Holly got together. I did *Me, Myself, and Irene* and Jim gets together with Renee Zellweger. I'm the inadvertent matchmaker," Irwin said wryly.

AN IMMEDIATE BOND

Since her scenes filmed first, Barrymore arrived before the rest of the actors. She also had a conflicting schedule with them once they did arrive; she was working while they were hanging out and rehearsing. This didn't leave time for her to join any of the gatherings, so her only meeting with the other actors was at Craven's dinner party. Once filming wrapped on her sequence, she left town—though many in the cast have met the actress in the ensuing years. For the rest of the cast, the connection was almost instantaneous.

"Just complete kismet. The script was great. You had the right script, the right director, the right actors," Maddalena recalled about the feeling going into production.

Many credit Craven with being the driving force of the atmosphere on set. Miller said that the director set the tone for everyone else to follow. Kennedy even remembers the director telling him, "Just because we're making a horror movie doesn't mean the process has to be horrific." The camaraderie extended beyond the cast to include the crew as well.

"Often times there's the cast and then there's the crew. But on this everybody was very, very tight," Mastandrea explained. "Anybody in the film business that has done this for a while knows that you're working long hours, close contract with people and if you have the opportunity to do it with people you love and people that can make it fun, it doesn't get any better than that. I think we all knew how lucky we were."

Mastandrea was able to see firsthand how much the cast had bonded at one point while riding in a van to set with Campbell, Cox, and McGowan, who was unable to shoot because she had fallen ill. Both of the other actresses stepped up to support her.

"They're both in my ear, saying you gotta change, you gotta change. We changed something, I redid something at the last minute and everybody rolled with it," the assistant director recalled. "Nobody bitched, nobody complained at all. We just changed [the schedule] and nothing was said about it. That was that."

Not only did the cast and crew get along on set, that camaraderie continued offset as well. When they weren't working, they hung out at the hotel, for better or worse.

"Oh my God, we took over the DoubleTree Hotel. It was a party. It was a party like in everybody's rooms. We all went to fancy restaurants on the weekends. We went to Sonoma, Calistoga," recalled Maddalena.

When it came to booking the rooms at the DoubleTree, the hotel didn't put the production's cast and crew all together, something that was rectified for the sequels. Everyone was located throughout the hotel, which led to complaints from the other guests about the production's shenanigans.

"We worked unusual hours, and I don't think probably any of the other guests were on our schedule. So, yes, we were a little crazy," Konrad admits.

To keep from creating a disturbance, the cast and crew started to hang out in a circular barn that was just a short walk from the hotel. Before they got into the thick of shooting, they would pack a cooler and trek the half mile to entertain themselves within the confines of the barn. Both the barn and the hotel itself ended up burning down a few years ago during one of the wildfires that have become an annual disaster in that area of California.

"We had an incredible time. It was the kind of experience that you just kind of explained that you have when you're making something you don't know if anybody's ever going to watch. You have to enjoy the experience because you have no idea if the movie's going to be seen by anyone," Plec explains. "It was just incredible, we would shoot until seven in the morning, get home on Saturdays, lay out by the pool and drink daiquiris and fall asleep in the sun at 11, get up after like five hours asleep, and go to some great Sonoma restaurant."

Adds Konrad, "Everybody was in the same sort of thing. I think the majority of the cast, with the exception of Courteney Cox, everybody was kind of at a similar level. Nobody was playing movie star diva tricks. Everybody was deferential to Wes and I think things are pretty good, you know what I'm saying? I think that we all had a good time. We were in a small town, we would take trips together, we would go to Sonoma and Napa and everybody kind of hung out. It was like a big party in that DoubleTree all the time."

BONDING OVER DINNER

One of the regular haunts for the production was a restaurant named Ca'Bianca, an Italian restaurant that is still open in Santa Rosa. Besser and Mastandrea found the restaurant while they were still prepping the production. They went there one night before the restaurant had opened and asked if the owner, Marco Diana, was willing to serve them. He obliged and in return they kept returning with the cast and crew once filming began. Maddalena recalls that they ate there every weekend.

"I stopped in, and it was late because we'd be prepping 'til late. I walked in and I said, 'Hey, if there's a few of us come in, will you stay open?' He said, 'Dude, I just opened, and I got nobody here.' So, we also had gone and that became our place, and we all became friends," Mastandrea explains. "By the time the movie was over, the place was huge and jammed. It was hard to get in and they just took off."

The cast and crew would call the owners to let them know what nights they were planning to come in so that the restaurant could prepare. They would close a little earlier on those nights, though Marco's wife, Karin Hoehne, mentioned that Santa Rosa closed a little earlier back then so the production would come in after they would have generally been closed anyway.

"They were so nice and friendly, and they were just like family at a certain point. Wes Craven was also very nice and just nice to talk to. The whole crowd was very, very sweet and they were very personable. It didn't feel like 'Oh, we cannot talk to them,' I think. They were one of us and that was great. They would ask us questions," Hoehne said. "They were just regular people that had questions. We also eventually befriended them in a way where we also would be invited to some of their functions, including when they did the first showing, the party, here in Santa Rosa, of the movie and also we were invited to one function at the Hilton hotel, where they were staying. Then, actually, some of those cast members came back years and months later to visit with friends and we would see some of them again."

Hoehne said that they told their staff they were not allowed to take pictures or ask for autographs with the cast, however, over the course of production the cast and crew offered to take pictures with them. She believes it was that ability to come and hang out together without having to worry about anyone interrupting or bothering them that was part of the appeal for the filmmakers and actors.

"We specifically never asked for autographs, asked for pictures. We just thought it was really great that they came because [we had] just opened," she explained. "I think they felt very comfortable in this place because it was just them and they didn't have to be so worried about any kind of people commenting on them or photographing them."

While she doesn't remember after all of these years if there were any favorite dishes that the group particularly enjoyed, she does remember that Diana would just cook things up for them to try and they always enjoyed those dishes. They also enjoyed having good wine with dinner. One thing she does remember is witnessing the start of the romance between Arquette and Cox. Hoehne recalled that after finishing dinner at the end of the night, the pair would sit in the corner and smoke Clove cigarettes together.

Everyone got along so well that the filmmakers invited the owners and many of the staff to appear in the film. Hoehne and her son, who was two years old, can be seen packing up their picnic basket as the town prepares for the curfew to go into effect. During the video store scene, many of the extras are staff members from Ca'Bianca as well. Diana filmed a cameo, too, but unfortunately, it ended up on the cutting room floor.

Hanging Out Together and Bonding

Among the ringleaders of the shenanigans were Arquette and Brown. Arquette decorated his hotel room with black lights and lava lamps and declared his room as one of the places for everyone to congregate. One night when the cast ventured out of the hotel, they went to play pool at a local billiards hall recommended by Barrymore. Since she had arrived before everyone else, the actress had scoped out many of the places in the area and offered recommendations to the remaining cast members.

"We would go there and shoot pool, and word kind of spread. So, it became the place everybody was going. People would mostly put their name on the chalkboard to play pool against the girl from *Friends*, or some of that shit," Brown said, referring to Cox.

On one particular night a misunderstanding almost led to a fight with some of the locals. Arquette was playing pool against a girl who was bi-racial and made a bad shot. In response, she made a joke to him about the shot.

"He said, 'What are ya, a troublemaker?' like a 1940s gangster," Brown explained.

However, due to the old-timey way that Arquette said it, the woman misheard and thought that he called her a racial slur. Things got heated. The girl's boyfriend came to defend his girlfriend and fight the actor, which only confused Arquette and Brown who didn't understand why they were so upset.

"Her boyfriend comes in and he is going to fight David for calling her that word. I am there and David is like 'Whoa, whoa, whoa, whoa, what are you talking about?' At first, we didn't know what... he didn't say anything to anybody," Brown continued. "I remember, what are ya, a troublemaker?"

Thankfully, they were all able to talk it out, explaining what he had actually said to the couple, and no punches were thrown. "That was the only instance of social upheaval [during production]," Brown said.

Another time, Arquette and McGowan went out crashing prom parties. The actors were bored the night of the local proms and began following limos to find out where the parties were happening.

"I was like let's chase the prom limos and crash their parties. So, we're crashing proms; I think we did like three that night. Any car that was dragging cans and had, you know, whipped cream on it, or something, we're like, let's go," McGowan recalled. Although, they didn't necessarily blend in with the other partygoers. "We were a bit older, right? And we're just also [wearing] our clothes. We're from Hollywood, we just looked different. So, they were kind of like, who are these weirdos? and we're like, 'Hey, we're the weirdos. What's up?'"

Having the weekends off from filming allowed the cast and crew to explore the surroundings outside of the immediate area. Kennedy recalled going to visit San Francisco with Campbell and Matthew Lillard, playing basketball with Ulrich, and going to Denny's with McGowan. He says that as an actor who was just starting out, he learned a lot during that time.

"One day I went shopping with [Cox]. It's kind of cool, it's one of the last times that I was the guy—not to toot my own horn—but I was the guy [who] they would hand me the camera and they go, can you take a picture with us, sir? So, I would be the picture taker for Courteney," Kennedy recalled. "She was pretty flooded, but it was still a small enough town that it wasn't so crazy. So gracious, so kind, and I just remember watching her and saying, 'That's how you handle yourself as a star.' She was always, like, 'always be gracious to people, take a picture.' It was a lot of school for me."

McGowan adds that despite Cox's resume, she never flaunted it to the other actors, "Courteney, she had a lot of experience, even way before *Friends*. She was an actress for a long time, but never came on with, like, I have more credits than anybody."

The peaceful tone on the set also allowed the actors to be comfortable with each other in case something didn't go exactly as planned during one of the scenes. Brown remembered that in his first scene with Cox—the scene in the alley outside of the police station where Gale infamously gets punched—he was supposed to catch her with one arm while holding a news camera in the other. During one of the takes, his hand grabbed in a different place than the stunt coordinator had shown him.

"I am here filming the thing, this arm is behind her, which I am just supposed to catch her. Well, on one take, I forget what it was, she fell, and I grabbed her right by the boob. My first thought was, oh shit; well, I couldn't let go because if I let go, she was going to fall. And I thought, oh my God, she is going to think I did this on purpose," Brown said about the incident. But the actress didn't even seem to notice. "I said, 'I'm so sorry, that was a complete accident' and she goes 'what?' It was that moment that I realized, oh she's cool. She's easy to get along with, she's easy to work with, and that showed throughout the rest of the movie."

CREATING A SAFE SPACE

Craven had created an atmosphere from the top that allowed everyone to feel comfortable, and everything grew from there. Maddalena says that this was the first experience where a lot of the cast had worked with a director that could make them feel safe and respected.

"You didn't have to yell or scream, it's not that environment. That's what Wes would demand, and we would all follow it. I think the actors all felt embraced. Everybody was equal," Besser explained. "You have actors who respect the director, and a director that respects them, a producer that respects them, and vice versa. So, it works."

"Marianne Maddalena is a very loving person and she always made us feel comfortable. Peter [Deming], the D.P., knew we were young, and he was always helpful. Patrick would say, man, your stuff looks great in dailies. Cathy Konrad would come in and you would say something, and she would laugh at your jokes," recalls Kennedy. "Everyone did their own thing, and I can't name a person on the set that didn't do something that was sweet or thoughtful."

Kennedy admits that when he had time off from production while everyone else was shooting, he would take day trips to San Francisco because he was sad about being away from them and needed a distraction. "When no one was around, I would take a cab and I would kind of wander the city. That was kind of neat. I was also sad sometimes. I was sad, just making this movie and being away from everybody, like when people were working and I wasn't on set," the actor said. "I would go to the city by myself and that was sad. That's how much I loved everybody."

Looking back, it's not lost on many of those involved with the production that they were lucky to work with Craven and experience the protected environment that he created for them as young professionals. "*Scream*, the first one, I was 25 years old and it's the first time I'd really been on a movie set, first movie ever made. I think about how lucky I was to enter this business and live in this industry under that safe umbrella of good people who treated each other respectfully, who supported each other, and the cherry on top, made a movie that was an absolute surprise, runaway hit, and was a zeitgeist hit, and a water cooler hit, and the pop culture hit, and has lasted now for 25 years," Plec said, reflecting on the experience.

In an industry where jobs might only last a few months, creating a bond and friendships that last over two decades is an impressive feat.

PEOPLE LIVE, PEOPLE DIE

AS PRODUCTION WAS ROUNDING home plate, the final weeks of filming were scheduled to be the finale of the film. Much of the third act takes place at Stu's house, where he is hosting a party, naturally, after the town issues a curfew. This leads to what *Scream 4*'s Charlie Walker would later refer to as the "third-act main cast blood bath."

Up until that point in the film, there had only been one death since the opening—that of Principal Himbry. Interestingly, his murder wasn't actually in the original script, but it was added after Weinstein expressed concern to Williamson that too much time passes without anyone succumbing to Ghostface's knife. In the third act, that all changes.

"Nick Mastandrea likes to come up with funny scene headings for all the scene numbers. Scene 114 was the entire sequence, like that entire ending sequence and so he just called it 'people live, people die,'" Plec explained. "We shot it for so long that our big crew photo at the end was all of us outside the house holding a sign that read 'people live, people die.' I just remember being there for weeks after weeks after weeks."

'SHIPPING' BILLY AND STU

In the final moments of the film, it is revealed that Billy and Stu are the killers, with Billy orchestrating the whole thing because Sidney's mother had an affair with his father, leading his mother to leave. While it's clear what Billy's motive is for the massacre, Stu only offers up peer pressure as his motive.

Fans, however, have theorized another reason for Stu's involvement. The popular internet theory suggests that the two were secretly lovers or that Stu went along with the plan because of his unrequited feelings for Billy. They point to the relationship of the killers in *Scream 4* (2011) as mirroring this, with one manipulating the other into helping carry out the plan by preying on his emotions.

The theory has gained so much traction that the book *Reading The Bromance: Homosocial Relationships in Film and Television* by Michael DeAngelis has a whole chapter, titled "Fears of a Millennial Masculinity: *Scream*'s Queer Killers," written by David Greven, that analyzes the subtext of the relationship between Billy and Stu. Greven's writing points to many instances in the film that he says not only suggest that the killers were queer, but that he takes a hard line in stating that they are.

Whether this was ever Williamson's intention, as a gay man himself, is unknown, but many have seemingly tried to read between the lines about what might have been going on with the two killers.

Adding Humanity to a Tragic Death

One of the most infamous scenes in the series is the death of Tatum. While being attacked by Ghostface in Stu's garage, she attempts to escape through the pet door—only to find herself stuck as the door rises.

From the start of the scene, many viewers took notice due a certain wardrobe malfunction that showed up on film.

"The famous scene in the garage, you know what I'm saying. It was really cold. The garage doors are open, so they could film inside, but it was like we were filming at night and even Southern California gets very cold at night, in Northern California certainly more so," McGowan explains. "Because it's the movies you're wearing not a jacket, you know, because those are the rules."

That was one of the few things that wasn't intentional about McGowan's portrayal of Sidney's loyal best friend. The actress knew her character so fully that when she showed up to set and the wardrobe and set dressing didn't match the character, she fought to correct the inconsistency.

"Every time I could inject some humanity into Tatum and be, like, no, care about me when I die. I want you guys to miss me when I'm not on the screen and it'll be that much more impactful when she does die," the actress explained.

This included the set dressing for her bedroom. Originally, the Indigo Girls poster that adorns Sidney's bedroom wall was in Tatum's room, but McGowan vetoed it.

"They put up a 90s lesbian, kind of granola rock band and they're called the Indigo Girls. And they were like, to me [who's] so young, they look like they're in their 40s. But they were just not; Tatum would not listen to these people. So, they had posters of the Indigo Girls, kind of like these Lilith fair, which was like a big kind of feminist music festival at the time, kind of rockers. And that was not her thing. No way," McGowan recalled. "When I go into her bedroom, I was, like, what, you just sold out my character. Like every piece of work I've done to make Tatum believable, you've just undone by putting these posters all over her walls. It doesn't make any sense."

A similar situation happened when it came to how Tatum would be dressed. When meeting with the costumer for the film, McGowan recalls that they wanted to put her in a certain type of shoe because they were popular at the time. The actress admits that her response had an edge to it.

"It was a very bitchy thing to say, but also kind of true because I just kind of had it. There's a point where, like, again, if the costume designer's putting you in stuff that's not the character, not the character that I saw in any way. And I was like, this will sink my character, like the wrong kind of musicians on the wall sort of thing. It doesn't match," the actress recalled. "So, she was like, you need to wear these white Keds. She's like,' They're very now;' I'm like 'They're very never.'"

Due to the costume disagreements McGowan went shopping for many of her costumes, including the outfit that she wore for her death scene. Having already seen the storyboards for how the sequence would play out, McGowan intentionally picked up a patterned skirt.

"I know they're going to focus on my butt. Because that's what they're going to do when I go in to get the beers from the fridge, because you got like a cute young girl, and that's what they do. So, I was like, I'm gonna get a skirt, with this weird swirl pattern that like points right at the nether regions on each side. And I was like, I'm going to corrupt American minds," McGowan said with a laugh. "I did it on purpose. Most of the stuff I do on film is very purposeful. Even that was very much like my kind of like f- you to kind of knowing the camera's [going to] be on my butt, I'm like, 'Okay, you want it, here you go.'"

When it came to actually filming Tatum's death, the actress didn't use a stunt performer. Knowing that the audience would be able to tell the difference in the physicality between her and the stunt woman, she climbed into the pet door herself. From previous experience she knew that she could already fit through one, so she had the crew nail her shirt to the garage door as a way to keep her from falling out the other side. Still, the sequence left her heavily bruised.

"They had a stunt double for me, but she's kind of markedly bigger than I was physically. I'm built like, 'where's my parasol?' But in reality, my brain is like Scrappy-doo that's, like, let's go! It's a bad mix. I have this delicate body, but my brain is like kill them all. So, I was like, no, I'll do my own stunts. I wind up going up and down in that garage door and I had bruises from like under my chest to like around the bottom of my thighs for like three weeks afterwards, just because the jolts of going up and down, you know, over and over," McGowan said. Despite the bruises, the actress did enjoy performing the stunt. "I knew, again, if I had a double it wouldn't look like me and at that point the audience definitely knew what I looked like. I was like, I clearly have to do this myself—and it was also fun. I like doing weird physical things."

However, based on the interactions with fans since the film's release it had the intended effect. "They'll literally [ask] was that really you getting your neck crushed? I'm like, would I be here to talk to you about it? Let's analyze that question."

Just before she dies, McGowan made sure to inject one last element of humanity into Tatum. The last word out of the character's mouth is a scream for her mom. By calling out for her mother, it was another way for the actress to show Tatum's innocence.

"I wanted one final thing that was like I refuse to let Tatum just be another, big-boobed blonde that dies for a body count number in a horror movie. I'd known enough about horror movies that was basically the thrust of it. I mean I know there's a lot of deeper layers to horror movies and all that stuff. I'm not a huge aficionado, so I can't really go into that, but I know that in a lot of the ones that I've seen. It's just like, oh, let's kill another hot chick, kill another hot chick or the hot guy, whatever, let's kill him and people don't really care," McGowan explained. "We all just brought it and made people care about us. I think that it was kind of like these are your friends. We might be dying, but we're your friends until then and hopefully you'll remember us. People do and that's amazing."

TENSIONS COME TO A HEAD

The house selected to be Stu Macher's house looked great onscreen and was on the market for sale—making it available to the production—but the location of the house presented a number of logistical challenges for the crew. It was situated on top of a hill, making it trickier to light the scenes. This also meant accessing the trailers required time-consuming trips down the hill. For these and other reasons, things took much longer than they normally would have at another location.

"It was a complicated location to shoot, and it was, in many ways, the wrong location to shoot. The nuts and bolts of my job is to fit a 12-hour day. I should say, fit the page count into the 12-hour day, or night in this case," Irwin explained. "I begged producers don't make this decision because the grunt time we need to move lights is the time you should be shooting."

Despite his protests, the production stuck with the location. In an effort to cut down on the commute time for the cast and crew, the producers asked Miller to help solve the problem so they wouldn't have to go back and forth down the hill to base camp. "Stuart Besser asked me to build something that would hide the make-up trailers up on that hill. Across the street from the house, we built a façade of barns that all the trailers were parked in so the actors could walk from their make-up trailers to the house," Miller said.

Building that barn cut the travel time for the cast and crew from 30 minutes by van to a five- or 10-minute walk. The production also added a fence and plants to the front of the house and painted the inside walls a deep red. Miller was later informed the color wasn't ideal for a horror movie filled with blood because it makes the blood harder to see.

The lighting was still an issue, though, especially since the scene took place entirely at night. "Normally, at night we'd put a condor, which is a big cherry picker kind of thing, up and put the lights on that and light everything we see because we're on level ground. Now we're not. How do I get a condor to light everything?" asked Irwin about the conundrum he was faced by the location's uneven landscape.

In the end, they found a way to hide the condor by putting it on the side of the house's garage, although it wasn't a perfect solution. Irwin notes that it is slightly visible in some shots during the film, and the complicated lighting process slowed down production. This only further exacerbated tensions that had been simmering between the director of photography and Craven.

Prior to joining the director's extended working family, Irwin worked in the genre with director David Cronenberg while living in Canada. After working on Cronenberg's classic remake of *The Fly* (1986), starring Jeff Goldblum and Geena Davis, Irwin moved to California.

Upon taking up residency in the United States, he continued to work in the genre on films including *Fright Night Part 2* (1988) and another remake, *The Blob* (1988). Among his other credits at the time were *Showdown in Little Tokyo* (1991) and *RoboCop 2* (1990). It would only be a matter of time before he and Craven would cross paths.

"Inevitably, that's what agents do, they hook up somebody's strength... supply and demand, you know? Wes was looking for a new camera man," Irwin said about how the two initially met.

Their working relationship extended from the *Nightmare Café* television pilot to Craven's film projects that followed, both *New Nightmare* and *Vampire in Brooklyn*. When the director signed on to work on *Scream*, Irwin was called in as well.

Scream was shot with an anamorphic lens, which distorts or stretches the image to recreate the original aspect ratio that you see on screen. This type of lens was created to help filmmakers to incorporate multiple different aspect ratios within a standard film frame. Prior to *Scream*, neither Craven nor Irwin had much experience with anamorphic lenses at that point.

"I think a lot of it was also Mark [Irwin] wanted to shoot anamorphic and really hadn't done a lot of it, nor had the A.C., Gary Ushino, done a lot of it. So, there were flare problems, focus problems, things like that," Mastandrea explained.

Lussier confirmed that there were ongoing concerns about the focus puller Irwin hired for the film, and those concerns were starting to come to a boil. As their title implies, a focus puller's responsibility is to maintain the camera lens's optical focus on whatever is meant to be the focal point of the shot.

"They had problems with the focus puller and those problems had been accumulating for three films," Lussier said. "The focus puller would sit when we watched dailies, and he would ride the focus the whole time, which meant it was really hard to tell when things were in focus and went out [of focus] because he kept sort of rolling focus while the dailies were being projected. To the point that used to frustrate Wes a lot and he would ask that that stop happening."

The issue came to a head during one of those viewings, although what actually happened in the screening room depends on who you talk to. Irwin says that when the lights came back up in the viewing room, Craven informed him that after speaking with Lussier everything shot up until that point had been out of focus and would need to be re-shot.

"My entire camera crew, which was sitting behind [Craven] was thinking, what I just saw was not out of focus. Everything we've seen has been in focus and you think it would take 35 days to tell us that everything from day one has been out of focus? I don't think so," recalls Irwin.

Following Craven's accusation, Irwin left the room to call Lussier back in Los Angeles, who confirmed the cinematographer's suspicions that nothing had been out of focus. After getting off the phone, Irwin returned to the screening room.

"Wes and Marianne, the producer, coming in from their side of the world, saying we just talked to the editor and he said, it's hopeless. It's all out of focus. We have to re-shoot the entire movie. I'm thinking there's either two editors, both named Patrick Lussier, one of whom has terrible vision and the other one, or somebody's not telling the truth," Irwin explained. "So, I said, 'Tell me again, you want me to fire my camera crew, my grip group, my electric group, get rid of the camera package, replace the camera package, and start shooting the whole movie again on Monday?' Yes, that's what we want you to do. I said, you sure you don't want another D.P. as well, because you fired everybody else? That was me jumping in front of the train, lying on the tracks, saying maybe you'll stop and not run me over."

While his effort to save the crew was noble, he said that Maddalena called his bluff and fired him on the spot.

Lussier explains his perspective, saying that it wasn't that the entire frame was out of focus or blurry. The issue was that the focus wasn't always zeroed in on the right aspect of the frame.

"When you have the right dramatic performance, but it buzzes— meaning it's soft for the moment you need it. You can often tell your focus is supposed to be on somebody's eye usually, and you can see the focus back in their hair around the wall or it's a head and you can see that the actor moved, and the focus puller just hasn't moved with the actor,"

Lussier said of the problem. This meant that while the individual frames may not have been blurry, there weren't as many options to choose from when assembling the footage because the focus wouldn't have kept up with what should have been the focal point.

Irwin maintains that there were no issues with the footage he filmed. Instead, he says that he was scapegoated because the film had fallen behind schedule due to the extra time required to film at the location for the finale. He said that Craven had a deal that if the movie went behind schedule, he would have to forfeit his salary. However, Konrad counters that claim, saying Irwin was dismissed due to the quality of the work that was being screened and not due to the director's salary.

"None of that's true. Honestly, Mark was a very nice guy. There were multiple issues," the producer explained. "There were issues of focus and there were issues of stuff that was presentationally causing a problem and that was the conversation. I think that it really was about that work, and it was really about several things that kept popping up in the dailies, which were question marks."

Still, Irwin maintains that his footage wasn't the problem and was used in the final product. "Everything I shot is in the movie. A hundred percent of what I shot was in the movie. Nothing was thrown away because, 'Oh my God, it's out of focus.'"

Upon returning to Los Angeles, he said that he even tried to go to the editing room to see Lussier and review the footage. When he arrived, however, he was stopped by security and told he wasn't allowed to enter. The day he was fired was the last day that Irwin and Craven spoke, though Irwin said that he tried to contact the director afterwards. "I tried every year on the day that I was fired. I would call Wes Craven Productions and call for him," Irwin said. The calls would all go the same way, he would be put on a short hold and then his call declined. "And 30 seconds [later], 'Yes, I'm sorry, he's not taking any calls today.' Just for years and years, that became the ever-expanding joke. I hadn't pegged Wes for being that kind of guy."

Despite the way that their relationship ended, Irwin still respects the filmmaker.

With Irwin no longer working on the picture, the production needed to quickly find a new director of photography. Irwin's crew stayed with the film through completion, but Peter Deming was brought in as his replacement. Deming would continue to work on the *Scream* sequels with Craven as well as *Music of the Heart*.

A Close Call

While all of the D.P. drama was unfolding, there was another close call involving one of the stunts. After the character of Kenny is killed, his body is hidden on top of the news van, only to be found when Gale gets in and attempts to drive away. Instead of using a dummy, they actually put Brown on top of the van for the sequence. "I almost went off the top of the van, on top of my head. I was up top with our stunt coordinator," Brown explained.

He was strapped to the top with only a clasp tying his ankle to the van's luggage rack. He also wasn't wearing a safety harness. The stunt driver, who was doubling for Cox, hadn't run through the stunt prior to filming, and when they called action, she hit the gas at full speed.

"When she hit the brakes, the camera fell backwards in the van and I went off the side of the van. The stunt guy grabbed me by the belt of my pants and my ankle," Brown recalled. "As I was falling, I grabbed the windshield wiper, I remember with this [right] hand because I was going off the passenger side of the van. I am hanging off the side of that fucking van staring at the ground. That was the only point; that was dangerous. Luckily, nobody got hurt, but yeah, that was a 'we survived that' moment."

Another incident that occurred while filming at the house occurred during the part in the climax when Sidney is hiding from Billy and Stu. She jumps out of a closet and stabs her boyfriend in the chest with an umbrella. During the first take, Campbell hit her mark. But in the take that is used in the film, she missed and hit Ulrich directly in the chest. The only problem is that Ulrich had open heart surgery when he was 10 years old to fix a congenital defect. Due to the surgery, he has metal wiring underneath the skin—the exact place where she made contact with the umbrella.

The pain and reaction that he expresses in the scene is genuine.

This wouldn't be the only time that Campbell would end up accidentally wounding a co-star. During the climactic battle in *Scream 3*, Sidney hides from Roman, played by actor Scott Foley, before attacking him from behind with an ice pick. Foley bellows in pain as he falls to the ground. It wasn't simply good acting, Campbell had actually missed the pad that she was supposed to hit with the prop and had actually stabbed his back. Like Ulrich, the reaction that you see in the film is him actually in pain.

Along with taking a photo in front of the house when filming wrapped, t-shirts were made for the cast and crew saying that they had survived scene 114. Metaphorically, Mastandrea might have been onto something with his cheeky name for the scene. Fortunately, the film wrapped production without any further incidents.

A FATE WORSE THAN DEATH:

AN NC-17 RATING

WITH PRODUCTION WRAPPED and the school board controversy behind them, the filmmakers were almost at the finish line. However, crossing home plate had its own hurdles, the biggest of which was a dreaded NC-17 rating on the original edit of *Scream* by the MPAA. This was often considered the kiss of death to mainstream movies because its restrictive rating prevents anyone under 17 years old from seeing the film in movie theaters, even with a parent. In fact, the year prior, the movie *Showgirls* (1995) was released with an NC-17 rating, creating an uproar and dismal revenue despite the controversy.

EDITING FOR AN R-RATING

"They don't give you really specific notes on where to cut eight frames from the shot, and we'll give you an R-rating, because they don't want to be seen as censors," explains Lussier. "So, you're going through and you're like wow, they say look at these areas. I guess they're talking about this."

The opening scene received the largest number of trims to address the NC-17 rating. Showing Steve's internal organs literally fall out of his body while he was duct taped to the patio furniture and Casey's dead body hanging from the tree at the end of the sequence were two shots that needed to be altered. For Steve's organs, they shortened the shot by a few frames. To rectify the issue with Casey's body, the filmmakers sped up the zoom in towards her by taking out frames from the shot. The original versions of those shots have been restored in subsequent director's cut releases of the film.

It wasn't just the MPAA who had a problem with the prop of Casey's body hanging from the tree. Some on set said that it was so realistic and horrifying that crew members would turn away from it whenever they had to pass it by.

The MPAA also had a problem with Kenny's death towards the end of the film, but the fix was a little less clear. His throat is slit by Ghostface while trying to help Sidney escape the masked killer.

"Wes told me this is too upsetting. The look on his face, because I am looking at my killer as if I can't believe; like I don't know what is happening and then I realize," Brown explained. "Wes said, I told them it's a murder, it's supposed to be upsetting. It's this human being whose life has been taken."

Kenny's death is pivotal within the context of the film because his dying act is to protect Sidney and help her escape even after his throat is slit. It's part of why his face is so distressing in the frames that the MPAA felt needed to be removed.

"His first thought in death was to save her because I cover my throat, I turn my back to him [Ghostface] to keep him away from her, and I'm telling her to get out the back," says Brown, the cameraman's portrayer. "Instead of the morbidity of his own situation or himself, he thinks of her."

To rectify the situation, they again had to cut frames from the scene in an attempt to make it less upsetting. Another trim initially requested by the MPAA was to one of the film's most iconic lines. At the end when Billy and Stu are stabbing each other, Billy tells Sidney that, "movies don't create psychos, movies make psychos more creative." That idea apparently didn't sit well with the ratings board.

"They felt that was probably too true an observation, that they just didn't want that concept out there, especially at the time, you know? There was all the talk of these movies are creating violence or causing kids to do this, that, and the other thing," suggests Lussier. "As opposed to these are a reflection as opposed to a cause."

Dealing with the ratings board has long been a source of confusion and frustration for filmmakers because the rules can seem arbitrary based on how the film is presented. In fact, Weinstein had to intervene to convey the intent of the film as satire versus an outright horror film.

"We only had to explain it to the MPAA. We really did get them on this is a comedy, this is a spoof. A little bit of cutting here and there and I think it worked," confirmed Maddalena about securing their rating.

"The argument we would often use after *Lord of the Rings* came out is, it's like dude, they have their catapulting heads over a wall, and you gave it a PG-13, come on!" Lussier said. "They'd be like, that's fantasy violence. It's just like, they're still severed heads, pal."

In all, *Scream* had to be submitted to the MPAA nine times before they were given approval to release it as a regular R-rated film at the end of the year. To avoid having a similar battle with the MPAA during the making of *Scream 2*, Craven and Lussier submitted a cut that had much more violence and gore than they intended to include for the actual theatrical release. They figured if they included more footage at the start, once they made the revisions to get the required R-rating, they would have the version they initially wanted.

"Wes had shot all this extra material for Randy's death and some of the other deaths. I went through and showed Wes a cut of the movie that was far more extreme, far gorier, so much extra blood. Omar Epps got stabbed in the ear four times," explained Lussier. "We sent that to them, and they gave it an [R-rating]. So, that makes no sense." The filmmakers proceeded to use the version they intended to release without the additional violence and gore.

Beltrami notes that in the original film, the music used during the chase scene through Stu's house between Sidney and Ghostface was called "NC-17," as a nod to the ratings debate. He adds, "I think the work was recorded well and I think that's probably one of my favorite sequences. I feel like that was mixed really well in the movie and it has a lot of punch to it."

A PUZZLING RELEASE DATE

Despite how much everyone enjoyed their time working on *Scream*, a common theme among those involved was a fear that no one would ever see the movie. In fact, throughout the film's production, another project was considered to be the big blockbuster that year. *Sphere* (1998) was a sci-fi film based on the book by Michael Crichton about a giant, mysterious orb discovered at the bottom of the ocean. However, that film hit several production hiccups and was shut down, delaying its release for another two years. During that time *Scream* alum Schreiber joined the cast. When it was eventually released, it bombed at the box office.

"I think we were all cautiously optimistic," Kennedy explained about the chances of *Scream* finding an audience. "I was reading a lot about VHS and oncoming DVD, and I thought, well, if we become a cult hit; the word cult was thrown around a lot. Cult, so if we can become this cool cult [hit], Hollywood will think we're cool."

Even Williamson began to second guess whether the movie worked while it was being previewed prior to release. "I remember Kevin saying, 'you know, the mystery works, but I'm not sure it's very scary.' But he knew every beat, right? He knew every turn. He knew everything," recalled Lussier. "When we previewed it in New Jersey in front of 400 people and two minutes in the killer says, 'I want to know who I'm looking at,' and 400 people [gasp], I think this might work. Then you realize it continues to work and continues to get better and better."

"I started thinking nothing like this had been out for a while. The kids didn't have their version of some of those movies [from the 70s] that we had, and I think that's just how it clicked. It was a unique take on it. Again, while we were making it, it was like let's just work hard and do it and have fun and see what happens," Mastandrea adds.

While most horror movies that come out at the end of the year might aim to take advantage of the Halloween season when people are seeking out scary fare, that was not the case here. Instead, the film was slated for release just before Christmas on December 20, 1996.

"Bob, for as big of an ass as he was towards Wes, still knew what he was doing. I mean, to release at Christmas—are you serious? You are releasing a horror movie at Christmas?" recalled Brown about his reaction to hearing about the release date.

Jackson, however, was not completely surprised by the release date. He was familiar with a tradition in Britain that gave credence to the seemingly risky release date. "In Britain there's a tradition of ghost stories at Christmas. So, every year on TV, they have ghost stories. For a long time, they tended to be M.R. James stories, but ghost stories at Christmas is a tradition," said the voice behind Ghostface.

Also opening that same weekend were two movies that had a little bit more brand recognition behind them. *Beavis and Butthead Do America* (1996), starring the popular MTV cartoon characters making their jump to the big screen, and *One Fine Day* (1996), a romantic comedy starring George Clooney and Michelle Pfeiffer, were pitted against the horror movie for their share of the pre-Christmas revenue. While *One Fine Day* (1996) was skewing towards a different audience, traditional wisdom indicated that *Beavis and Butthead Do America* was playing for the same audience as *Scream*.

"It was almost Christmas Eve, so there weren't a lot people going to the movies anyway," Maddalena explains about their apprehension towards the release date. "We thought *Beavis and Butthead* was really going to kill us."

Konrad puts it even more succinctly, "Nobody was banking on this. No one saw this coming."

It didn't ease their minds that some of the industry trade reports were calling *Scream* D.O.A. at the box office on opening day. Even a fortune teller hired by the studio for the film's post-premiere party predicted the film would quickly fade from theaters.

"The last line she said, that was the last in the [*Los Angeles Times* article of the film premiere and party] said this movie will go poof at the box office. I predict this movie will go poof at the box office," McGowan recalled. With a laugh, she adds, "And I'm like a-ha! How do you like me now, fortune teller?"

THE AUDIENCE REACTS

Those fears seemed to be confirmed when the filmmakers went to a movie theater that night to check out audience reactions to the three films. Craven and Maddalena went from room to room. She said that in the *Beavis and Butthead* theater, the audience was engaged with the film, laughing and throwing things at the screen. When they left and walked into the *Scream* theater, it was—no pun intended—dead silent.

Dejected, they went their separate ways to celebrate the holiday. "Wes and I just said, okay, we didn't nail it. I went up to Carmel and Wes went off to Hawaii, feeling so sad and we had a flop," explains Maddalena. Then a funny thing happened. "Bob Weinstein called us and said congratulations. We were like, why? I guess the exit polls were amazing."

Those exit polls led to word of mouth about the film, and when the weekend numbers were released, it beat out *One Fine Day* by more than $125,000 despite playing in 500 fewer theaters. In that first weekend, it grossed $6,354,586.00.

"I remember the initial excitement around [*Scream* being released]. I remember going to see it and thinking it was amazing, then going to see it, I think, three more times in the theater," recalls Amie Simon, of ILoveSplatter.com, a website written by women for women who love horror movies. "It's also, I think, one of those movies that's an experience when you see it, especially on opening night. But even at other screenings. It's just like people don't know what's going to happen; they're surprised. They're like yelling at the screen."

Konrad had gone to Colorado for the holidays with a friend, who was an executive at Fox, the company that produced *One Fine Day*. She got the news about how the film was performing while at the airport. "I was at the airport in Montrose and I was at a payphone getting word that the weekday numbers, the good news about the weekday numbers, which is where the word of mouth began. After the weekend, despite not opening at the top, we did something that others were not, which was growing as the days progress and I was so excited and enthusiastic. I was like, 'Oh my God, my movie's doing really well,' and this man looked around the corner at me and he's like, 'What movie's that?' I said, 'It's called *Scream*,' and I looked at him. I'm like, Oh my God, you're Normal Schwarzkopf. It was Stormin' Norman on the other side of my payphone. He was very excited for me."

The following two weekends, an even more unexpected thing happened. Its box office revenue grew. The second weekend grossed over $9 million. And the third weekend, it made over $10 million and was the third highest grossing film. To achieve any of those feats is highly unusual in Hollywood. Most films see their highest box office receipts during opening weekend and then decline; some will decline more slowly and thus stay in theaters longer, but rarely do films actually increase their performance in subsequent weekends. It had officially become a word-of-mouth success.

"Seeing it with audiences after the movie opens and it gains more momentum, not less. Even though it opens not so well opposite *One Fine Day* and *Beavis and Butthead*, I think *Scream* is the movie that people will remember as opposed to those two," Lussier says.

Adds Konrad, "To know that it was just growing because people really enjoyed it and talking about the postmodern components of it and how fresh and unique it was, it was really exciting."

"*Scream* really revitalized the slasher genre and did it quite well because it was kind of dead before Wes Craven and Kevin Williamson picked it up," said O'Dell, who was covering film and the entertainment industry at *Access Hollywood* at the time. "I think Wes's and Kevin's brilliance and using the humor and the wit involved with it...worked for such a big audience because it wasn't so scary. There was that kind of humor and wit in it that made it okay for you not to be too terrified."

Weinstein's idea to counterprogram all of the holiday cheer with a little bit of blood and gore paid off. While nearly everyone thought it was a risky move, Maddalena is willing to give credit where credit is due.

"That was all Bob Weinstein and we thought he was crazy. I mean, we thought he was nuts. I got to say, Bob, you did it," Maddalena said. "That was his brilliant marketing move. That was all Bob."

"Bob Weinstein did something kind of atypical, which is he took a movie like this in this genre and decided it was a Christmas release. For patterns that people usually program their release and distribution, that was a crazy move, in our opinion, and we certainly weren't shy in trying to express our fear about having a release at that time," Konrad explained. "But he was bullish about it, and obviously he was right for a lot of reasons. But again, I think it was a paver for that counter programming idea that if you have something that's a little bit different than what everybody else has, maybe there's enough of the holiday fluff and fair. You know, why burn it on Halloween, or one of those typical windows."

The surprise success also led to a windfall for the producers.

"We all had these deals where we got box office bumps at $40, $50, $60, $70, $80, and $90 million. We never thought we would get there. Then all of a sudden it went $40, then $50, then $60. It capped out at $100," Maddalena explained about the deal they had with Dimension. "So, we made a lot of money after the fact."

With all of those profits, it also meant that a sequel would be inevitable.

SECTION 2

SEQUELS SUCK!... BY DEFINITION ALONE, SEQUELS ARE INFERIOR FILMS!

Actresses Elise Neal, Portia de Rossi, Rebecca Gayheart, Sarah Michelle Gellar
and actor Jamie Kennedy enjoy a night out while filming *Scream 2*.
(Photo courtesy of Jamie Kennedy)

BUILDING
A FRANCHISE

SCREAM WAS SLICING and dicing its way through the box office competition, thanks in part to the successful word-of-mouth from fans, for the first half of 1997. The film remained in theaters until almost Memorial Day, an unprecedented six-month run. The success also meant that planning for a sequel couldn't be far off. As Stu tells Sidney at the end of the first movie, "These days, you gotta have a sequel."

In addition to raking in the money, the film touched a nerve in the general consciousness. In June 1997 at the MTV Movie Awards, *Scream* was awarded the coveted Golden Popcorn statue for Best Movie, beating out *The Rock* (1996), *Independence Day* (1996), *Romeo + Juliet* and *Jerry Maguire* (1996). Campbell was also nominated for Best Female Performance, though she lost to Claire Danes. Campbell, Craven, and most of the cast members were on hand at the award show to accept the award.

Perhaps more prestigious than winning the award, the film was included as one of the award show's famous parodies. The skit used clips from Barrymore's opening and infused new dialogue from the caller. At the end, it was revealed to be *Saturday Night Live* cast member, Mike Myers, terrorizing the actress. Speaking of the classic late-night show, Campbell was invited to host in February 1997.

Going all in on the film, MTV held a contest that would give one lucky viewer the chance to win a walk-on role in *Scream 2*. The winner was Paulette Patterson, who played the role of the theater usher who hands

Jada Pinkett Smith and Epps the Ghostface costumes at the beginning of the film.

With the success of *Scream*, every studio in town was looking to release their own horror film. Many followed a similar formula in an attempt to cash in on the bloodlust that had begun. From Williamson-penned films like *I Know What You Did Last Summer* (1997), to *Urban Legend* (1998), to attempts to re-invent dormant franchises with *Bride of Chucky* (1998) and *The Rage: Carrie 2* (1999), there were suddenly a lot more screams happening at multiplexes.

Further cementing the cultural impact of *Scream* was the fact that just a few years later a spoof was made, heavily relying on the *Scream* series for its plot. It even recycled a familiar title: *Scary Movie* (2000). Upon its release, *Scary Movie* grossed over $157 million at the domestic box office and spawned another successful franchise for Dimension with four additional sequels.

In just a few short months, the cast and crew went from wondering if anyone was ever going to see the film to watching it become a cultural touchstone. There might be no direct correlation, but it is coincidental that the use of caller ID in the United States tripled in 1997 versus the previous year.

GETTING THE BAND BACK TOGETHER

The hardest part in making a sequel is often coming up with a worthy story to further the franchise. Fortunately, when Williamson sold the original script, he also provided an outline for the sequel. Development on that idea was quickly set into motion.

"When I first sat down with Kevin, in his mind there was a trilogy here, and even though he didn't elaborate fully on what each thing was, in his mind there were legs to this idea that extended beyond just a one-off," Konrad recalled. "I think that it was very quickly, within a month or two the conversations were ramping up about the enthusiasm and the excitement about that and how to capitalize on that and to do something slightly different, which is to not wait. Again, to puncture kind of the old ways of thinking about how long you have to wait to do something after one. What if you just plan the other one right away?"

However, with so much hype and excitement around the follow-up, the pressure was on to create a film that lived up to its predecessor.

"We also were very much like, oh boy, let's make sure we don't drop the pooch here," Kennedy said, adding that despite the expectations of wanting to live up to the success of *Scream*, he felt more comfortable the second time around.

Development for the sequel began early in 1997, targeting a release at the end of the year. Since the film was fast-tracked, a few of the original collaborators were already committed to other projects, meaning Craven couldn't quite get the entire band back together. Bruce Alan Miller was in Chicago working on *U.S. Marshalls* (1998), the follow-up to *The Fugitive* (1993), when he received a call from Maddalena in January about the impending sequel. Producer Stuart Besser was also prepping another project and couldn't join. However, both would return for *Scream 3*.

"I was working. We were doing a big movie; it had a lot of effects. I hadn't heard a thing [about *Scream's* success], and I couldn't leave my designer that had hired me," Miller explained. "That's why someone else did *Scream 2*. They did a beautiful job too. I loved *Scream 2* actually."

One person that wasn't asked back for the sequel was producer Cary Woods, whose production company Konrad had been working at during the development of the original film. The relationship between Woods and Bob had soured during the making and release of the first film, which then left Konrad in the middle.

"That is really between Cary and kind of his relationship with Miramax. I mean, I think Cary had a different idea of what he wanted out of Harvey and I think Harvey had a different idea of what he wanted out Cary. I think at the end of the day, what those two wanted really had nothing to do with why one makes movies, to be frank, or why one has a production company," Konrad said. "All these things were gestating at the time, and for me, because I was the one [with] boots on the ground, developing all this stuff, for me, as a producer, I wanted to see those through. I was given an opportunity to do so, and whether that served Harvey's purpose, then it served Harvey's purpose. But really, I wasn't out to satisfy either of those people's agenda. I was out to just get the best deal for myself and make the most out of a pretty tricky situation between two guys that were kind of having a clash of the titans, so to speak. I tried to stay on the side."

She adds, "When I realized that I was in the middle of something that I really didn't want to be in the middle of, to be honest with you, I just want to make movies—and, of course, I'd like to be recognized for the work. I was realizing that, in the midst of this, I was really being discarded and marginalized in a way that you; as we in this Time's Up, MeToo world, like there was a different time back then. It's like when do you advocate for yourself? So, when it was presented to me by the legal team at Miramax if I had intentions of going with Cary on whatever adventures he was going on—to which I really wasn't privy to, nor to be spoken to because it was really all about him—I was like I have no plans. Make me an offer."

Konrad signed a new production deal with Miramax and has continued with the franchise since.

The actors had also moved on to new projects. Campbell and Cox were in the midst of filming their television shows when *Scream* was released and exploded onto the cultural landscape. Kennedy and Ulrich re-teamed with roles in the James L. Brooks film, *As Good As It Gets* (1997). Williamson had written *I Know What You Did Last Summer* and was beginning work on the pilot for his show *Dawson's Creek* (1998). Interestingly, Kennedy had auditioned for a role in Williamson's horror follow-up but lost out on the role of Max to actor Johnny Galecki.

Kennedy was on vacation in Mexico with his girlfriend when he got the call about the sequel being greenlit and the possibility of coming back to reprise the role of Randy. "I was in Tulum in late February and then they're like, 'Yeah, they're probably going to commission a sequel,'" Kennedy recalled. "Then I ended up getting in [the film] and I kind of was going right back to *Scream*."

It was important for Craven and Maddalena to surround themselves with people that they trusted and liked. They were loyal to their collaborators and vice versa, which is why so many of the filmmakers kept reuniting film after film.

"Our philosophy was that we spend so much time at work, because we loved it, that we wanted to be around people we liked, and we wanted to have a really good time. That was kind of our company philosophy and everyone talks about how our movie sets are so easygoing. We'd have dinners, parties, you know we had the coffee truck, the ice cream truck," Maddalena said. "Wes never yelled; you hear all these stories about directors who scream and yell. Wes treated everyone the same. It didn't matter if you were President Clinton or the janitor. We just tried to have a really calm set."

Mastandrea, who had already worked on a handful of projects with Craven before *Scream 2*, adds that, "Timing always worked out that I was always around when he was doing his movies. That was the case with a lot of us quite honestly. I mean, there was a whole group of people. It just worked out that we all were available. We all stuck together, and it was a great time; it was a great run."

Back then, Miramax was known for signing their talent to holding deals for multiple projects. When he negotiated his return for *Scream 2*, Craven signed a three-picture deal, and many of the *Scream* franchise's actors signed similar deals. Craven's deal, however, allowed him to choose a non-horror film of his choice to direct for the company. The project he chose for his next film was *Music of the Heart*, starring Meryl Streep and reteaming him with Bassett. It would be his first non-genre film. All he had to do was direct the *Scream* sequel first.

Williamson wasn't left out of the windfall, either. Miramax signed the writer to a $20 million exclusive deal.

QUICKLY WRITING A SCRIPT

As pre-production began there was just one key element missing. Williamson had created the outline, but the script wasn't finished. Maddalena and Plec paid Williamson a visit in North Carolina, where he was filming *Dawson's Creek*.

"Julie Plec and I flew down to North Carolina to see what he was up to because the script was late," Maddalena said. "He and Julie got along so well, she stayed behind to help finish the script."

Plec and Williamson had initially become friendly during the filming of the first film. She said they "were the ones with the least amount of work to do" on set, allowing them time to get to know each other. "We had a really good time. We've famously said we'd sit in his car with the heat on, smoking cigarettes, and talking about the stories that he was going to tell," Plec remembered. "After that movie wrapped, he started calling me every now and then and saying, 'Oh I've got the script, do you mind taking a look at it and giving it a read for me?'"

In fact, the pair got along so well that they eventually formed a partnership and worked together on the television drama *Wasteland* (1999) before launching *The Vampire Diaries* (2010) universe.

While in North Carolina, they worked together to talk through the story for *Scream 2* with Williamson using Plec as a sounding board. "He and I were just a unit where we would talk about the story, we would talk about the scenes. We would work them out, you know, speak them out loud and then I was more of like a bouncing ball or a soundboard and support system," Plec said about the collaboration. "I might be the one typing and we're talking about it. I'm putting words on the page, but by no means would I point to any of that script and say, that was me."

Part of the concern about getting the script out of Williamson was that in order to strike while the iron was hot, they had to film over the summer of 1997. Campbell and Cox's television schedules meant that the film needed to shoot while they were on hiatus. Any delays would lead to them racing the clock to finish before they were due back to their respective shows.

Scream 2 fast-forwards two years after the Woodsboro massacre. The action takes place at Windsor College, where Sidney and Randy are now attending, instead of Woodsboro. Everything is going swimmingly for the survivors until someone decides to make a real-life sequel, coincidentally timed around the release of *Stab*, a movie-in-a-movie based on Gale Weathers' best-selling book about the events from the first film.

Adding the meta *Stab* film was always part of Williamson's plan from when he wrote the initial outline included with the original script.

"When Kevin sold the first script to *Scary Movie*, he already knew that the second movie would begin with a movie-within-a-movie big set piece," Plec recalled, though she added that the name of the fake movie might not have been created at that point.

Every good sequel needs to provide new depth to the existing characters and expand the world they live in. One way Williamson achieved this was by establishing Courteney Cox's Gale Weathers as the secondary lead to Campbell's Sidney Prescott. In expanding Gale's role, Williamson softened some of the reporter's edges while retaining her sharp tongue and quick wit.

"I think because [Gale's] a powerful character from the first movie, they wisely increased that for the franchise," Ziembicki said.

The filmmakers also decided to explore the characters further through the score. In the first film, Beltrami had created Sidney's theme; the sequel gave him an opportunity to create one for Arquette's Deputy Dewey Riley.

"There was a chance to explore the character of Dewey and come up with a theme for him. I viewed him as a sort of Western sheriff lone guy and that's something that I was able to carry on in his theme throughout third movie as well," the composer explained.

Schreiber also saw his role as Cotton Weary grow exponentially in the sequel. Cotton was an important character in the first film, but he was referenced more than seen. Now he was being brought into the mix as a fully realized supporting character. While filming his brief part in the first film, the actor was clued into the plans that Williamson had for him in the then hypothetical sequel.

"I met Kevin, who is hilariously funny, who was writing it and he had told me that he had more plans for my character, which I was thrilled about," Schreiber recalled. "He had all sorts of crazy plans; that was what was so great about Kevin. His mind would just build layers, and layer on layers of arcs and narratives."

Although Schreiber shouldn't have been surprised by his eventual return and expanded role, Cotton's portrayer was grateful for the amount of material that both he and the character were given, especially with the expanded cast.

"I felt they were very generous in what they gave Cotton and I. There was a huge company to spread the love around to and they did a really masterful job, I think particularly in the second one, just spreading it around," Schreiber said. "Kevin, Marianne, and Wes, all of them, they loved Cotton. They were fully 100% Cotton. They loved Cotton. I never felt like I got short shrift at all."

Schreiber admits that he knew that one of the bigger aspects of his role in *Scream 2* was to act as a red herring in the mystery. Cotton certainly makes a viable suspect, considering his history with Sidney and his yearning to get his 15 minutes of fame.

"That's the thing about the genre; the character, in a funny way, is not really as important as the role they play in the film, in the genre—at least that was my experience of it. So, the reality of who I was, which was an innocent man, had to take second position to a kind of potentially crazy characterization that could feel threatening and dangerous. You want the audience to play that really fun suspenseful game of which one is it," Schreiber said. Even after the killers are revealed, and Cotton isn't one of them, viewers still aren't sure what side he is playing. It was an added layer for the actor. "That was the fun of the writing and the fun of acting it, walking that tight rope."

One of the scenes in the film that helps to skyrocket Cotton to the top of the suspect board is the library scene where Sidney gets a message sent by the killer that is coming. From. Inside. The. Library. Detectives Andrews and Richards swiftly rush Sidney to safely— by putting her next to an open doorway—while they search for the mysterious messenger. Cotton approaches Sidney to propose doing a joint interview with Diane Sawyer but he doesn't take it well when she declines his offer.

The scene has also long been rumored to feature a cameo by returning cast member Rose McGowan in the background, similar to Matthew Lillard's at the mixer. The actress confirms that she is not in the scene, saying that she had already begun to be blacklisted by Harvey Weinstein by that point. However, Craven used to tease actor Phil Pavel about his acting in the scene.

"Wes used to joke with me because, of course, I was excited. It's my first part. When Liev Schreiber's character, Cotton, confronts her in the library and I'm supposed to escort him out, I really milk it. If you watch it closely, I make a scene that should take two seconds last like six, 'cause I'm looking around and I'm like bringing it," Pavel said. "Definitely the young actor in me was trying to milk the scenes for everything I possibly could. But at the same time, I was there as a supporting role, really to be in the background."

In addition to the film continuing to explain and then break the rules of horror movies, Williamson expanded his scope to poke fun of another trend that was popular at that time. Midway through the film, Derek, Sidney's boyfriend played by Jerry O'Connell, declares his love through song.

"It could have been Wes making fun of, at that time, every rom-com had that scene where someone sang to a vintage song," explained Pavel. "That was another Hollywood trope that was being trotted out in a way that Jamie's character would have made fun of."

Lussier said that while the scene wasn't hard to edit together, there is a downside to having those types of scenes in a movie. "The *I Think I Love You* thing, it was just sort of annoying, right? The song, I find anytime I cut songs and things like that, is the music gets in your head and you dream it. You're hearing it all day and it just stays fixed in your skull," the editor explained. "Wes had covered it really well. There's a lot of different cutting angles to us and different cutaways, so you can always manage to make things in sync there. It wasn't a big challenge to do and then often when we were at the cutting process, once we had that version of what we liked, we would skip it."

Another iconic song almost appeared in the film but was cut due to a rights issue. *Bittersweet Symphony* by British band The Verve was supposed to play over the closing shot of the film. However, according to Plec, due to the issues with the song sampling The Rolling Stones' *The*

Last Time it became too expensive to use the song. Instead, Collective Soul jumped in with the song *She Said* serving as the closing song.

BIGGER BUDGET, LESS ISSUES

With the returning cast and crew in place, Craven and his team had to fill out the rest of the behind-the-scenes crew to replace those who weren't able to return. That included finding a new production designer to step in for Miller. Although he wasn't yet fully familiar with the original film, Bob Ziembicki was one of the candidates interviewed for the position.

"Not really sensing what the zeitgeist is, it's like at the time why does this work? Why did it capture a movie audience's imagination when it did?" Ziembicki said about the research he did prior to the interview. "I was aware of it because I prepared for the interview. So, I was familiar with it, at least familiar with the principles."

Another designer was initially selected for the job, but creative differences led to a parting of the ways and the team circled back to Ziembicki. Once hired, Craven and Maddalena let him know that he had actually been their first choice.

Since this was the second film in the series and the production designer that they originally hired had already gotten the ball rolling, some of Ziembicki's work was already done.

"They've gone through it from the first *Scream*, so I was kind of real impressed," Ziembicki said about the process that was already in place. "They were already a well-oiled machine from the first show. I just had to step in and keep that continuity and don't ruin a good thing because they knew exactly what they wanted."

Based on the success of the first film—it made more than seven times its budget during its box office run—the filmmakers were given a larger budget for *Scream 2*. In fact, the promotional budget alone for the sequel was larger than the original film's entire production budget.

"The first movie had been released already, was a big hit. I think Dimension kind of let us alone. Ironically, I had more money in my budget than I would have guessed for that kind of movie, but they didn't really care," Ziembicki said. "It's like the first one was a hit and now we can kind of lavish a little more on it. So, that was rare."

"On the first one, I think, I had maybe 30 or 40 players tops, and then not even for that many sessions. By the third movie, I mean, we were having huge orchestras, like 90 musicians, choir, and singers, and all kinds of stuff," Beltrami explained about how the budget grew through the series. "They almost outgrew themselves; you know. By the end, I was sort of missing the intimacy of the first one. But I think that was just the nature of projects. Everything was bigger."

Having proven themselves with the first film, along with receiving the increased budget, the filmmakers were also given more autonomy while making the sequel. "The second one, it was pretty much our movie at that point. The first one had been such a hit, Bob kind of trusted us," noted Maddalena.

There would still be a few unforeseen hiccups as the production found its legs. But once the filmmakers got past the initial hurdles, the production ran smoothly, allowing the film to be released in theaters less than a year after the first film debuted.

"They didn't start shooting it until I guess June, end of May, beginning of June, something like that. We were in theaters in December, so it sped along. I think our director's cut on that was 11 days. I think on *Scream* one we spent three to five weeks before we showed them," Lussier recalled.

BUT I WANT
TO BE IN THE
SEQUEL

DUE TO THE SIZE of his role in the first film, Schreiber didn't bother telling people that he was in the original *Scream*. However, he soon found out that it was hard to escape the movie after it became a phenomenon.

"I didn't really pay attention to it because I had such a small part," Schreiber said. "Suddenly, it was everywhere. I am reading about it everywhere. It's this huge movie. I was almost embarrassed to tell people I was in it, because if you blink you miss me."

He wouldn't have that problem with the sequel, though. Not only was Schreiber's role expanded, but he plays a pivotal role in the sequel's finale, and he lives to be in the third film.

All the surviving main cast members agreed to return for the film: Arquette, Campbell, Cox, and Kennedy joined Schreiber along with a new cast of potential victims. Eagle-eyed viewers can also find a returning cast member who didn't survive the first film's blood bath. Matthew Lillard, who played Stu Macher, visited the set while the sorority party scene was being filmed and he can be glimpsed in the background behind Murphy, the sorority sister played by Portia de Rossi.

Beach and Katzman were again hired to cast the film. Things were even easier the second time around because everyone in Hollywood was dying for a part in the film. Beach described their work on the sequel as being the most fun of the three films in the series that they worked on because they didn't have anything to prove. The world was their oyster in terms of casting.

"The first film, we didn't know where it was going to go. The second film was more of, we had a hot property that people want to come in on," explained Katzman. "It was a different vibe. It was a different feel."

The script delays weren't a factor when it came to casting because as Beach notes, actors were so eager to be in the film they would take any role. She said, "Everyone wanted to be in it, so they didn't really care what it was. They knew it would be that kind of quality."

While the initial casting process itself wasn't affected by the delayed delivery of the script, Beach and Katzman did stay with the film longer than their usual casting sessions just in case. "*Scream 2,* I also think that took a while. We had overages. It wasn't just a 10 week, I think it was a longer process," Katzman explained. "It just took a little bit longer."

CREATING A MORE DIVERSE WORLD

Since Barrymore created such a splash in the first film, the filmmakers looked for another recognizable actress to meet her end in the opening minutes of *Scream 2*. She would come in the form of Pinkett Smith. Omar Epps joined her in the beginning sequence as the boyfriend who drags her to the premiere of *Stab*. Similar to the first film, the actors were cast without having to audition. This became a custom that would continue with *Scream 4*; Liev Schreiber obviously didn't audition for *Scream 3* as he was already established within the series.

In the opening, Pinkett Smith and Epps offer a blistering critique about the depiction of race within the horror genre, specifically how black characters don't tend to survive long. This theme is carried throughout the remainder of the film. With that social commentary already baked into the script, it made sense to diversify the cast from the all-white actors in the first film. This meant using color blind casting for characters that didn't have an explicit ethnicity written into the script, such as Joel and Hallie.

"They wanted Jada to open it up, so that's what made us realize let's really diversify the cast and go for it, and it totally worked and felt totally organic," Beach recalled. "Also, it opens it up to a whole new audience. I think we realized that audience was so broad. It wasn't just white women over 45 going to see *Scream,* which I know wasn't the demographic anyway. It just opened it up."

It's something that actress Elise Neal, who portrayed Hallie in the film, applauded in a 2020 interview with the website *Too Fab*. "At the end of the day, representation is important. But I think one of the biggest lessons about equality is you could be blue, black, white, whatever and if you're right for the role, it should be yours. If you're right for a job, it should be yours. If you're right for anything in the world in terms of equality, it should be yours for the getting."

Production designer Ziembicki notes that the diversity extended beyond the primary actors. "One of the things that was striking is just how contemporary it looks. If you look at even background extras too, there's women, there's black people, all of that stuff. It was shooting in the later 90s; that was kind of novel in the time, for one thing."

With every actor beating down their doors, the casting directors remember some of the good times they had during casting sessions. "[It] is so much fun when you are casting. It's a blast. Totally love our jobs," Beach proclaimed. Beach specifically recalled when she, actress Paget Brewster, Orlando Jones, and Katzman had a McDonald's party in the office. Interestingly, Beach knew Brewster in boarding school; Brewster's parents were teachers at the school and were her "dorm mother and father" when Paget was a toddler.

Sometimes casting a film can feel a little bit like playing the classic video game Tetris, making sure you have the right pieces so they fit together into a cohesive unit. That often means shuffling around actors who auditioned for one role into another character that might be a better fit.

"Sarah and I are often the ones to say, within an age range, or within an ethnic range or what, you can always say, if this isn't right for this, what about trying that. Sarah is usually really good at saying, you know what, maybe you'd be better for this if they tried it that way," Beach said.

Katzman noted an example from *Scream 2*, "That's a case where both Portia and Rebecca [Gayheart] audition for other roles, but Wes really liked them, and they were, like, hey, would you do the sorority sisters?"

A Brush with a Real-Life Serial Killer

As with the first film, some of the parts were cast through connections the actors had with Craven. That was the case with Pavel, who attended Northwestern University with Craven's son, Jonathan. The two worked on the university's popular Mee-Ow comedy show, which previously starred actors such as Julia Louis-Dreyfuss, Dermot Mulroney, Stephen Colbert, and Seth Meyers during their collegiate years. Pavel was a performer in the show while Jonathan was a producer.

After graduating, Pavel moved to Los Angeles and the two teamed up again for a comedy improv show, this time with Jonathan directing. Craven and Maddalena attended the show to support Jonathan, enjoying what they saw. Pavel recalled, "When I moved to LA, anyone who was vaguely related to show business were super intimidating. So, the idea that Wes Craven came to our little crappy improv show was a really big deal and I was flattered that he thought I was funny. He brought me in for an audition for *New Nightmare* and I was so nervous."

He didn't get the part; however, Lou Thornton, another actress from the show, was cast as an ICU nurse in the film. A few years later, Pavel wrote Craven a letter asking the director to keep him in mind for future projects. Craven brought him in to try out for the role of Sidney's theater director in *Scream 2*. When he received word about the audition, Pavel hadn't yet seen the first film. He made plans to see it prior to the audition and ended up having a brush with a real-life horror story the day he intended to see it.

"I was like, okay, I'm going to finish my shift at work and I'm going to go see this movie *Scream* by myself. While I was at work, my boss, the general manager at the Chateau [Marmont], called me into her office and she said, 'Look, I want you to know that the FBI has been here today and there is a serial killer on the loose. His name is Andrew Cunanan, and he just checked out of the Chateau, but he's been on property. He targets gay men, so you need to be really careful," Pavel recalls about the man who would become infamous for killing fashion designer Gianni Versace. "I'm easily excitable because I'm in my twenties. So, I'm suddenly told that there is a serial killer that targets gay men and now unbeknownst to me, I'm going to see *Scream* by myself in a movie theater. In the opening scene, where Drew Barrymore gets the knife through the chest, I freak the fuck out."

When he relayed the traumatizing experience to the director, Craven found it amusing. Pavel thinks that little anecdote might have helped him get cast as Detective Andrews, one of the police officers assigned to protect Sidney once the murders happen again, instead of the much smaller role that he had originally been brought in to read for.

CHANGING THE PERCEPTION OF TELEVISION ACTORS

The *Scream* series helped change the Hollywood bias towards television actors transitioning to the movies. Unlike today, when the first two films were made in the late 90's, there was a clear delineation between television and film actors. However, with box office grosses of over $100 million and lead actresses best known for their television roles, *Scream* inspired other television actors to spread their wings into a more lucrative big screen career. *Scream 2* continued this trend, adding Sarah Michelle Gellar, known for her role on *Buffy the Vampire Slayer* (1997); Jerry O'Connell, who had been a child actor and was starring on the show *Sliders* (1995); and Laurie Metcalf, the Emmy-winning actress from the sitcom *Roseanne* (1988).

"There used to be a time when I first came out here where there was a big pecking order in terms of a huge gap between whether you were a television star or a [film] star," Pavel said. "Occasionally in pop culture, you would see a television actor who was able to break out, but it was always, there are the film actors and there are the television actors. Then suddenly in popular culture to have Neve Campbell and Courteney Cox who are mainly seen as TV stars suddenly get big movie careers as a result of *Scream*. You had every TV actor dying to be in this movie to try to get to the next level."

Scream 2 also continued a common horror movie trend of casting relatively unknown actors. From Tom Hanks to Jennifer Aniston, and even earlier Steve McQueen and Jack Nicholson, the genre has a long history of casting actors before they hit it big. For *Scream 2,* that actor was Timothy Olyphant.

The actor had a small role as a film director in *The First Wives Club* (1996) the previous year, but it was Olyphant's theatrical work in the off-Broadway play, *The Monogamist,* and David Sedaris' *The Santaland Diaries,* that caught the eye of the executives at Miramax. They pushed Beach and Katzman to bring the actor in for an audition, and he snagged the role of Mickey, "the freaky, Tarantino film student," who ends up being revealed as one of the killers. He almost lost the role, though.

"The producers were nervous that Tim Olyphant was signaling too much in his acting that he was the killer, because it was supposed to be the surprise, and they thought that he was acting too much like a psycho for each of his scenes early on," Pavel recalled. "Because I was friendly with Wes and Marianne, I would kind of maybe be within earshot of some conversations that I remember there being a lot of concern over whether Tim needed to be replaced early on. Thankfully, that didn't happen. I think he was great in it, but I remember that came up as one of the things while they were shooting."

Ziembicki was also a fan of Olyphant's performance, adding, "Watching it, I realized, not that it was a star-making performance, but I saw there was a lot more there than I recall when we were shooting it."

GETTING IN ON THE JOKE

As previously stated, everyone wanted to be in the film, and not just for the main cast. Big name actors like Luke Wilson, who played the *Stab* version of Billy Loomis, agreed to make a cameo in the film. "It became an easier process because everybody seemed to want to be in it. Anybody we asked about were either interested and, yes, let's get this offer for them as far as even the cameo things," Beach said.

The best casting was based on a joke from the first film. When asked who should play her in the movie of her life, Sidney responds "With my luck, I'd get Tori Spelling." Despite the script's joke, Spelling auditioned for Campbell's role in the original film. While she didn't get it, when it came time to cast the *Stab* version of Sidney, the choice was obvious. Along with the scene with Spelling and Wilson re-creating the Sidney and Billy's run-in at school after his arrest, she shared they were supposed to create a *Stab* version of the original's finale with the kitchen scene. Even though the filmmakers had gone so far as to cast someone to play Stu, the additional scene ended up being cut due to scheduling issues.

Nancy O'Dell appeared together with Spelling for the actress's cameo but said that the joke never came up while filming, but often afterward.

"We did talk about it on the show [*Access Hollywood*]. How great was that? That was the perfect thing about *Scream*, and why it worked so well, is that it could crack its own jokes," O'Dell explained. "And, Tori, she's a great sport. She always has been. She was very much up for the game. She thought it was funny too and gave a great interview about the fact that that was why she was a character in the next movie."

Though she had been working as a reporter for years, *Scream 2* marked the first time that O'Dell acted. Her cameo came about when Craven called her agent to offer her the role. "When Wes Craven asked me to be a part of number two, I was just so flattered because I thought he had done such a great job in utilizing humor and wit and stuff in the midst of something that also was [a] slasher film," O'Dell said. "Then, oh my gosh, he was such a nice person. He was loyal to you, and I think that's why I wound up in number two, three, and four, because it was like if you're in my number two, I want you in my number three and I want you to be in my number four. So, it was just a good guy who was very talented in what he did."

The reporter learned firsthand about Craven's reputation for being especially good at working with newer actors. During the filming of her scene in *Scream 2*, she quickly found out the difference between her day job and how movies are made, stating that he was patient and willing to help walk her through the process.

"Here I am with Tori, who is at the height of popularity within her TV show that she was doing, and it was kind of the first movie that I had really ever done," O'Dell recalled. "I remember them saying, 'Okay, we're ready to shoot the scene. I just started with my lines and I just went. Then I remember Wes going like, 'Nancy, you need to wait for us to slap the board and go action.' I was like, 'Oh.' But the way he did it, was so kind and nice. It was just so quiet and mild mannered."

She adds, "He was by far the best first director to have, period. I mean, just so nice and continued on to be throughout his success with the movie and it being the number one horror movie in all the world for the longest time. You just didn't think that this director was that because it never went to his head. He was just super kind and very loyal."

Regarding her character in those films, O'Dell remembers, "I went from being a reporter, to like on the street, like on the fly, to having my own talk show." The real-life reporter ultimately decided they should be the same to demonstrate a character arc between the films. She adds that she wasn't initially sure whether to play the character closer to herself or more like Gale Weathers. "I always thought, like am I playing what would be a Nancy O'Dell character? Am I supposed to be a different, more tabloid-y like Gale was, you know? Which one am I supposed to be?"

With a killer new cast assembled, the film headed into production.

10

THE INTERNET IS SCARIER THAN GHOSTFACE

WITH WEINSTEIN TRUSTING the filmmakers, it was smooth sailing for the production of *Scream 2*... almost. Because the film was so highly anticipated, the filmmakers increased security protocols in an effort to keep any of the major plot points from being leaked prior to the film's premiere.

"It was all very clandestine and kind of very dramatic. But there was a lot of interest in preserving the 'who's the killer?' idea," Konrad explained. "You're going back to the time of the day where [the script is printed on] like red paper, you know blood red papers that nobody can even read anything, to codes, to P.A.'s dispatched with four different versions going to five different houses, to someone's parked outside your driveway and you can't have it. You have to read it and give it back."

KEEPING THE CAST IN THE DARK

Since she had a role in the film, one might think that the producers would have given O'Dell some inside information about the making of the movie. However, she said that wasn't the case. "We were allowed to report on the movie, but we weren't given the future script; like I never knew the ending. I don't think a lot of the cast members knew the ending of what was going to happen," said the journalist. "I'd watch it along with everybody else when the movie came out. I'm like, who is the killer? I'd be going crazy, and it would drive me nuts. I'm, like, I thought I'd have a little inside scoop. But they won't give you that ahead obviously, especially if you are a reporter."

A lot of films start with the cast and crew gathering to read through the script together. For this film, they did the table read as usual, but stopped before the finale. The cast as a whole were only given partial scripts; only those actors who were in the finale received those pages. Everyone else was left in the dark about who were the killers.

"They held the end back or they held who the killer was going to be. I really didn't know. I thought Timothy was the killer. Then I thought Liev might have been the killer, and I didn't know if Sarah Michelle was going to be the killer. There were so many different people," Kennedy said. Although he began to notice something that tripped up his suspicions about one actor. "I don't remember knowing who the killer was, but I remember just Timothy being on set longer and longer and longer. I'm like, okay, I think Tim has something here."

Kennedy shared that the cast was only given the first 40 pages of the script, and then anything after that was given to the cast as production moved along. In an effort to keep the audience from being able to guess the identities of the killers, Craven made a point to fill the film with paired-up characters. Since the first film had two killers, he assumed many viewers were expecting that again and would be looking for clues; having characters paired together in many of the scenes was a way to throw viewers off-guard.

"I was so grateful because [Craven] had this idea that with *Scream 2* there was going to be all these sorts of pairs of characters throughout the film, whether it was Rebecca and Portia as the sorority girls, or if it was going to be me and the other police officer. There was going to be this idea that there were two killers working together, and you weren't sure which pair it was going to be," Pavel explained. "A lot of people don't realize that about him; [he] is super smart and super funny."

Along with the cast being kept in the dark, some of the crew wasn't clued into the twists either.

"Obviously like the costume department, they would kind of know, the people who needed [to know the ending], or props or something, they would know. But everyone else was left in the dark," confirms Ziembicki.

"Security got really, really tight by the time we finished. I remember the brown [script] papers; first time I'd even seen that. We couldn't xerox them because the color was too dark. You could barely read the letter."

To quickly be able to trace any scripts, the production had copies watermarked with everyone's names and were numbered. Along with those measures, the scripts were also printed on a special paper that had a large bar running vertically down the middle of it. This not only made it nearly impossible to photocopy, but it also presented issues when it came time for the actors and crew members to try reading the copy on the page. Kennedy notes that the only other script that he saw at the time with similar measures taken was *Titanic* (1997), which would be released a week after *Scream 2* and go on to become the highest grossing film at that point.

"Such a pain in the ass to try and read them and print them with that and they would put some big gold thing across the page. It was a total pain in the ass to try and work with those things," Mastandrea said about the security measures.

KEEPING SECRETS WITH A CROWD

The larger budget and scale of the project meant many more extras could be included in the scenes. This left the filmmakers vulnerable to possible leaks from those hired to be in the background, despite all the efforts they had implemented. The opening scene, in particular, included a theater filled with extras for the sneak preview of *Stab*. Almost immediately after they filmed the scene, photos from the set ended up on the internet, providing spoilers about the movie.

"I do remember that. We tried hard. But in the end, it doesn't really matter. We tried hard. What can you do? It doesn't really hurt your box office," Maddalena said, adding that sometimes leaks can actually even help pique the curiosity of some fans.

"I never did a poll and go, hey, did you guess and are you upset? Nobody said, 'Oh my God, I'm so bummed I knew.' People were just happy to see Ghostface again up to his mischievous little shenanigans. It was like they were happy to take the wrapper in the color it came," Konrad said in agreement. "A movie like this, oftentimes what's interesting is sometimes all the conversation about what is or isn't [in the film] accentuates the success, right? It actually creates more of a fervor for what could be. It's a little bit of a busted P.R. model, but I think that it never hurt us per se."

Another element in *Scream 2* that lent itself to possible leaks is that many scenes take place outside, including the initial press conference where viewers are re-introduced to Gale, or Randy's death scene and the car accident near the end of the film. Since they were out in the open, the filmmakers didn't have as much control as they did in the empty theater where the finale takes place. They weren't too concerned about onlookers during the filming of those scenes, especially since this was before the days of smart phones with cameras in everyone's pockets.

"I can't think of anything that was more difficult or extraordinary," Ziembicki said. "That's kind of what you were used to. If you have to beef up security, because you're shooting in a bad neighborhood at night, you would do that."

Being that they were filming on a college campus over the summer, they had more access to buildings. Ziembicki remembers that while in Georgia, the college had an entire dorm floor that was deserted, so they were able to use it as if it were their own movie set.

"We all worked on other things, too. I've done a lot of movies; J.P. [Jones, the prop manager] had done a lot of movies. Peter's done a lot of movies, so that stuff didn't change for us at all," Mastandrea explained. "It was great for us to go out and we got better and came back and gave more to the party, too."

A Bigger Leak Happens

If the photos from the opening created an initial headache for the filmmakers, they got a much bigger headache when the entire movie script ended up online. "I remember hearing that and everyone shit their pants," Kennedy said. "That was a big deal."

While unfortunate, Plec says it might have actually been a blessing in disguise that the leak occurred. Williamson had to re-write a large portion of the script, giving the pair a chance to regroup and fix parts of the story, mainly in the finale, that they weren't completely happy with initially.

"We were like, oh that's good because we hated it anyway. So, it just made us go back and re-break basically the second half of the movie," Plec said. Though she recalls that, "It wasn't the script. It was a long outline."

One of the changes from that original script was the identity of the killers. An early version of the script had Derek and Hallie as the culprits behind the masks. The initial, leaked version of the script also ended with Sidney dying from stab wounds as the film faded to black. Even though those two ended up being victims, Debbie Salt was always planned to be the mastermind behind the massacre. It's revealed that she is actually Billy Loomis' mother, exacting her revenge on Sidney. The seeds for this twist were planted all the way at the beginning of the first film. While being quizzed by Ghostface, Casey incorrectly answers that Jason Voorhees was the killer in *Friday the 13th*. The menacing voice informs Casey that it was actually Jason's mother, Mrs. Voorhees, who is the villain. She too is looking for revenge for her son's death.

With the script leak and re-writes, Beach and Katzman had the timeline on the project extended. The process generally takes 10 weeks to complete.

"I feel like they had the script, then we didn't have the script. Then we had to stay on for overages while they were re-writing the script," Katzman said. "I remember being in the office [and] there isn't much to do today, except hang out and eat McDonald's."

Despite the major changes happening, not everyone was fazed by the script re-writes. For some of the actors, like Schreiber, the leaks and changes added an electricity to the production.

"Some things may have been re-written, and I don't remember, but that was the fun of it. We were, to a degree, just kind of staying in the pocket and the thing felt alive," the actor explained.

Indeed, all of the attention being paid to the production meant that the audience was interested and excited for the new film to be released. Fans were salivating for any morsel of information about the sequel. This was a double-edged sword when trying to keep the twists a secret so they would enjoy them when the movie was released.

"There's the storyteller in you that wants the story to be a surprise and you don't want people to know. But then you also realize that there is this industry around our industry, which is the tabloids, and people who are interested in what you're doing," Schreiber said. "To me, it felt like heat. It felt like a good thing. It felt like, wow, everybody is really interested. That's exciting."

To this day, no one involved with the production knows exactly how the script or outline got leaked. That hasn't stopped conspiracy theorists on the internet from pointing the finger at different people, including

Williamson himself, over the years. Despite all of their efforts, the filmmakers say that the list of suspects would have included anyone who had access to the production offices. Mastandrea says that there was a "bootleg" script floating around that was used to easily make photocopies that could have led to the leak.

"I think obviously a bootleg existed. It didn't have that [bar down the middle] on there. We all just copied it so we could actually read it. That's probably how it got out, I'm sure," Mastandrea said. "I'm sure everyone said *fuck this*. I mean, give us a script we can read, somebody had a clean copy and it's just okay, here it is, but don't give it to anybody else and who knows where it actually went."

Maddalena adds, "It could be anybody, anyone in your production office. So, we changed the ending."

11

GRUESOMELY KILL YOUR DARLINGS

IT'S AN UNFORTUNATE FACT that some of the characters in horror films won't make it to the end credits. As Mastandrea put it while filming the finale to the first film, "People live, and people die."

Dewey was initially meant to meet his maker in *Scream 2* but escaped the Grim Reaper's grasp. It wasn't his first time escaping death, however. The character wasn't originally meant to survive the first film, either, but was given a reprieve because Craven—rightfully so—thought that he might be a fan favorite. Williamson again planned for the character to be killed off in *Scream 2* after getting sliced and diced in a recording booth, but instead he is seen at the end of the film being carried out on a gurney giving a thumbs-up to Gale. Though his frequent brushes with death have become somewhat of a joke in the series, his continued survival was due to his real-life relationship with Cox.

"I think just the chemistry between Gale and Dewey was so strong, it would be too heartbreaking to take Dewey from Gale," Maddalena explained. "There's no reason to do it because we could injure him and have him recover."

Let's Bloody it Up

One of the other surviving characters from the first film wasn't as lucky. After offering up the rules for sequels, Jamie Kennedy's Randy gets a call from Ghostface and eventually dies after speaking ill of Billy Loomis. Interestingly, the star wasn't given a heads up about his character's demise prior to reading the script for the first time.

"I remember reading it in the table read and I was like, *ohhh fuck*. I knew that someone was going to have to go, and I knew that Neve and Courteney were the big two, they were the anchors," Kennedy remembers. Although he does make a case for why Randy should have survived, "It could be a quattro, all four of us on the cover of *Entertainment Weekly*. You need the voice of the people."

Even with that realization that someone had to die, it wasn't any easier for Kennedy to accept. Although now removed from the situation, he has a more philosophical outlook at Randy having to die and its impact on the rest of the film.

"Rose said it beautifully, what makes the movie so great is you kill your darlings. You gotta kill your darlings," Kennedy said, referring to a quote from the actress during a livestream reunion in November 2020. "What makes *Scream* so powerful is the angst that people feel. At least once a day, when people hit me up on the internet or see me at the grocery store, [they] just say, man, you never should have died. They just say it and it's because they were so connected."

When the big day to film the scene finally arrived, it was made even more eventful because Kennedy's parents were visiting the set that day.

"I think they wanted to be there and wanted to see it. They were also worried. They're like, you're going to die? They know it's a film, they were like, I don't want to see my dead baby," Kennedy recalled.

Craven and Jackson used the visitors to their advantage as a way to further torment the star, though. While in the midst of filming the scene, Jackson and Kennedy's mom found their way to each other.

"Roger, he's so good. He's so method and he knew I'm young and impressionable, I would still be like this. He really called me on the phone. So, when I'm filming that scene, he's really calling me on the phone. I didn't know where he was, and he was also saying some very personal things to me to elicit a reaction, which I didn't know he was going to do.

Then he was with my mother, and he put her on the phone," Kennedy said. "Now, whether that's Wes or Roger, whatever, but that fucked me up. He had my mother, so it was really cool."

For his death, Randy is pulled into a news van and killed off-camera, so viewers only see the van shaking back and forth with glimpses of a struggle occurring inside before seeing the gruesome aftermath. To design what Randy would look like when the body is revealed to audiences, Kennedy expressed a desire for a more is more approach. After Craven had gotten the shots he wanted for the scene, Kennedy told him he wanted to take things further.

"I was like, you know, let's go for it. He's like, yeah? What do you want to do? I'm like, you know what, man, I don't want to die, and I don't think you want me to die. But if I'm going to die, I want the audience to really see that I'm dead and feel for that," Kennedy said. "I just got blood and I just took that blood and put it everywhere. He's like, yeah bloody it up, bloody it up! He was with me. My mom and dad were on set that day. They were like, man, you're really bloody and I was like, I'm dead and I'm going to go for it."

Kennedy says that what is in the film is the version he created with Craven, something that the actor is proud of to this day. "He showed it mangled, and he went with it and he didn't have to. So, I thought that was awesome."

Audiences certainly did feel his death. Maddalena and Kennedy both said that over the years they have heard from fans about their disdain that the beloved character was killed off in the film.

"Whatever the reason is, you have to kill people that are important in the story and that's what makes the story good. But maybe people didn't know the impact," Kennedy explains. "I mean it is a movie, but people really do seem quite perturbed that Randy died, because I think it was, in a way, taking the audience's voice away."

However, his death also serves as the catalyst for Sidney to fight even more to avenge her friend's death at the end of *Scream 2*.

"I think that plays along the lines of realness of the movie and why, yeah, it helped her be not just a movie character, but a real character who wanted to avenge the death of her friend," Kennedy said. "They always tried to really ground it in what a real person would go through if they could see this. That's one reason why they work."

CREATING A HORRIFIC DEATH

The deaths in *Scream 2* were much more elaborate than many of the ones in the first film. Possibly one of the most ambitious deaths in the series is the opening of the film. In that 11-minute sequence a lot happens. Unlike the Drew Barrymore scene, this opening had more moving parts with multiple settings in the theater and dozens of extras that needed to be controlled.

Scream 2 opens with Pinkett Smith playing college student Maureen Evans, and Epps as her boyfriend, Phil Stevens. The couple, unaware of what is waiting for them inside, is in line to get into a sneak preview of *Stab*. They discuss the merits of Sandra Bullock movies and the role of race in the horror genre.

They then walk into a theater filled with rabid moviegoers and it looks like something out of the 1950s with cheap gimmicks being used to heighten the fun and scares for the audience. In fact, Ziembicki added the giant arm stabbing through the air outside of the movie theater as a way to play up the atmosphere of the scene.

"I thought then it gets [into] William Castle territory. So, that was my excuse, the big stabbing fists outside on the marquee—which, other than having a nice budget to kind of come up with that idea, I thought that tie-in, it was that kind of '50s or B-movie genre spectacular movie premiere," Ziembicki said. "That was just, I had the money for it and time for a change. So, I thought, how about let's put one of those up there. That just came out of my head. The marquee seemed like an obvious place too because I knew it is going to be a big wide establishing shot."

After Maureen and Phil settle into their seats, *Scream 2* begins to offer viewers a perspective that visually connects Maureen to what is happening on the screen in *Stab*, the movie-within-a-movie depicting a "fictional" version of the events from the first film. Heather Graham plays Casey, with many of Barrymore's lines from the first film closely mimicked in the new version. Figuring out how to display the *Stab* footage that the characters were watching onscreen became a concern for the filmmakers.

"There's another cut of that opening which has every shot of what's projected on the screen, every time you see the *Stab* movie you're always over the audience. You're never inside the movie," Lussier explained. "Then when Wes came in, he felt we were too removed from the Heather Graham section of that. So, we created this thing that really anytime we went from Jada Pinkett's character, from Maureen, into the movie, we would go full frame from the audience or anything like that would be removed. But from her, we would go inside, so that you had a much stronger emotional link between Maureen and the Casey character onscreen, Heather Graham's character."

Further marrying the two characters' fates is that as Maureen tries to escape from the killer inside the theater, she ends up standing on a stage that has part of the film projected onto her before collapsing. Maureen's dramatic death was partly Pinkett Smith's idea. While appearing on the *Couch Surfing* video series from *People* magazine, the actress said she had a specific request for her death.

"I remember saying to the director at the time, I want to die the most horrific death that has ever happened in a horror film and I want it to be long and excruciating and he was like, cool," Pinkett Smith told host Lola Ogunnaike. "Let me tell you, he let me have it."

While the opening of *Scream 2* might not be as downright brutal or have as many jump scares, it offers a more visceral reaction. Maureen is attacked in front of an entire theater of college students, but due to the atmosphere, the other filmgoers think that it is just an elaborate prank for their enjoyment. Only after is she stabbed multiple times do some of the theatergoers begin to realize she's actually being killed. However, no one jumps in to help her from the masked assailant, who slips out as their victim feebly climbs the stairs to get on the stage.

Pinkett Smith's death in the film becomes the most meta in the series, with multiple layers of the self-referential commentary that the series was known for baked into it. It's hard not to see the underlying meaning between the death of Pinkett Smith and Graham's characters being entangled with each other.

Dying with My Eyes Open

Pavel also had a specific request for his death scene.

"I got to be murdered by the Ghostface killer. That's what you want in a Wes Craven movie, especially in a *Scream* movie. I was like, 'Wes, can I die with my eyes open?'" Pavel remembered, "By the time I get to the end of the night and I die, I got to do a dead eye stare on the fake rubber glass. It was super fun. But I remember I just ate up. I was like a kid in a candy shop because I was experiencing behind-the-scenes Hollywood for the first time."

Growing up, Pavel played guns with his siblings and his favorite thing was to do a dramatic death scene, ideally from the top of the stairs so he could roll down them. He fondly remembers filming his death scene, and not just because his underwear was filled with fake blood.

In the scene, Andrews' throat gets slashed by the killer while transporting Sidney and Hallie to a secure location. To show the blood coming out of his throat, the props department used movie magic in the form of a sponge filled with the fake blood kept in his hand. Thus, when he reacted and raised his hand to his throat, he'd squeeze the sponge and release the blood through his fingertips. The effect didn't give them enough blood squirting out, though, so they resorted to another method.

"We did the first shot and Wes said, I want more blood. Suddenly, the crew—what's so great when you're working on a multimillion-dollar big budget Hollywood movie is that the set people, props instantly pulls together—they have a huge three-gallon jug of karo syrup that's red, that's for fake blood, and they do a pump. They cut a hole in my jacket and they ran a tube and they taped it to the palm of my hand. So, when I would bring my hand up, then it was going to squirt out while they pumped it. We had done one shot and they hadn't wiped down my hand enough, so it was still really sticky. As I brought my hand up [for the next take], the tube fell into my jacket and they pumped three gallons of karo syrup into my underwear. For continuity, I had to sit in that red karo syrup all night. But I was happy to do it."

Coincidentally, Pavel's death scene had another change from the initial script. Andrews' partner, Officer Richards, dies in the final film when Ghostface hits him with the car and a construction pipe goes through his head. The stunt was choreographed for the pole to go through the character's chest, but when it went through the head during filming, the props department had to adjust and go with it.

The scene is also notable because of the allusion to Officer Andrews' sexuality. Just before the infamous "*I Think I Love You* Scene," Sidney is describing him to Hallie as a "Gemini, but I think he is gay." That suspicion is all but confirmed when Hallie asks him where they were being taken and Andrews' cheeky response is, "Don't ask, don't tell."

Addressing homosexuality was a big deal. Nineteen-ninety-seven was also the year that Ellen DeGeneres came out publicly. It was also a few years after the military had adopted the "Don't Ask, Don't Tell" policy. The policy was adopted by the military in 1994, during the Clinton administration. It prohibited closeted homosexuals or bisexuals from being discriminated against or harassed while also prohibiting openly gay, lesbian, or bisexual individuals from serving in the military. This meant servicemen and women couldn't openly talk about their sexuality, if homosexual or bisexual, and that superiors couldn't launch an investigation into their sexuality without having first witnessed acts that weren't allowed. It was repealed in September 2011.

Throwing that line in addressed the character's sexuality without having to come right out and say it, while also poking fun at a topical issue that was going on in the world. The actor, who is openly gay, believes that the character was gay—something that was brought into the script partly because he was in the role.

"I think that when Wes had the idea for the character, that was sort of a nod to all of that. He shaped Officer Andrews and that was a dialogue that was going on with 'don't ask, don't tell'. He always liked to keep things topical and always liked to have something that was of the moment," Pavel explained. "I would like to think that was part of what ended up shaping the role. [Craven] would punch up the script that maybe some of those elements were brought to it because of my involvement."

Still, over 20 years later, Pavel is amused when one of his employees recognizes him from his role in the film. "It just blows their mind that they can't believe that their boss, that they see walking the hotel in a suit, got killed and is gagging with fake blood in the late-night movie they saw the night before," Pavel says with a laugh.

12

ENJOYING THEIR SUCCESS

FILMING ON *SCREAM* 2 kicked off in June 1997 at Agnes Scott University, located just outside Atlanta, Georgia. The production spent the first half of its schedule down south before transferring to California. The Georgia locale was used for a lot of the college campus exteriors and some of the interiors, like the cafeteria serenade scene and Sidney's dorm room.

Other scenes, such as the car crash and Cici's murder scene were filmed on the West Coast around Los Angeles. In fact, the location selected for the Omega Beta Zeta house had been used in multiple other films, including the cult horror favorite, *The Midnight Hour* (1987). Known as the "Crank" house in Altadena, it was also featured in *Hocus Pocus* (1993), *Matilda* (1996), and *Catch Me If You Can* (2002).

The cast excitedly assembled down south in anticipation for cameras to start rolling. It might not have been exactly like summer camp–though there was still plenty of fun to be had–this time around, everyone was there to work as well as enjoy themselves. "They were still riding this wave of insane success and anticipation for the sequel. Here was this group of people who had worked together on the first film and a lot of people were sort of Wes's people, who had worked on [his] other movies. So, I think they'd been through the highs and lows of his career with this," Pavel described. "Suddenly, to be working on this project where there was so much heat and so much recognition and so much anticipation, there was a real joyful celebratory mood on set; like we'd won the lottery."

HOTEL ENCOUNTERS

Off set, much of the cast and crew were again staying together at the same hotel, leading to some innocent shenanigans and run-ins. Roger Jackson admits that one of the only times he unexpectedly came face to face with a fellow cast member was in the hotel while filming *Scream 2*. Fortunately, when the voice actor met Kennedy in the hotel's laundry room, Kennedy was none the wiser to who he had just met.

"One night I sort of had the munchies and I went down to the concession machines to get something to nibble. In the same room was the hotel laundry, guest washing machines and dryer. I walked into the room and there was somebody leaning into a machine. I walked in and they turned around really quick. It was Jamie and he said, do you know how to do fabric softener?" Jackson recalled, adding that he responded in the negative and proceeded to get his snacks before returning to his hotel room.

In response, Kennedy said, "Yeah, sure. He was messing with me. That's hilarious. It was like a dorm, man. We would just act during the day; do our laundry at night."

In a risky move by production, Jackson also once rode to set with Arquette and Cox, but they also weren't aware of the identity of the other passenger in the car.

Arquette, meanwhile, continued his usual hi-jinks while filming the sequel. Ziembicki remembers the actor running around the hotel in his underwear.

"I've worked with him after that, since then a couple of times, but that was a weird time in his life, I know,—let's just say that—when we were shooting in Georgia," the production designer recalls. He adds, however, that when it came to the onscreen role, Arquette created a lovable character in Dewey. "I thought some of his choices as a character were kind of weird, but they kind of play really well. I could see people loved that character. He's very charming."

Unlike the first time, there were no issues with disturbing the other hotel guests. However, there were plenty of nights out, dinners, and parties for the cast and crew to enjoy during those initial weeks of production. The new additions to the franchise had no idea to expect all the socializing.

Ziembicki recalls celebrations for crew birthdays at restaurants and open bar nights. As a newcomer, he noted that they helped maintain the already high morale on set. But he also saw it as a way for the returning cast and crew to celebrate the success they had.

"When we were on location in Atlanta for the first four weeks, it was like every weekend there would be a big party. I mean it's definitely fun," Pavel said. As much as everyone got along, he admitted that a few cliques formed, though he chalks that up to being young. "Look, when you get a bunch of actors together, there's always going to be a hierarchy."

"We went out a lot, I remember that," Schreiber also recalled about the experience. "There was a lot of eating and drinking, that's for sure. But I remember having a really good time."

WELCOME NEW ADDITIONS

Many of those involved talk about the addition of actor Jerry O'Connell to the franchise and how he impacted the vibe during production. The actor, who gained fame as a child actor in *Stand by Me* (1986) and made a comeback in the 90s thanks in part to a role in *Jerry Maguire* (1996), joined the film as Derek, Sidney's boyfriend. Having been in Hollywood since he was a child, O'Connell acted as an old sage on set with a laidback aura. Mastandrea likened him to having the same type of vibe as the cast did while making the first film.

"Jerry kind of fit in, like Jerry would have been part of *Scream* one, that kind of vibe. He fit in probably more so than the rest and hung out with us all more so than the rest," Mastandrea said.

When talking about O'Connell, Pavel described him as "couldn't be nicer, super lovely guy, super fun, and funny and jovial."

O'Connell and Kennedy also became close on set. When the two weren't filming, Kennedy recalled they would fly to New York City and hang out there. Still relatively new to the industry, Kennedy got advice about the perks of Hollywood and how to handle the upcoming press circuit before the release of the film.

"Jerry O'Connell was always taking me to the gym. He's like we got to look good, we're going to have magazine shoots. We're going to have photo shoots, we have to look good," Kennedy said. "He was like, don't eat that biscuit—biscuits were big in Atlanta. That biscuit is not going to look good in a *Rolling Stone* article. Take that biscuit off your plate. So I would do that."

O'Connell was also one of the lead organizers for cast outings. When he and Kennedy weren't jetting off to Manhattan, they were going out to clubs in Atlanta. The cast frequented one club in particular, and it turns out that they weren't the only notable people there at the time. Two future Hollywood players were getting their careers started in the city back then, too.

The first, Scott Budnick, was a club promoter at the time. He eventually became a producer, teaming with director Todd Phillips on many of his early films, such as *The Hangover* (2009) trilogy, *Starsky and Hutch* (2004), and *Due Date* (2010). Coincidentally, Phillips also worked with Mark Irwin as his director of photography on *Road Trip* (2000) and *Old School* (2003) after Irwin was fired from *Scream*. The second, Scooter Braun, was a DJ at the club. He is now known for managing Justin Bieber, Ariana Grande, and The Black-Eyed Peas, as well as for his feud with Taylor Swift.

Braun reminded Kennedy of their history years later when their paths crossed again. Kennedy recalled, "I did an event with [Scooter] and Justin [Bieber] probably about eight years ago. He was like, dude, remember I was the DJ when you're doing *Scream 2* in Atlanta."

Screaming for Love

By the time *Scream 2* started filming, Arquette and Cox were officially an item. Giving credence to Irwin's theory that he was something of a matchmaker, *Scream* co-stars Campbell and Lillard were also dating by the time that the sequel started filming. This explains, in part, why he was visiting the set when he filmed his sorority mixer cameo. Franchise newbie O'Connell was also bit by the love bug, though during a 2018 interview the actor stated that he and Sarah Michelle Gellar didn't start dating until after the film wrapped.

O'Connell wasn't the only person enchanted by Gellar during production. When the cast and crew gathered for the first time at the initial table reading of the script, the actress, who played sober sister Cici Cooper in the film, was one of the most popular attendees. Pavel remembers sitting next to her at the reading. "I sat next to this petite blonde girl, who I just thought was like a child actor or a teenage actress. I didn't recognize her, but she had like fierce attitude that she was giving," Pavel recalls, adding that he was intimidated at that first meeting. "I realized it was Buffy, the Vampire Slayer, it was Sarah Michelle Gellar, playing the part. So, it was super intimidating for me to be around because everyone else was a working actor and I was the newbie. But everyone was super nice to me and I made a lot of long-term friendships."

Kennedy also took notice of the actress during that reading, saying, "I remember seeing her at the table read and I was following her around, but she's so sweet. She was only there for like a week, and she was so busy."

13

RECORD SETTING CARNAGE

MUCH OF THE FIRST ACT of *Scream 2* is spent skewering sequels. There's even an entire scene early in the film where the characters specifically discuss how most sequels end up being inferior to their predecessors. By doing so, the film was treading into treacherous waters. If successful, as the sequel ended up being, it would serve as a knowing wink and comical send up to a Hollywood system that churns out sequels for financial gain rather than artistic endeavors. If the film failed on any level, the filmmakers would have served up on a silver platter the opening punchline and lede for every film critic in the country.

In the horror genre, sequels can also be tricky with audiences because you have established certain characters that might be seen as untouchable, which dulls some of the suspense.

"There's something about in sequels, the second you've established who your hero is for your franchise that's going to go on from the first movie and arrives in the second movie, the odds are far less likely that you're going to kill them—as witnessed by [Sidney], Dewey, and Gale are now in the fifth movie," Lussier explains. "That level of them becoming untouchable in that way, that removes a certain amount of jeopardy when you watch it."

RECORD SETTING OPENING

Fans couldn't wait to find out if their favorites from the first film were going to survive the sequel. *Scream 2* was released on December 12, 1997, just 357 days after the first film debuted. This time, there were no D.O.A. predictions upon release. In fact, both *Titanic* and the latest James Bond film, *Tomorrow Never Dies* (1997), shifted their release dates to get out of the way of the horror behemoth.

Scream 2 got rave reviews from critics and grossed $32.9 million at the box office during its opening weekend. Any fears that the sequel wouldn't live up to the hype were quickly squashed. Opening to such an impressive number meant that the film was front-loaded in its grosses, unlike its predecessor that chugged along for months. Nevertheless, the final results were almost the same. Its box office gross was just $2 million shy of the original.

During its opening weekend, the film also set a record for the biggest opening for a December release. It held that record until *What Women Want* (2000), starring Mel Gibson and Helen Hunt, was released. At the time, sequels would generally make about two-thirds of what their predecessors made at the box office, so setting a record and nearly matching the first film's numbers showed the fan power for the sequel.

"You can look at the opening numbers for *Scream 2* versus *Scream 1*. So many people just went off the bat, you know, within the first two weeks because they knew it was a proven commodity. They wanted to see the sequel and so you had sort of a bigger rush right at the beginning as opposed to this slower build, which to me makes sense for a hotly anticipated sequel," explained author Chris McKittrick. "The goodwill and the fanaticism from the first film had a major role in that. The fact that it came so quickly afterwards, you know that was pretty unheard of that a movie sequel to a major hit with much of the original cast, you know the ones that are still alive, comes out immediately like within a year. That doesn't happen too often, so the fact that Dimension Films was able to just to get everything together on not just a script, but all the talent together to shoot this thing while the original is still in theaters was huge."

"Like talking about no sequels are as good [as the original], that's what you're thinking about for *Scream*. The only thing that set [*Scream 2*] apart from the first one is it wasn't first. It's such a good movie. It's an incredible movie," Kennedy said. "It's to me, almost equally as good and it's just, it's so hard to do."

Most studios would be happy with the numbers that *Scream 2* earned during that first weekend, but Miramax and Dimension are not just any studio and the Weinstein brothers are not typical studio chiefs. When the first weekend earnings were initially reported on Sunday, the numbers were inflated by the studio to $39.2 million. It wasn't until the following Friday, a week after it opened, that they conceded that the reported numbers had been incorrectly enlarged. They blamed an extraordinary last-minute demand from theaters to show the film on multiple screens at cineplexes, thus artificially increasing both the number of screens and the revenue.

At the time, Harvey Weinstein blamed the mistake on the company's inexperience with handling films as popular as *Scream 2*, but you have to wonder how innocent of a mistake it was for executives with a history such as theirs. It was especially fishy because the reported grosses and the actual grosses simply reversed two digits. In spite of this minor controversy, no one could take the box office achievements away from the filmmakers. In fact, many people were lining up to congratulate them.

In the late '90s, Craven lived next door to comedian Pauly Shore. The two neighbors weren't exactly close, with Shore sometimes throwing parties that annoyed the director. Despite their differences, when the film opened at number one, the comedian put up a banner in his yard to congratulate the filmmaker on his achievement.

"It said, 'Congratulations! Number one movie in the world. Number one movie, you did it,'" Kennedy recalled. "Wes was so touched by that. I remember asking Pauly that years later, I'm like why'd you do that. He goes, 'Because it's hard to do, buddy. It's an achievement.' That's the beautifulness of our business, you know, whatever people think, or you read. It's not. Pauly was having parties, keeping Wes up; but he still admired him and did that. Wes was so touched by it. I just love stories like that."

Scream 2 Offers Career Boosts

Kennedy says that despite the success of the first film and the steady work he enjoyed, he didn't really see a career boost until after *Scream 2* was released. It probably didn't hurt that the sequel also gave him even more memorable speeches than the first film; he has another 'rules' speech, and his death scene was really a showcase for his talents.

"I was kind of on the same train and then it was really not until *Scream 2* came out, they were just like this is a thing and this is really happening," the actor noticed. "Then I would just get an audition and book the movie. Pretty much audition for a movie and then get the movie, and I'd be busy. That's what kind of happened. Maybe it was just they liked me, and I just had to read. It wasn't offered, but it was a pretty easy audition."

Ziembicki, who only worked on *Scream 2* in the series, also sees the film as a personal milestone. He notes that the film is the highest grossing film on his resume. Plus, the film holds a special place in his heart because it got him into the union.

"I feel very fortunate. *Scream* was my first union job. I got in the union for *Scream*," Ziembicki said, who has started to step away from the industry. "I'm really delighted. I had a great career. I was glad to be part of this one."

In the ensuing years, Pavel continued to add more credits, including working with Craven and Maddalena on additional projects, but his career took a different path as a hotelier. He would still run into his former castmates at the hotel and reminisce about their summer spent working in Atlanta.

"Having ended up running a place like the Chateau Marmont in Hollywood, I would see all of these people as their career would go. My life path took me to being a hotelier as opposed to being an actor, but it's funny because these people would still come in and out of my life," Pavel explained. "The Chateau, for a long time, was a place where a lot of casting directors did castings. So, they would take a meeting and Tim Olyphant would be coming in and he'd be like, oh yeah, I just got this new TV show. So, yeah, it was cool. I'd see Jerry O'Connell; that would be sort of fun. We'd always recollect about what a blast we had on that movie."

Casting director Lisa Beach, in character as a reporter for her cameo in *Scream*, with director Wes Craven. (Photo Courtesy Lisa Beach)

Lisa Beach, producer Marianne Maddalena, Wes Craven, actor Skeet Ulrich, screenwriter Kevin Williamson, and casting associate Sarah Katzman. (Photo courtesy of Sarah Katzman)]

Wes Craven, producer Cathy Konrad, and Marianne Maddalena imitating Lisa Beach during a casting session, who is known for doing high kicks. (Photo Courtesy of Lisa Beach)]

Actress Courteney Cox, assistant director Nick Mastandrea, and Skeet Ulrich on the set of *Scream*. (Photo courtesy of Nick Mastandrea)

Solar Prods., Inc. **SCREAM the sequel** *Feature Call Sheet*

Director: **WES CRAVEN**	Nearest Hospital:	**Date:** THURSDAY, JUNE 26, 1997
Producers: **CATHY KONRAD/MARIANNE MADDALENA**	DEKALB MEDICAL CENTER	**DAY** 10 OF 48 DAY
Co-Exec. Producer: **KEVIN WILLIAMSON**	2701 N. DECATUR RD.	LA Crew: **7:00A Lv. hote**
Co-Producer: **DANIEL LUPI**	404-501-5200	Local Crew: **7:00A @ Lo**
Sunrise: 5:29A Sunset: 7:52P Weather:		Shooting Call: **8:30A**

PRELIMINARY

THERE WILL BE NO FORCED CALLS WITHOUT PRIOR APPROVAL BY UPM (no exceptions) ALL CALLS SUBJECT TO CHANGE BY UPM AND/OR AD'S
NO PERSONAL VIDEO CAMERAS ALLOWED OR USED ON SET. ABSOLUTELY NO NON-WORKING MINORS ARE ALLOWED ON SETS OR STAGES

SCHEDULE

DESCRIPTION	SCENES	CAST #'S	D/N	PGS.	LOCATION
					AGNES SCOTT COLLEGE CAMPUS:
INT. LIBRARY					
SID GETS AN UPSETTING E MAIL	90	1,5,37,42,43,A	D3	1 3/8	MCCAIN LIBRARY
INT. LIBRARY					
COMPUTER MESSAGES	91, 91A,91B,91C	COMPUTER SCREEN	D3	4/8	MCCAIN LIBRARY
INT. LIBRARY					
COTTON GETS BUSTED	92	1,5,42,43,A	D3	2 0/8	MCCAIN LIBRARY
					AGNES SCOTT COLLEGE
					141 EAST COLLEGE AVENUE
					DECATUR, GA 30030
		TOTAL:		3 7/8	PARK PER MAP

K = Minors under 18

TALENT

#	CAST AND DAY PLAYERS	STATUS	ROLE	PU/LEAVE	MAKEUP	SET CALL	REMARKS
1	NEVE CAMPBELL	W	SIDNEY	6A	6:15A	8:15A	P/U @ EMORY LOBBY
2	COURTENEY COX	H	GALE	HOLD	HOLD	HOLD	HOLD
3	DAVID ARQUETTE	H	DEWEY	HOLD	HOLD	HOLD	HOLD
4	JAMIE KENNEDY	H	RANDY	HOLD	HOLD	HOLD	HOLD
5	LIEV SCHREIBER	W	COTTON	6:30A	6:45A	8:15A	REPORT DIRECTLY TO LOCATION
6	JERRY O'CONNELL	H	DEREK	HOLD	HOLD	HOLD	HOLD
7	ELISE NEAL	H	HALLIE	HOLD	HOLD	HOLD	HOLD
8	TIM OLYPHANT	H	MICKEY	HOLD	HOLD	HOLD	HOLD
19	DUANE MARTIN	H	JOEL	HOLD	HOLD	HOLD	HOLD
20	REBECCA GAYHEART	H	LOIS	HOLD	HOLD	HOLD	HOLD
21	PORTIA deROSSI	H	MURPHEY	HOLD	HOLD	HOLD	HOLD
37	COREY PARKER	WF	LIBRARY GUY		6:45A	8:15A	REPORT DIRECTLY TO LOCATION
38	JASON HORGAN	H	FRATERNITY JOCK #1		HOLD	HOLD	HOLD
42	CHRIS DOYLE	W	OFFICER RICHARDS	6:30A	6:45A	8:15A	P/U @ EMORY LOBBY
43	PHILIP PAVEL	W	OFFICER ANDREWS	6:30A	6:45A	8:15A	P/U @ EMORY LOBBY
XX	TONY CECERE	W	STUNT COORD.		N/A	7A	REPORT DIRECTLY TO LOCATION

+ ATMOSPHERE AND STANDINS	SPECIAL INSTRUCTIONS
BRING PENS & RAIN GEAR, SI'S PARK WITH CREW	SPECIAL EQUIPMENT: 1 70'CONDOR(BLACK) W/ STRAIGHT
SI'S FOR #1, #5, #37 @ 6:45A	ARM,1 60' CONDOR(BLACK) W/ STRAIGHT ARM,
SI'S FOR #42, #43 (PULL FROM CROWD)	
THESE EXTRAS REPORT CAMERA READY:	
45 STUDENTS @ 6:45A	
1 MATRONLY LIBRARIAN @ 6:45A	
	LIBRARY SCENES. MUSCO, 24 FRAME PLAYBACK
	SET DRESSING: COMPUTER TERMINALS,HANDCUFFS,
	POCKET KNIFE , WALKIE TALKIE
	NOTES: AC UNIT, COMPUTERS ON SEPARATE POWER
	VIDEO: COMPUTER SYNC 6 SCREENS, COMPUTER IMAGING
	MATERIAL, 24 FRAME PLAYBACK
TOTAL SI'S =3	
TOTAL EXTRAS= 46	

PARK & REPORT PER CYNTHIA STILLWELL
770-460-2020

ADVANCE SHOOTING NOTES

Date/Description	Scenes	Cast #'s	D/N	Pgs	Location
FRIDAY, JUNE 27					
EXT. MILTON CANDLER DRIVE	43PT	2,3,19,A	D2	7/8	THE BREEZEWAY BETWEEN
DEWEY BESMERCHES GALE					AGNES & REBEKAH HALLS
EXT. MILTON CANDLER DRIVE	114 AV	2,3,19,A	D3	1/8	THE BREEZEWAY BETWEEN
DEWEY BESMERCHES GALE			VIDEO		AGNES REBEKAH HALLS
IF TIME PERMITS:					
INT. SCHOOL OF FILM	111	2,3	N3	4/8	BUTTRICK HALL, 1ST FLOOR
DEWEY & GALE SNEAK DOWN HALL					
ALSO DO:					
INT. SIDNEY'S DORM ROOM	69 RESHOOT	1,6,7,8,A	D2	1 5/8	AGNES SCOTT BLDG.
POST SLEEPOVER					2ND FLOOR

UPM: DANIEL LUPI		First Asst. Dir.: NICK MASTANDREA
Prod. Ofc. Phone: (404)378-9646	LA Prod. Ofc. Phone: (213)464-7207	Second Asst. Dir.:LUC OUYANG/ DAN ARREDONDO
Prod. Ofc. Fax: (404)378-5854	LA Prod. Ofc. Fax (213)464-8630	Phone #: 404-712-6006 LUC'S HOTEL/404-371-0204 DAN'S HOTEL

A call sheet, dated June 26, 1997, used during the production of *Scream 2*. The film was simply known as *Scream: The Sequel* at the time. A call sheet is created by the assistant director to inform cast and crew members when and where they need to report for filming on that specific day. (Photo courtesy Phil Pavel)

Wes Craven, Lisa Beach, and actress Neve Campbell (Photo courtesy Lisa Beach)

The badge worn by the cast and crew on set while filming *Scream 2*. (Photo courtesy Phil Pavel)

SECTION 3

NOT A SEQUEL, PART OF A TRILOGY. COMPLETELY PLANNED.

Actor Liev Schreiber and Marianne Maddalena on the set of *Scream 2*.
(Photo courtesy of Lisa Beach)

14

CREATING A KILLER CONCLUDING CHAPTER

WHEREAS *SCREAM 2* WAS TURNED around in under a year, the concluding chapter to the original trilogy didn't arrive in theaters quite as quickly. Everyone had other projects that they wanted to work on before tackling the third film. For Craven and his team, that was *Music of the Heart*, the movie starring Meryl Streep as an inner-city music teacher. During that film's production process, the Weinstein brothers were back up to their old tricks.

"They did a re-cut of *Music of the Heart* and brought it to the set and showed us. That wasn't too cool," Maddalena said.

Being known for his horror films and wanting to break out to other genres, Craven felt the weight of what the success of the film could do for him.

"I think Wes felt the pressure more than the rest of us because he's the horror guy. Now he's doing a movie with Meryl Streep," Mastandrea said. "I treated it as another movie that I was working on for Wes. I worked hard all the time and try to make it the best I could and help them out wherever I could. I think he had the pressure as opposed to the rest of us."

"Wes was kind of ashamed of doing horror. He really felt like it was second rate. Plus, he felt he really was kind of an erudite English professor. He wanted to be doing drama. He always felt a little ashamed of horror, I think," adds Maddalena. The director might have seen *Music of the Heart* as his possible exit plan from the genre. "Wes really did not want to do horror. He wanted out of horror. No one knows that about Wes. People don't understand that he did not want to do horror. So, they made a deal that he could do a drama if he did *Scream 2*."

While the film didn't perform well at the box office—this was prior to Streep's comeback as a box office draw in the mid '00s—it did net the lead actress an Academy Award nomination. It was the first time Craven had directed a performance that was nominated for an Oscar.

Quickly after finishing *Music of the Heart*, the filmmakers knew that they had to circle back to the *Scream* franchise because they had specific windows to work within due to their cast's availabilities.

"I can't remember at what point that the timeline started ticking, if it started ticking right away, or a year later. But I remember that we had Neve Campbell and Courteney Cox, who could only work during their hiatuses. So, it was always that May, June, July window," Plec described. "That was the window and so they were pushing really hard to get the movie ready and to get the script ready."

Meanwhile, Williamson's career was firing on all cylinders. Shortly after the release of *Scream 2*, *Dawson's Creek* premiered on The WB network and became an instant hit. He would later leave that show to launch the drama *Wasteland* (1999), a short-lived show on ABC starring Gayheart, with Plec serving as a producer. Additionally, he wrote the alien invasion sci-fi film *The Faculty* (1998) and helped produce Jamie Lee Curtis's return to horror with *Halloween: H20* (1998). If that wasn't enough, he also made his film directing debut with *Teaching Mrs. Tingle* (1999)—which was the script he wrote prior to *Scream* that had languished in development at Focus Features. The film was re-titled from *Killing Mrs. Tingle* before its release due to school violence that was happening in the country at the time. Before the Weinstein brothers would let him helm the movie, he had to direct a test scene. He used the bathroom scene from *Scream* for the test, with McGowan appearing.

With all of these projects, plus others on the horizon, it started to become apparent that he, too, had limited availability to write the concluding chapter of the planned trilogy.

"There's a psychology, always, to the relationship between studios, when they want something, and creators and creatives, when they want to deliver something," Konrad said. "I think there was a lot of pressure on Kevin personally and professionally to continue to one upmanship himself. I mean it always is the case when you have a huge success that the high bar gets raised, even if everybody's happy with what was [already done]. I think that Kevin really had ambitions, and still does, and has proven that he can write many other kinds of things. I think it was hard for him to be stuck as that guy doing only that one thing."

A Real-Life Tragedy Causes Production to Pivot

The initial idea for the concluding chapter of the film was something that Williamson and Plec originally came up with during production on the first film. The fight with the Santa Rosa school board sparked the idea.

"Having been in Santa Rosa and have all the parents be so strict about their kids that their kids actually were the troublemakers. We wanted to basically tell the story of Woodsboro 10 years later after everything had happened and the town had gone up into like a curfew lockdown. The kids that were too young to know the teenagers when *Scream* happened were now teenagers themselves and had lived in the shadow of that and were fucked up as a result," Plec explained. "They're coming back to shoot a *Scream* reboot in the town. So, that was the basic premise, and then Columbine happened."

That original premise would have also brought back one of the previous killers as the big bad for the film. The character of Stu was last seen in the first film when Sidney dropped a television onto his head, seemingly crushing his skull and/or electrocuting him. Williamson's plan entailed the character having survived his brush with death by television and now acting as a puppet master to the teenagers of Woodsboro from his prison cell. Lillard has spoken in multiple interviews over the years about his proposed involvement in the sequel, and his willingness to be involved in any other sequel.

Lillard isn't the only actor who said they might be interested in returning to the series. McGowan said that over the years fans have been intrigued by the fact that Tatum had two beds in her bedroom, which could have led to the actress' return.

"I always thought like if [Miramax] hadn't been, you know, the worst company in the world to work for and what had happened to me hadn't happened, I think it would have been very smart to have her twin come back and seek revenge," McGowan muses. "Everyone's always had all these conspiracy theories about that bed."

However, all of those ideas came to a screeching halt just before production was scheduled to begin when tragedy struck in real life.

The Columbine school shooting occurred when a pair of high school students ambushed their classmates in Littleton, Colorado on April 20, 1999. During the attack, 12 students and one teacher were murdered and nearly 25 more were injured. The gunmen died by suicide in the school's library. It was a wake-up call to the nation.

"Columbine happened and then all of a sudden Wes decided he didn't want to do a movie where kids were killing kids, probably smartly. That basically killed the entire concept," Plec said. "They were still trying to move the movie forward, but Kevin wasn't available to do it and they chose to move forward anyway because of the actors' window."

The ensuing reaction to the school shooting was to point a finger at violence in entertainment. Video games, films, and musicians like Marilyn Manson were called out for being causes of the violence. The idea that the media was making people more violent wasn't a new argument; both *Scream* and *Scream 2* reference it, with Mickey even suggesting it as his defense if he got caught in the sequel. However, the backlash was different this time, perhaps because there was video showing kids trying to escape the school during the massacre. Hollywood stood up and took notice of the product they were releasing and was aware they would have to answer for it at some point.

"There's the issues that came forth with Columbine and the perception of media's influence on certain actions and everyone was looking for an easy answer, I think," Konrad said about the time.

However, defending the horror genre was nothing new to Craven.

"Wes spent half of his career defending horror, about how you work it out in movies, you don't work it out in real life, like nightmares. You go back, all the poor guy has to do is defend horror in all the interviews and people attacked us for doing horror movies," Maddalena explained. She adds that in the aftermath, "All horror movies had to really question themselves at that point."

Along with the delicate political climate, Maddalena said that the initial idea was also rejected because Williamson wasn't there to shepherd it through to completion. Williamson left the film as a writer but stayed on in a producing capacity.

"Kevin just was so busy on other projects. We had a slot, and when a director has a slot, you know, he is making $4 million dollars, he doesn't want to wait," Maddalena explained. "I think Kevin just said I'm sorry, I am not available, and you have to wait. Bob said, well, we're not waiting."

Even though that *Scream 3* storyline might not have been used for that film, shades of the idea were saved and re-purposed for both Williamson's television show, *The Following* (2013), which ran for three seasons on Fox with Kevin Bacon in the lead, as well as for *Scream 4.*

With Williamson relinquishing his writing duties and the initial outline out the window, Bob Weinstein turned to a new writer. Ehren Kruger wrote *Reindeer Games* (2000) for Dimension Films and had previously scripted the paranoia thriller *Arlington Road* (1999). Based on that work, he was given the job of writing *Scream 3,* but there was a catch. He only had two weeks to deliver the script.

"Bob would do that; he would give you somebody for two weeks and we would be making *Scream 3.* You know, we are spending $50 million dollars, but we only got Ehren for two weeks," recalled Maddalena. "Don't forget what Bob does, he would find a good writer and he would work them to death and put them on 20 projects and they'd have nervous breakdowns."

At the end of the two weeks, Kruger did indeed turn in a draft. Instead of returning to Woodsboro as Williamson had intended, the film was set in Hollywood. The sequel now revolved around the making of *Stab 3,* a sequel to the *Stab* film introduced in *Scream 2,* with the cast of the film getting murdered in an attempt to lure Sidney out of hiding. This took the meta takes to an all-time high and allowed *Scream 3* to make fun of itself and all of the behind-the-scenes drama under the guise of *Stab 3.*

While a draft of the script was handed in, Maddalena says it wasn't quite where they needed it to be for production to begin before he got pulled from the project. The producer doesn't fault the writer, though, acknowledging that he had a learning curve in getting to know the characters and the franchise as a newcomer.

To finish the script, they brought in a ghostwriter, Laeta Kalogridis, who would continue her work while the film was in production. The jokes in the film about the ever-changing *Stab 3* script were grounded in reality, and to make matters worse, Weinstein's calls again became a daily part of the routine.

"He would call us every morning before shooting and scream at us for two hours about the script and then Laeta would go off in her trailer and write," Maddalena recalled.

As if that wasn't enough, during the development process, Williamson filed a lawsuit against Weinstein. Williamson spoke briefly about it while on the *Shock Waves* podcast in May 2020, noting that the reason for the lawsuit was because he owned the rights to the franchise.

"When all was said and done, he didn't write the script. But the whole franchise that sort of led to that moment and he had all the ideas and it led to that moment. Then they moved on due to mitigating circumstances. I think it was just about like, you don't get to make that movie for free even if I didn't write it," Plec explained. "I remember they paid him. They paid him and they paid me, so he won, I guess."

Maddalena doesn't remember the particulars of the lawsuit, but she adds, "I know there is a big love/hate relationship between Bob and Kevin."

FINDING THE RIGHT TONE

Along with the many other moving parts regarding the script, another wrench was thrown into the mix during contract negotiations with the cast members. Neve Campbell agreed to come back to finish the trilogy, but her contract stated that she would only film for three weeks. She had signed onto another project for her hiatus, *Drowning Mona* (2000), starring fellow "scream queen" Jamie Lee Curtis, which had many fans blaming scheduling conflicts for the reduced role. However, that wasn't the reason.

"That was a drag. I think it was her price tag. It would be like $250,000 a day if we needed an extra day. But it was all her choice, but I don't think it was because of availability. I'm not sure what her reasoning was there," Maddalena said. "I don't think she realized that you really can't be the lead if you are only in it for a certain amount of days, so maybe that wasn't such a good idea."

This wrinkle required a shift to happen in the script, leading to Gale and Dewey stepping up to be more of a focal point than they had been in the previous films. To be ready for their increased roles, Cox and Arquette—who married in June 1999—cut their honeymoon short to come back and jump right into production for *Scream 3*.

The heightened reality of their Hollywood-filled storyline caused a disconnect in the film. Sidney's story, featuring her initially living in seclusion, is a much more grounded movie that shows the effects that being terrorized multiple times can have on a person. Meanwhile, Gale and Dewey, wrapped up in the filming of movie-within-a-movie, *Stab 3*, is a more comical tale.

Over the years, many of the cast and crew would complain about the plot of the film seeming to be something out of an old Scooby-Doo cartoon. It didn't help that, like those cartoons, the climax took place at the spooky old mansion where Ghostface gets unmasked.

"No one was ever happy with the story. It kept being worked on while we were filming it. It just wasn't a passion project for anybody," said Besser. "It was painstaking to get the script and to get it where everybody was on the same page about it."

The increased reliance on comedy in the film has actually been a sticking point for many fans over the years. "I think leaning into the humor in the third film has far more to do with trying to cope with the shortcomings of the script. The script works, but it just works. It was sort of vamping its way through some of that stuff," Lussier said. "I think part of that is it lacks that real sort of edge that Kevin Williamson and Julie Plec [brought], especially in the second one, and then Kevin in the first one. So that the script was far more... it was a little more ordinary."

Maddalena also says that Craven was a fan of adding comedy into scripts whenever he was given the option. "We did a series called *Nightmare Café* and he torpedoed it because he wrote one of the episodes and directed it. It was called "Aliens Ate My Lunch" and it was so silly. I think Warren Littlefield thought that he was mad and cancelled the show. It was three little aliens that come in and their spaceship puts out a giant hairball. It is the silliest," recalled Maddalena. "It was just his instinct and that's what he really was dying to do, so I think *Scream 3* just let it go."

Lussier notes that the type of humor utilized in *Scream 3* sets it apart from the other films in the series. The first two films had a biting humor to them, but that type of razor-sharp wit was missing with Williamson off of the project.

"You can tell that Kevin didn't write it because it didn't have his edge to it. I think that was a constant challenge," admits Lussier. "Ehren Kruger's a really good writer, but he was committed to other things, so he wasn't available for as much as they wanted during production. Wes did a bunch of the rewriting himself. They had other writers come in, but I think Wes did most of the better writing."

Lussier points to the dream sequence where Sidney is visited by her mother, Maureen, as one of the scenes that Craven added to the script. The editor adds that it wasn't just the humor that was missing Williamson's touch, it was the depth that he gave to each of the characters. Case in point: Jenny McCarthy as Sarah Darling. On set everyone loved the actress, with Beach and Katzman both singing her praises for her audition.

"She had done the MTV show, she was hosting on that. She was actually really funny," Katzman said about the actress. "She had that mixture of being attractive as well as really funny. She has that personality that was just spunky and funny. It worked well."

Adds Beach, "We had a great time with her in the audition room."

But onscreen, her character is one of the most forgettable in the series. Sarah is one of the *Stab* actors, only appearing in two scenes before she's "cut into fish sticks," to use a phrase from the character herself. Unlike the previous movies where Henry Winkler and Sarah Michelle Gellar had similar roles, McCarthy isn't given enough character depth to impact the audience when she's in peril.

"The Jenny McCarthy sequence, her death, I think it's fine. It feels a little bit routine. You don't really care about her as much," Lussier said. "She feels a bit like stunt casting, but not the way Drew Barrymore was, which was really successful."

Seemingly echoing Lussier's thoughts, when summoned to the fictional director's office to discuss her character in the fictional movie, Sarah states "What character? I'm Candi, the chick who gets killed second. I'm only in two scenes."

"Even Cici's death [in *Scream 2*] is very intense and very scary. So, I don't think you care about [Sarah]. She doesn't seem connected with our main characters in a way that means anything to them, you know? Cici is, we understand, she's part of the [Greek system] that Sid's part of and everything like that," Lussier continued. "There's a relationship there that we can understand, whereas I don't think we get that with Jenny McCarthy's character. She's just, it's almost like you're watching a short film where she dies."

One thing that wasn't apparent at the time, but in hindsight has become eerily unmistakable, is the reveal about producer

John Milton, played by actor Lance Henriksen. He's exposed for having secret drug-fueled parties that led to Maureen being taken advantage of and losing her innocence. The party leads Maureen to leave Hollywood and return to her hometown, forever changed. It seems to be more than coincidence that the character has such a predatory backstory similar to that of Harvey Weinstein, especially in a film that he helped produce. More than 80 women have come forward with allegations against him, including McGowan, who detailed her rape by Weinstein at the 1997 Sundance Film Festival and the aftermath in her book *Brave*. In February 2020, the producer was found guilty of two felony charges and sentenced to 23 years in prison in New York.

A Cut Above the Rest

Something else that fans have been vocal about over the years is Gale's bangs in *Scream 3*. Cox was heavily involved in curating her look over the course of the films, always a little over the top with Gale's look and making sure that it matched her attitude.

"Cox had her own idea, sort of, how flamboyantly she wanted to dress and play that character, including the streaks in her hair," Konrad explained about the actress's involvement in developing the look of the character in the earlier films.

But when it came to her hairstyle for the third film, Cox deferred to her husband. Arquette has said that the initial inspiration for the mangled bangs was Bettie Page.

"That was my fault. Totally, I'll take full responsibility. I mean they're, you know, a professional hairdresser's fault, of course, and they didn't really do Bettie Page kind of really blunt bangs. Like, that's what the idea was," Arquette told *Entertainment Tonight* in 2020. "They tried to mess with them. You can't. You have to go fully in. You can't, like, halfway those kinds of things."

Cox, for her part, has poked fun at the bangs and the horror they have caused fans over the years. She even posted a video to Instagram in celebration of Halloween in 2019, defending the bangs and even playfully cutting her hair to recreate them.

A Killer Theory

Scream 3 holds the distinction of being the only film among the first four to have a single killer. During the development process, the filmmakers threw around the idea of adding a second killer into the mix. The suggestion was to have Angelina Tyler, played by Emily Mortimer, secretly be Roman's girlfriend and his accomplice in the murders. Though the idea was quickly abandoned, the rumor is that Angelina would have also been a classmate of Sidney's back in Woodsboro, jealous of the notoriety she achieved after the events of the first film. This was revisited in *Scream 4*, when Deputy Hicks, played by Marley Shelton, mentions being a former classmate of Sidney's and even appearing together in school plays.

"There was a debate; the other writer wanted to try and have Emily Mortimer's character be one of the killers as well," Lussier said about the conversations. "It's often when you're in those situations, you're going, what are the pieces I have still in play and how can I use them differently than they're being used now. It's like, well, here's a piece if we don't kill a killer here, even if we see her dragged around the corner we can say that's like Billy's death—death number one—in the original. That in and of itself was the reason not to do it."

Revealing that Roman was the murderer in *Scream 3* was one of the biggest twists in the series. Not because he was the killer, even though he was supposedly dead in the basement. It was the motive behind his murderous rampage that audiences didn't see coming. He was revealed to be Sidney's half-brother from the brief period when Maureen had been an actress in Hollywood. Once he was grown, he attempted to connect with his mother, only to be rejected by her. As a result, he set out for revenge and orchestrated everything behind the scenes since before Maureen's murder.

This also has led to one of the biggest theories with some fans believing that Roman is actually in the first two films watching over everything to make sure his plan is being carried out successfully. In *Scream*, after school is cancelled following Sidney's attack in the bathroom, Ghostface can be seen stalking Sidney and Tatum throughout Woodsboro. First, watching them outside of Tatum's house and then in the grocery store while they pick up snacks for Stu's party. Fans have long said that with Stu and Billy terrorizing Randy at the video store, neither of the killers would have been able to be in both places at once.

The theory picked up more steam with the knowledge that at one point, the filmmakers were going to have Ghostface in the closing shot of *Scream 2*. The aerial shot pulls back from campus as Sidney walks away from the crowd of reporters and the camera pans past a bell tower that was originally going to have Ghostface standing inside. Add all of this to the fact that Roman had apparently been stalking Maureen in order to record her motel trysts with both Cotton and Mr. Loomis, the theory isn't as farfetched as it might seem.

If nothing else, it explains away a possible plot hole in the original film about Ghostface running around in broad daylight.

15

FINDING A NEW CROP OF VICTIMS

WHILE THE SCRIPT was being polished, Beach and Katzman were hired to begin their process to find potential new victims for Ghostface. Again, they could build the cast around many of the surviving cast members who would be returning, including Campbell, Cox, Arquette, and Schreiber. However, this time around Cotton would be the star of the opening sequence.

Despite an extra layer of meta humor, thanks to the movie-within-a-movie conceit established with *Stab 3* as a central part of the film, the process wasn't affected in how the casting gurus set out to look for actors. While the humor might have been more plentiful for the concluding chapter, it was always baked into the script.

"It's a send up of a movie-within-a-movie. It was always a send up, all of these. It's a send up for a quintessential horror movie. So, I think we always had comedy in mind because I think our feeling is that comedy actors can go into drama a lot easier than drama actors can go into comedy," said Beach. "When we are doing a drama, we can look all over the board as opposed to [comedy]. We can look at comedy people who might want to go into drama, just because it would give them something different to do, whereas it's a lot more difficult to get a purely dramatic person into a *Horrible Bosses*."

As with the second film, keeping as much of the film a surprise to fans was important. This meant that actors had to come to the casting office and sign waivers, the pages—known as sides—used for the auditions were watermarked, and actors were watched while they read them. This also meant the actors spent an increased amount of time in the office, leading to more parties with some of those waiting to audition.

"We ended up having a pizza party with Topher Grace and Rebecca Romjin because they were there reading the script and we're like we're starving, we are getting pizza," recalled Katzman. "They were like, yeah, we want pizza too. So, we were, like, okay. We all had a pizza party while they read their sides."

It wasn't all fun and pizza parties though. There was drama when one actor took the sides with him as he left the office. The casting directors say it wasn't purposeful, as the actor quickly threw them in a trash can while still on the CBS studio lot. The casting offices for *Scream 3* were located on the CBS Studio lot across from where the original *Big Brother* (2000) set was being constructed. Nevertheless, they had to track him down and dig the pages out of the garbage.

"We had them all numbered, one, two, three, four. Whoever took it out had to sign. He accidentally walked out of the office with them, took them, and put them in the trash, and we had to actually get it out of the trash," recounts Katzman, who remembers who the actor is but didn't out him.

Beach added, "Yeah, it was a big drama."

Along with numbering all of the materials, actors auditioned with pages from the previous movies. This was done because the script was top secret—so much so that neither Beach nor Katzman received a complete script. For the *Stab* actors, they used previous scenes from the characters they were playing in the fictional movie. For other characters, the casting directors used scenes that would be like that character from the other films.

"I actually got a scene from *Scream 2*. I actually got Jamie Kennedy's part when he was talking to the killer on the phone, when he got sucked into the van. I read from that," Foley said at the time the film was released. "Cold reading is never fun. I prefer to know. It helps to know the story and the character you're playing. You don't want to overdo it on a character."

Since this was the concluding chapter and the previous two films had been so successful, every actor in Hollywood wanted a part in the film. Along with Grace and Romjin, other notable actors who auditioned for the film included Naomi Watts, Eric Stonestreet, and Paula Marshall.

"We could pretty much get anybody in that we wanted, who's available," explained Beach. "But the ones we did get in, I think there really was an embarrassment of riches from whom to choose."

A Second Chance to Join the Franchise

Scream 3 offered actor Matt Keeslar a second opportunity to join the franchise after previously auditioning to play Billy Loomis in the original film. While he didn't get a part in that film, he had since signed one of Miramax's three-picture deal contracts, leading to his audition for the new film. Echoing Beach and Katzman, Keeslar notes that when he walked in, the long hallway was filled with every young actor in that age range trying for their chance to get into the movie.

"Literally everyone that you could possibly imagine from young Hollywood that you had seen at the bowling alley, at the bars, at the clubs, they were all just sitting there. I went in, signed in, and sat down. It was probably two hours sitting in the hallway. I mean literally sitting on the ground in the hallway. There were no seats or anything, it was so crowded," Keeslar remembered about the audition. "They finally called me in and what Wes Craven said was, 'I guess I have to pay attention to your audition.' I guess what that meant was I had this three-picture deal, I had done an indie movie that had caught the attention of Harvey Weinstein at that point in time. Either they had, I don't know what they do exactly, dog-eared my resume or something, to be one of the people that they wanted to pay particularly close attention to in the audition."

Katzman says that for their part, Keeslar was given the role based on the strength of his audition.

"I also think for all of those roles, I'm sure we had lists put together and we were checking availability on the parts. They would say, let's put an offer out to them, then we would also let agents know there is an offer out on this role, but still want to read them as back-up and would do exactly what we would normally do," Beach explained. "Sometimes they would just say, he's not going in with an offer out. I'm sure it was a combination of the two, it just happened that the best man got the part."

So many actors were jockeying to be in the film that some were touted for being in the film without ever getting cast or even being in contention. Prior to breaking out in *Almost Famous* (2000), actress Kate Hudson appeared in a small movie titled *Desert Blue* (1998). When released on home video, the back of the movie's box offered a description of the plot. As is customary for newer actors, a recognizable film credit is listed next to their name to help audiences place them. Listed next to Hudson's name was *Scream 3*. She never appeared in the film nor, according to Maddalena, was she ever seriously considered for the film. Still, the DVD release of *Desert Blue* immortalizes the actress as having been a part of the sequel.

DRIVING ACROSS THE BORDER TO GAIN A WORK VISA

Meanwhile, British actress Emily Mortimer was cast a week prior to the start of filming as Angelina Tyler, the actress who wins a national casting contest to play Sidney in *Stab 3*. However, there was just one problem that the filmmakers and casting directors weren't aware of when they cast her: Mortimer didn't have a valid work visa in the United States. It was a revelation that took the production by surprise, Katzman remembered, "We were surprised, and we were like, oh my God, how is this going to happen?"

The casting directors said that the situation never reached the level of panic where anyone thought they were going to have to recast the role. Since it was 1999, before the requirements became more stringent following 9/11, the solution was a fairly easy one. The remedy required her to first leave the country and then someone from the production had to driver her back into it by car.

"Emily was hired on a Thursday, I think, and had to be on set Monday. I think my assistant at the time, or somebody I can't remember who, flew up to Vancouver and met her and drove her back down," Besser recalled about the situation. "It is something that we never, in the day we are in now, we can't do that anymore. But back then, you were able to get a visa within 24/48 hours at that time. I'm thrilled that I was able to claim that I was the first one that got her here to work."

"They tricked us. They didn't tell us she had that issue," adds Maddalena. "So, we cast her, and we're committed to her. Then they say, oh by the way. Actors do that. Agents, they trick you."

In the end, Besser took it all in stride, seeing it as all in a day's work. "Your job is to get it done, whatever is thrown at you. So, there it is. It's Thursday, and ok, let's figure it out," Besser said, before adding that he had one stipulation, "Please don't have her start time or call time before 11 a.m. on Monday, just in case there is traffic."

RETURN OF THE LIVING DEAD

Scream 3 also saw the return of two dearly departed characters. Maureen Prescott, who had yet to appear in any of the films except in photos with Sidney, was brought back into the fold as the mystery would focus heavily on her this time around. After the outcry over him getting killed in the previous film, Randy was also brought back for a cameo. Neither Kennedy nor McRee were expecting the call for a return engagement since they figured their time with the franchise was finished.

"I thought I was dead, but I had fun doing it," Kennedy said about filming his cameo, which was completed over the course of an afternoon.

The cameo served as a way to continue sharing the rules the characters must follow in order to survive. This time he shared the rules for surviving the concluding chapter of a trilogy via video. During his video, Randy lets the characters know which of the cardinal rules he broke, leading to his death.

Kennedy found out about the cameo through his agent, though he tried taking credit for the role. "The funny thing is, at the time, my agent was like, 'Yo man, so I got this role.' I'm like what? He's like, it's a horror movie. I'm like, what is it? *Scream 3*. And I'm like, *you* got me the role? Yeah, well you don't have to work for it. I'm like what are you talking about," the actor recounted how he found out about the offer. "That's when I was over agents. But he was, like, I got this role for you."

At one point in development, the filmmakers toyed with resurrecting Randy back from the dead, but that idea was abandoned for the video cameo that appears in the film. There was also a change to how Randy's sister, Martha Meeks, would appear in the film. Martha is on the lot working as an actress and runs into the Woodsboro trio.

"There was an earlier version of Randy's scene where Randy's sister shows up and she's a contortionist and is like contorting. It's a different actress, doing all of these sorts of, you know, legs behind her head. It was so weird," recalled Lussier. "Ultimately, that was thrown out and it was redone with the woman who plays Randy's sister."

McRee was at work in an annual American Airlines re-certification training session when the call came in from a production assistant to gauge her interest and availability in returning to the role.

"P.A.'s don't call actors a year later to say, how's the weather," explained McRee. "She said, so, listen, I don't have a lot of time, but Wes asked me to call you. He's got this crazy idea he's throwing around in his head, like, the idea is something like Maureen comes back to life in this dream sequence of Neve's. Now he's not committed, he's just tossing it around. Maybe it will happen and maybe it won't. He asked me to give you a call; it's been a year, see how you are doing, see what's up, see, if he decides to go this route, would you be available?"

The actress said her heart started pounding from the excitement of the call. She wouldn't have to wait long to hear from her agent regarding whether they would go forward with the dream sequence. She received a call a few days later with the details. Along with the dream sequence, her role expanded to include voiceovers in a few scenes and footage that was meant to have been filmed before her character was killed. Because McRee was a model in the '70s, she was also able to provide the production with actual photos to be used as Maureen's headshots from her short, ill-fated acting career.

"They were so jazzed. I probably brought down to L.A. two dozen, maybe more. Some were 8 x 10's; some were 11 x 14's; carried them in my little portfolio that I used in Manhattan. So, those were the originals. I was 19, I weighed 99 pounds, five-feet-seven," explained McRee. "Some were from jobs, and again some were headshots."

AN AWKWARD REUNION

Scream 3 served as a reunion of sorts for Parker Posey, who was cast as fellow *Stab 3* actor Jennifer Jolie, and multiple actors. Before 2000, Posey had made her name by starring in a slew of well-received independent films. She even earned the title, "Queen of the Indies" for her work. During her time on the independent circuit, she had appeared in *Party Girl* (1995) with Schreiber (the two also appeared in *Mixed Nuts* (1994), but like *Scream 3*, didn't have any scenes together) as well as Christopher Guest's cult favorite, *Waiting for Guffman* (1996), with Matt Keeslar. After that film wrapped, the two didn't stay in touch in the intervening years, partly due to an incident with the rental car they shared.

"When we were in Austin shooting *Waiting for Guffman*, we shared a rental car and we split it because we were both poor and needed a car. Parker basically completely trashed the car, cigarette burns on the dashboard, garbage all over the floor," explained the actor. "She turned it into the rental car company and there was like $1,000 worth of damage, which at the time was significant… and then she tried to get me to pay my half of $1,000 of damage."

He found out about the damage while in Canada after she had told someone that Keeslar hadn't paid her for his half of the fee. Afraid that the ordeal could wind up with the actors fighting in court, he agreed to pay her. Because he didn't have a checking account at the time, the actor had to get his agent to write Posey a check, who he then reimbursed.

"I don't think that she remembered that when she got to set for *Scream 3*. But already, we were not best friends at that point," Keeslar recalled.

Posey also created a stir among fans when she was quoted in an interview prior to the film's release saying that she only signed on because she needed a paycheck. Many viewers saw it as the actress dissing the film as well as making them worried that the film's script wasn't great. However, in an interview celebrating *Scream 3*'s 20th anniversary, the actress provided a little more context around her controversial comment.

"I was nervous to take on a part where I'd have to be scared and on the run. I'd been out of the country for over a year and landed in Hollywood to hopefully get a paying job—and I did. So, I was happy to fit into the studio system. We talked about why people wanted to scream together in an audience—what the films held a place for—that catharsis," Posey told *Too Fab*.

16

A NEW ON SET DYNAMIC

WHILE THE FIRST TWO FILMS were mostly shot on location outside of Los Angeles, the third film stayed in Hollywood for its filming—appropriate since so much of the film deals with Hollywood. This changed the dynamic on set, though. Craven still maintained a calm set for the production despite all of the script changes, but since everyone went home at night, there wasn't the same sense of bonding that the other films experienced.

A COG IN THE WHEEL

To Matt Keeslar, it felt like two groups had formed among the cast members: the indie actors and the more established actors, though a few of the actors were able to jump back and forth. Part of the disconnected feeling on set was due to the increased demands on the cast compared to previous films.

"By now all the actors had other obligations. So, we had to work around that. It wasn't camp. Somebody needed to be on another show or a film for these days or those days, so you are working out a schedule to accommodate that," said Besser, who returned for the third film after missing *Scream 2*. The script issues didn't help either. "Pages are coming in that day or that morning. So, it wasn't the fluidness of the first one."

Keeslar described his time working on the set as feeling like he was just a small part of a much larger machine. Scott Foley agreed that the film set held a much more serious tone than the way the previous film sets had been described.

"It was a very serious set for the most part. Now, of course, when you're that serious all the time, you can't help but lose your mind every now and then and fits of laughter were not uncommon," Foley said. "For the most part it was very serious. It's good work, but that's our job."

For some of the returning crew, production staying in Los Angeles this time around actually helped them be closer to the filming. Beach and Katzman said that it was during the third film where they felt that they had crossed over into feeling like part of the family. Another close member of the group, Lussier, also enjoyed working nearby because it allowed him to visit the set.

"It was also nice that we were cutting right across the street from where they were shooting so we could go for lunch and have lunch from catering," Lussier explained. "*Scream 3*, it felt like there was a lot of returning people from different things. Josh Pais, who was in *Music of the Heart*, showed up as one of the cops, as Patrick Dempsey's partner. People who they had worked with before and wanted to bring back. So, I think it was a lot more fun that way."

Even with the proximity allowing for the filmmakers to be closer to each other, Besser admits that the third film just didn't have the same feeling to it.

"It just wasn't a passion project to anybody, actors or Wes. It just didn't have all the things *Scream* one had, and not because it wasn't original. It was just it was painstaking to get the script and get it where everybody was on the same page about it. It just seemed forced," he said about the film. "I think we all go into the process and the film having that bar. Whatever movie it is, I think you need to set the bar that high otherwise I don't think you're fulfilling what you're supposed to be doing. My personal opinion was no, it never did hit that bar. It just didn't."

KEEPING THE PLOT SECRET

Like the previous film, security was important. Whereas the actors in *Scream 2* were able to get a mostly complete script, the actors on *Scream 3* were only given their scenes. The script pages still had the red anti-photocopying bar down the center, making it difficult to read. But the real problem for the actors was the lack of a full script because they weren't able to fully contextualize what was happening in the film.

"I never had a full script. So, I don't know how the story comes together," Foley said at the time. "It was really hard to do because I usually like to know the whole arc of the character, where he begins and where he ends. Without knowing that, it's just really hard to play a character."

Adds McRee, "Every day I was given five-to-six pages of what was happening before the scene I was involved in; my scene, of course; and what was happening after so I could follow the character and where we were, the pulse of the scene."

Keeslar says that the plot was so locked down that he didn't even find out that Roman was the killer until he saw it at the premiere. Unlike the initial read-through of the *Scream 2* script where the cast read to a certain point prior to filming, Keeslar said that during the *Scream 3* read-through there were "still huge parts that were missing or blacked out." Whether that was completely due to keeping things secret or because the script wasn't fully ready isn't clear. Foley himself didn't find out that he was the killer behind the mask until after filming had been underway for a few weeks.

There was one actor, however, who remembers getting the whole script.

"I want to say they shared the whole script with me, but that may be because I want to say that. I would have remembered, I think I was pretty tight with those guys at the time, and I don't think I ever would have leaked anything," Schreiber said. "I had been in the other movies and we had hung out when we weren't working. Wes and Marianne, we had become sort of close."

During production, the cast and crew also weren't allowed to have cameras or take pictures. Keeslar saw more security on the film focused on that than anything else. This also could have been to keep the paparazzi from taking pictures of the cast—another instance of life imitating art.

"There was always still a fair amount of security on set, just making sure that there weren't people taking pictures," Keeslar said. "Which could have also been to help the actors as well. It was a weird time when things were getting to the point where the paparazzi had become so powerful. There were so many more ways for things to get leaked online, and so forth, that I think they had started to see that they needed to be much more careful about where they were filming, how they were filming."

In fact, while the production was filming on location in Runyon Canyon, they completely blocked the area off so no one could walk or drive by. The parking lots were even closed to people who just might have been trying to go hiking in the area.

To further keep the film's plot twists under lock and key, no test screenings were done except to those who were connected to the film. Plus, a special note was attached to the *Scream 3* press kit asking film critics not to spoil any of the big reveals in their reviews.

"The power of the internet had grown, so times had changed again. It was a different world," Maddalena said. "I think they had confidence in the movie, just felt they didn't need to do that. We probably had quiet test screenings, 30 or 40 friends and family. But we didn't need to go put it out there where you could film it."

Foley thought cloaking the film's plot in secrecy was a smart marketing ploy, despite the frustration it might have caused during production for the cast. "What they're trying to do is drum interest and suspicion in the hopes people will go see [the film] and find out the secret, which I think is a smart move," the actor explained while making the rounds promoting the film.

ADJUSTING THE CHARACTERS

With the script in flux throughout filming, changes were made throughout the production process. One of the changes included trimming the roles of the *Stab* actors. The fictional actors apparently came off too callous and narcissistic for the audience to really get behind them, which is necessary in a horror film. But Keeslar, who estimates at least half of his scenes got cut, says that is how the script portrayed them.

"It seemed on the page that's how they were written. It was a very dark commentary by these young Hollywood actors," the actor explained. "We did them as we would, and we weren't directed otherwise. But I can say, just looking at the page, it came off as very dark commentary on young celebrity at the time, which is why I think those scenes got cut out. When they ultimately screened them, they were like, wow this is really casting this group of young actors in a pretty negative light."

Conversely, one actor who saw their role continually increase during the film's production was the future McDreamy, Patrick Dempsey. He was a late addition, cast as Detective Kincaid the day before he was due on set with multiple dialogue-heavy scenes to be filmed right off the bat. His first scene was with Campbell at the police station. Based on how well he handled himself, he was added into more scenes.

"Dempsey, not having read the script and not knowing where his character was going, played it. That is still one of my favorite scenes in that movie because he plays it so specifically of both: I am the romantic lead; I am the killer. I am this, I am that. I am just the red herring. If you watch all the weird little nuances of his performance, it's really intriguing," Lussier explained. "I think his role got bigger because of the strength of his performance in that first scene."

His role expansion also included the final showdown between Sidney and Roman. In the original version of the ending, Kincaid doesn't show up to save her. However, when the filmmakers went back to rework parts of the scene, he was added into it. This presented another issue, though. As explained in the audio commentary, Dempsey had to wear a wig because he cut his hair between when the film originally wrapped and the sequence was reshot.

A-List Treatment

The budget almost doubled again for the third film from the second film's budget, which allowed some of the actors to get the star treatment for the first time—fitting since it was a movie about pampered actors. McRee, who was still living in Northern California while *Scream 3* was in production, was in awe of the treatment that she received from the time she was picked up from her house in a limo.

"The limo picked me up at my home in Sonoma, drove me down to [San Francisco International Airport]. It's about 75 miles away from my home. He said, I'll be here to pick you up when they finish shooting. When is that? I don't know, but they will let me know. Don't worry, I'll be here," McRee recalls about the experience. "I flew first class down to L.A., short flight, one hour. At the end, the driver was there at the gate holding the little sign with my name on it. The driver took me to the hotel, I checked into my suite. There was a fruit basket, a bottle of wine, a welcome note."

While getting the red carpet metaphorically rolled out for her, McRee said the experience made her realize how some in the business might lose touch with regular, everyday life.

146 | It All Began With A Scream

"I understood why some A-list actors have such huge, overblown egos. The reason that is, is because everything is done for us. Everything. The clothes are put on, the zippers are zipped, the buttons are buttoned. Our make-up is applied, our make-up is taken off. Our hair is done, from shampoo to finish. Our feet are picked up and placed in the shoes. We are escorted to our limos. We are escorted to our trailers. Whatever we want, we ask for and it magically appears," the actress said. "Actors don't live in what I call reality. It's crazy the stuff that big budget films allow."

Keeslar takes it a step further, saying that in some ways Hollywood infantizes its stars. He recalled one time on set when Arquette had just gotten a motorized scooter and was riding it around in the parking lot.

"I remember looking at him and thinking, this is a multi-millionaire who's buzzing around in a scooter like a 17-year-old or a 14-year-old and thinking to myself, this is the funny thing about the infantilization of young Hollywood, that we get so much of our lives dictated by agents and managers and business managers and publicists that he has this arrested development of a young teenager, who is the star of this huge movie," said the actor. "I think that is a common theme that I saw throughout, this kind of behavior of an adolescent being played out by these people who actually had lots and lots of money and lots and lots of influence and 'power.' I think that is also what *Scream 3* is lampooning or characterizing in the young Hollywood."

With the extra money in the budget, the filmmakers were also able to use some of it to throw Craven a 60th birthday party in August of 1999. The party was held at Konrad's house and included not only cast members from the trilogy, but also actors from their previous films like Bassett.

"We had a $20,000 birthday dinner for Wes's 60th. I remember them calling us and saying what's this? We were like, too bad!" Maddalena said. "Cathy Konrad had this beautiful house; we got a tent in the backyard and we had this incredible French provincial dinner with sunflowers and catered. We just had a great time. We had a sit-down dinner for like 30."

A FAMOUS LOCATION FOR THE CONCLUSION

It seems only fitting that an iconic franchise would find an iconic location to film its climatic ending. That came in the form of the Canfield-Moreno Estate, now known as The Paramour Estate, in Los Angeles. The mansion was built in the 1920s for silent film star Antonio Moreno and his wife Daisy Canfield-Moreno, the daughter of oil pioneer Charles A. Canfield. After the couple died, the mansion was operated by the Catholic church as a home for unwed mothers and over the years its legend has only grown.

"It has a whole other history of horror movies; you know, what's happening in the basement of the Catholic home for unwed mothers. So, it had a horror movie-esque history to it," Miller explained about the location. "It was a spectacular house. It had been bought by this woman who was restoring it slowly. It had a lot of work to be done. It had great, old Hollywood rooms in it."

Not everything seen in the film during the last act is actually part of the house, though. Some of the more salacious aspects were created by the production team. Miller clarifies that Milton's bedroom with the mirrored wall had to be built, as did the secret door behind the closet that led to the back hallways.

BAD BREATH TRYSTS

The ending of the film takes place in a screening room located in Milton's mansion, where Roman is unmasked and has his final showdown with Sidney. At the beginning of the scene, Sidney sees home video footage of her mother that Roman had taken leading up to Maureen's murder. This is followed by footage of Maureen meeting various paramours at a motel for affairs. Among them are Cotton Weary and Mr. Loomis, Billy's dad from the original film, played again by C.W. Morgan.

McRee notes that while Schreiber was a complete gentleman and professional on set, the same couldn't be said for Morgan, who got a little too zealous when going in for a kiss with the actress.

"You know we are there to have sex, and the scene called for a kiss. Just lips touching right outside the door before you race into the bed. Oh, my goodness, the cameras are down below, we're up above. He thrusts his tongue in my mouth and he has the worst breath. Yuck. The cameras are rolling, so I can't react the way I would normally react under circumstances," explained the actress. "I tell him after that experience, do not put your tongue in my mouth. He tries, I kind of clamp my lips. It obviously showed on film, so we had to do it a few more times. I couldn't wait to get away from him. I ran down the steps."

Noticing that she was distraught, some of the makeup department crew came over to check on her. She told them what happened, and they quickly sprang into action providing gum and breath spray to help her.

"They are so compassionate and so caring," McRee said. She had forgotten Morgan's name in the ensuring years, though, adding, "I tend to forget the names of people who rub me the wrong way and that is a perfect example."

17

UPPING THE
BODY COUNT

MIDWAY THROUGH *SCREAM 3,* Randy delivers a video message from beyond—or more specifically, filmed prior to his death at Windsor College—offering the rules to survive a trilogy. In the video, Randy warns that in the concluding chapter of a trilogy anyone is vulnerable to being killed off. It's a prophecy that doesn't necessarily come true in the film, but the filmmakers decided to go bigger with some of the kills in this concluding chapter of the initial trilogy than in previous films.

ADDING ACTION TO THE OPENING SEQUENCE

The opening for *Scream 3* is different than its predecessors in a multitude of ways. The stakes were raised by having a known character, the beleaguered Cotton Weary, caught in the crosshairs of Ghostface. Also, unlike the previous two films, the sequence wasn't contained to one location. The film opens with Cotton Weary stuck in infamous Los Angeles traffic when he gets a mysterious phone call from Ghostface and must race home to save his girlfriend, Christine.

The opening wasn't always planned to include Cotton. During development there were many different ideas on how to start the film. At one point, the opening sequence was going to center around a new character named Ben Damon.

"It's a spoof on Ben Affleck and Matt Damon, who were obviously very popular at the time, you know coming off of *Good Will Hunting*," explained Lussier.

It also kept with the trend of characters named after popular actors from that time, such as Angelina Tyler and Jennifer Jolie referencing Angelina Jolie, and Tom Prinze, whose name is a mash up of Tom Cruise and Freddie Prinze, Jr., the latter of which starred in Williamson's other horror hit *I Know What You Did Last Summer*.

The idea for Cotton to be terrorized by Ghostface in the opening minutes was a suggestion from his portrayer, Schreiber. He saw the opening of *Scream 3* as a way to give Cotton an epic send-off from the series. "I thought the opening kill was the funnest kill and if I was going to go out, I wanted to go out big," explains the actor.

While he might have requested to be in the opening sequence, the idea that Cotton Weary would have become the host of his own talk show, titled *100% Cotton* in the film, originated from a joke in the editing bay during *Scream 2*. Lussier and his team got the idea from the scene in the sequel where Cotton is interviewed about being exonerated in the murder of Maureen Prescott. That interviewer was played by none other than Williamson, making his only cameo in the series. The editors told Craven about the joke and lo and behold it ended up coming true in *Scream 3*.

Once Cotton was established as the main victim in the opening sequence, the filmmakers set out to give him the best scene possible. That meant setting him up as the hero, racing through the city of Los Angeles to get home to Christine before Ghostface got to her. Driving through Los Angeles added a new element that audiences hadn't seen before in an opening death.

"I think that was just Marianne, Wes, and Kevin loving Cotton. They just loved Cotton, and I got the benefit from that. It seemed like they were giving him this whole action sequence," Schreiber recalled, adding, "But I also think that was part of the rule, or the game, of the movie. You open big and then you had to get bigger every time. I think part of the struggle with a sequel is how do you re-do something that you've done already? One of those answers sometimes is just throw more stuff at it. To a degree, that's kind of what my opening was. It was like, well, let's make it an action sequence. He's probably going to buy it, and they probably are going to know he's going to buy it, so let's try to make it as exciting as possible."

On a deeper level, after the killer's motive is revealed at the end of the third film, it made sense to have Cotton as the focal point of the opening.

"Once you discover who the killer is and what the killer's motivation is, and I think often you forget, but that's why Cotton died. Cotton had an affair with Maureen, with both the killer and Sid's mother, right? So that's why Cotton is chosen specifically. He makes total sense, given who the killer is," adds Lussier. "He was the catalyst in the beginning as well. He was the one who was originally accused. He was the one who should have saved Maureen but did not."

Even after Cotton was selected as the opening victim, multiple versions of it were filmed. In the initial version, Cotton arrives home while talking to Christine on the phone, who seemingly has escaped and is safe at a coffee shop. However, he quickly discovers that the person on the other end of the phone isn't his girlfriend. Upon arriving at their apartment Cotton finds his girlfriend dead in a closet and Ghostface has been using a voice changer to impersonate her the whole time.

While Williamson didn't write the script for *Scream 3* he was still involved as a producer and offered notes. One of those notes was about the handling of Christine. "Kevin had the note of when he saw it, he's just like, don't have them rushing to save somebody who's just a body falling in a closet. That has no meaning," recalled Lussier. "It was a huge improvement. It was a great note."

With that note, the filmmakers began casting for an actress to play Christine. It is the only opening role in any of the films that required an audition process. Kelly Rutherford, who at that point was most well-known for the hit television show *Melrose Place* (1996), was selected to make her feature film debut with the role and was excited about taking on the character.

"When I auditioned for it, I knew it was kind of a thing to get this beginning of the movie. Drew Barrymore had just done it, so I thought, oh this has got to be really cool," the actress recalled. "I just thought I better be able to scream. That was the key. So, I just went in and did my best."

During the audio commentary for *Scream 3* Craven mentions that not only can the actress scream, but it was her ability to do so that won her the role. She wasn't aware that she had such an impressive scream. "My kids will probably say that too," Rutherford said with a laugh, before adding, "I don't know where it comes from. I don't know. I don't usually yell in my personal life very much."

The actress, who doesn't typically watch horror movies, was a fan of the *Scream* franchise because it was more of a murder mystery than a typical horror film.

"I hide under the covers with movies like that. But the way they had done *Scream* was so good. It was just the way they did it, with a little bit of a twist, made it so much fun," explains Rutherford. "That was sort of one of the first that I went, oh I can watch this. This is fun and the cast was great."

She didn't have much time to prepare before she was due on set, but due to the nature of the scene she didn't have to memorize much dialogue. Along with it being her first film, it was also a change of pace for her to play a more physically demanding role. Over the course of her few minutes onscreen, Rutherford is chased through an apartment (falls and all); fights to defend herself against Schreiber's character, who she thinks is attacking her as part of a game; and is ultimately killed and thrown down a hallway.

"I remember being very tired at the end of the day, and just like whoa, because between the yelling and the physical aspect," recalls Rutherford. "It was a very physical role, but it was fun. Again, it was not something I had ever done before."

The pace of filming was also an adjustment for the actress. She got her start on soap operas, where they filmed an entire script each day. When she transitioned to primetime television, the pace slowed a little bit; instead of filming a full episode in a day, they film a 42-minute episode over five days. Filming her sequence in *Scream 3* was an even slower process.

"You go on a film set and it's like molasses. It's just really, you're sitting there, really can we do this, can we do this? It's a different pace for sure," Rutherford said. "My role, it was nice because they did it over two days and it was two full days, so it really did go by fast. We did a lot of work in two days."

Despite only shooting for two days, the two actors got along quite well. "I didn't even remember that Kelly was ever not in it. But I loved hanging out with Kelly," Schreiber said. "I honestly don't remember her ever not being in it."

Rutherford says the admiration is mutual. "Liev is such a cool guy and I just admire him so much as an actor. I think those are the things that you take away, 'wow what an incredible experience I had on set and the people I worked with I really respect,'" said the actress. "[He] is so great. I think he was on set, preparing to do some Shakespeare play at the time, it was kind of funny that we were doing this type of genre and meanwhile he is over in the corner preparing for Shakespeare. That's so him."

"He was just adorable, you know. I was just so happy to do it with him because I think he is such a strong actor. I think as an actress, you feel so safe with him, he would catch you. You know what I mean? It sounds almost romantic. But it's more just, he's such a solid actor that you just feel safe to do anything. It's a comfort zone," Rutherford continued, who admits that it helped having Schreiber and Craven to guide her in the role. "Between Wes Craven being this calm guy that could have almost been a meditation teacher and you have this solid rock of an actor and a man; it was such a nice experience."

Rutherford's newness to films helped with her role because she was playing such an innocent character. Christine is targeted by Ghostface simply because she is in a relationship with Cotton. Through much of the opening scene, she actually thinks that it's her boyfriend who is chasing her as part of some kind of *Stab*-themed sex game. Even when he is trying to explain to her that they are in danger she doesn't believe him until it is too late as Ghostface stabs her from behind.

"I thought when they cast Kelly, that was an excellent choice, both in casting and creatively for the story," said Lussier. "That opening actually works really well and is very intense. It's good that it's about a character you care about and is a good sleight of hand of making the victim think that the person she loves is actually trying to kill them. It sets up a lot of very cool stuff in that opening."

That scene essentially redeems Cotton. Initially perceived as both Maureen Prescott's killer and a fame hungry ex-con, he's now cleared his name and gone on the straight and narrow to host his own top-rated daytime talk show. He is then targeted by Ghostface and sacrifices himself in an effort to save his girlfriend. He also doesn't give the killer information about where Sidney is hiding, even though it's unclear if Cotton actually knew that information or not. Schreiber sees the arc of his character throughout the series as a mirror to his own life—minus the murdering, of course.

"It was kind of following the arc of my own career actually. In the first one, I just had been a glorified extra. By the second one, I was making a legitimate run of things with a movie career. By the third time, I was already ready to talk about my post celebrity experiences," Schreiber says with a laugh. "That was part of what was so great about *Scream*, it poked fun at and it dramatized real contemporary life and issues. I don't know that a horror movie had been kind of socially hip up 'til that point and *Scream* really did that. We were all, kind of in a funny way, poking fun at ourselves with those characters. I know I hear Cotton was this sociopath who really just wanted to be on TV. I guess that sort of sums me up."

When it came to filming her cameos in the films, O'Dell used the context of her scene as clues to find out the larger story and who might be the killer.

"I remember so hard trying to deduct like, okay, what can I deduct from this scene that's going to happen. All I knew was certain people that [appeared in] the scene were still alive at that point. That's all I knew," O'Dell said. For *Scream 3*, that meant that she knew that Cotton Weary had been murdered early on as she was the television journalist Sidney sees reporting on his death.

AN EXPLOSIVE DEATH

The death of Matt Keeslar's character, Tom Prinze, is a unique killing in the series and one that truly acts as a time capsule for that specific moment in time. The scene begins with many of the main characters gathered at Jennifer's house when production is shut down after Sarah's death. Ghostface calls, but not on a phone this time—instead, he reaches out via fax machine. The fax, which Tom reads alone inside the house, says that the killer will give leniency to whichever person smells the gas. Then on cue, the entire house blows up with everyone else watching from the backyard.

The scene is probably one of the most digital effects heavy of any in the series; the first two films barely used any. In fact, the only digital effect in the first film was the reflection of Ghostface's mask in Henry Winkler's eye after Principal Himbry's murder, at a cost of $1,500.

In order to achieve the explosion effect, they had to take two shots and overlay them. It included having to take a plate shot of the house, to provide a reference between the two shots for the compositors. As far as direction about his death, Keeslar didn't receive much from Craven about what he was supposed to do while being blown up.

"I don't think we did it more than a couple of times, but I think what he said was like, you got to look like you are blowing up now," Keeslar recalls. "That's when I did that weird, *waaaa* type of thing and that was me trying to get into the method acting of how a person would feel when they are being blown up. But I don't know, I think I just tried something, and he was like, oh, that's fine."

It is partly due to that scene that Plec has never seen the final, completed version of the film. "As much as I love and admire all of those people that made all those movies and they're my family and I shouldn't speak critically, I just felt like that movie was not in the voice of the other two," Plec said. "I thought that when the house blew up, when the message came in on the fax machine and the house blew, in my head I was like, are you kidding me? How did we get here?"

As much as Plec might have been confused while watching it, the cast was just as perplexed about what was happening while making it. Keeslar said he found out that he was getting killed just prior to filming the scene. He knew that he wasn't the killer, but beyond that he didn't know how his character might be offed.

"I don't even know that I knew when I was supposed, or how I was supposed, to die. Obviously, I knew I was not the killer. I didn't get that script. So, yeah, I had no idea when I was going to be taken out," he explained. "I don't think that I, now kind of looking back, I don't remember when I got that scene necessarily. It seems like I was still figuring it out, even on that day. Oh, actually this is, I'm getting blown up here. This is the end of my character. I think I was just putting together as I was reading it. It could have been 24 hours before that, but literally, it was a new thing to me."

A CONTROVERSIAL DEATH

One of the most beloved aspects of *Scream 3* is the introduction of Parker Posey's Jennifer Jolie, the neurotic actress playing Gale Weathers in the *Stab* movies. Jennifer is a thorn in the real Gale's side throughout the film, but by the end the two form an unlikely partnership to solve the case. It's really a case of self-preservation, though. As Jennifer sees it, if she's with the real Gale Weathers, they won't kill her because the killer really wants to kill Gale.

The onscreen chemistry and banter between Cox and Posey is a highlight of the film. Posey was a direct offer and didn't have to audition for the role. The chemistry came through naturally between the two actresses.

"So brilliant, they were both amazing," Maddalena said about the pairing.

Adds Lussier, "I think that the Parker Posey stuff is great and it's really fun anytime she's onscreen."

Being that Jennifer became so beloved during the film, her death in the final act was met with jeers from fans. But unlike the reaction of other fan favorites like Tatum and Randy, fans were upset with the way that Jennifer died, not just that it happened, because it seems to occur because of a need to simply get rid of the character.

During the sequence that sees much of the remaining cast get butchered in quick succession, Jennifer ends up in a secret passageway behind Milton's bedroom. Inevitably, Ghostface finds and chases her into a closet that has a row of two-way mirrors. Frantically, Jennifer starts banging on the mirrors to get Dewey and Gale's attention—which she successfully does, as they quickly notice the mirrors shaking. However, rather than starting at the pane that is shaking, Dewey methodically starts at the opposite end of the mirrors, thus giving Ghostface enough time to trap Jennifer and murder her. When he finally shoots the pane she was behind, her lifeless body falls onto the floor.

Many fans have taken issue with why he would have done this, other than the mere fact that it allowed Ghostface to attack Jennifer—Posey, however, isn't one of them. She told *Too Fab* that she liked her character's death and the symbolism it holds. When asked, Lussier said that it is something that would have probably gotten fixed if they'd had the opportunity.

"I think in the land of infinite visual effects dollars, that would have been fixed. But that wasn't where we were at that time," the editor explains.

Although he does say that there was one death that did get altered in post-production—that of Jennifer's bodyguard, Steven Stone, played by Patrick Warburton. During production they had the phone conversation recorded one way, but then went back during ADR (automated dialogue replacement, when actors re-record dialogue after filming is complete) to change the tone.

"Patrick Warburton's death, her bodyguard, was interesting. The first version of that was quite different. Dewey's voice that's recorded is really aggressive, really like attacking and again is a bunch of crescendo, and then he's attacked. So, you can feel it coming. Then during ADR, Wes did this other version, which was just so strange, the version that's in there, so that when the attack comes, it makes Warburton even a bigger dick, you know, his character is even more because he started laughing at this guy who's almost in tears at the other end of line," Lussier said. "That was a real example of just ADR completely changing the tone of a scene and making the scare so much more successful."

18

THE END OF AN ERA

SCREAM 3 WAS SCHEDULED to be released at Christmas in 1999, but delays forced it to be pushed back. Rather than waiting an entire year to continue the trend of being released around the yuletide holiday, it became the first in the series released at another time of the year—it hit theaters on February 4, 2000. This trend would continue with the later films in the series.

At the turn of the century, the early part of the year was generally seen as a dumping ground for films that studios weren't sure would do well in other times of the year. However, studios would occasionally schedule films there to help them clean up at the box office since there was less competition. That strategy worked for *Scream 3*; the movie opened up to a franchise record of $34.7 million in its opening weekend, and almost entirely made back its budget in those three days.

That impressive number set a record for a February debut, and was the biggest ever opening for Miramax. That record was short lived— lasting just a year, until *Hannibal* (2001) grossed over $58 million the following February. The film also set a record for opening on the most movie screens for an R-rated film. It held that record for three years, until it was broken by both *Terminator 3: Rise of the Machines* (2003) and *The Matrix Reloaded* (2003). Keeslar learned about the film's stellar opening while in the Czech Republic filming a television adaptation of the book *Dune* (2000).

"It came out and it was number one at the box office that weekend. There was very little recognition or fanfare in the Czech Republic, and most of them were Brits, or Czech or Russian actors, German actors. I do remember the guy who was playing the lead in *Dune* was like, hey, his movie just was number one in the box office and everybody going like, oh interesting," Keeslar recalled. "I think it was probably the only movie that I was ever in that made money, like actual money at the box office and probably made back its budget without having a lot of weird overseas sales machinations and DVD and cable sales. That was different and new."

Also new was that *Scream 3* was the first film in the trilogy to not cross the $100 million dollar mark during its box office run. Domestically, it topped out at $89 million. Internationally, it did slightly better than its predecessors, earning $72.6 million. Regardless, it's a run that the producers were happy with.

"A lot of it was Bob paying to keep it in theaters and paying for publicity. Even the other numbers we reached was a lot of Bob really working hard to keep it in theaters," Maddalena said. Among the ways Weinstein extended their runs was through re-releasing the previous films. "Love that. But he probably decided not to do it, but you can't be disappointed at that number. No, we were thrilled with it."

The combination of *Scream 3* and *Scary Movie*, which was released the following summer, meant big things for Dimension Films, as it surpassed its parent company for box office grosses that year and led to a shift in power between the Weinstein brothers. About the drop at the box office, Besser believes that the audience had outgrown the series in the years between the sequels.

"Their lives changed. Their parents weren't dropping them off to the theater, or their one friend who had a car and a license would drive to the theater or had an older sibling who could take them. You are now talking about an age group that is in relationships. Some are married. They're working, it isn't going to school and being able to party," the producer explained. "The maturity of those years gives you a different life that you fall into and it isn't going to *Scream 3* when it opens on a Thursday."

INCREASED RECOGNITION

After production was finished on *Scream 3*, McRee returned to her everyday life, working as a flight attendant. She estimates that prior to the release of the film she might have gotten recognized once or twice a year by passengers, though they wouldn't exactly be able to place where they knew her from; they often suggested it was from a previous flight. That increased exponentially after the movie was released.

"All of a sudden *Scream 3* comes out and, you know, I walk through the terminal in my little flight attendant uniform, and I feel people looking at me and I feel people pointing at me. One day, one particular flight, [a pair of] boys were in high school, maybe first year of college. We land at JFK and it's a wide body 747, I'm in a jump seat facing AFT and these two boys across the aisle, are in the aisle going, psst, psst, psst, and they are kind of pointing and looking at me," said the actress. "On the way out, they go, 'You know, has anyone ever told you, you look exactly like the girl from *Scream*?' I just smiled and I said, 'Wow, gosh, what a compliment! Thanks. Hey, thanks for flying American. Enjoy your time in New York.' That is how I handled that. I felt giddy inside. I felt seen, heard, recognized. All those things that humans love. It was really sweet."

McRee adds, "That's when I realized the power of the flipping media, especially films, especially popular films made by well-known directors."

While the film may have raised the profile and recognizability of the cast, it didn't necessarily translate into boosts to their careers like the previous films had done for the actors.

"I think it was more about the franchise and less about the actor at the point. I think that there was no breakout star, right? They could have put anyone in those parts and it still would have been the same movie that it was," hypothesized Keeslar. "Unfortunately, it's kind of like white noise when you have that many young actors all in the same movie. It's a little bit like, yeah, he was in that, but so was everyone else. Big deal. It's not going to necessarily put you over the edge."

A MIXED REACTION

When the first two films were released, they were met with both critical acclaim and box office success. Upon its release, *Scream 3* might have done well at the box office, but the word of mouth wasn't as strong, and critics didn't love it as much as its predecessors.

It's long been a polarizing film, with some critics claiming that the franchise was running out of gas and fans taking strong positions on whether they liked the tonal shift or not.

"*Scream 3* is a funny thing. It's not a bad movie by any means, it's just a different *Scream* movie. It's often referred to as the Scooby-Doo *Scream*," explained Nick Meece, webmaster of the oldest *Scream*-dedicated webpage, Scream-Thrillogy.com. "Purists who are whole-heartedly Team Williamson loathe *Scream 3* simply because it's written by a different scribe. It's not the third and final entry that we were supposed to [get], and many fans can't accept the twist in *Scream 3*, feeling it comes out of left field. Can't say I completely disagree. Needless to say, the people that love *Scream 3*, really LOVE *Scream 3*."

"I think people, even during the making of it, there's a little bit more complacency, right? There's a little more okay, we're making this one, we've been successful two times before," Lussier admits about the criticisms that fans have had regarding the film over the years. "You could feel [Williamson's writing] missing in the third, and that Ehren was only available part-time and was on other projects and then the other writers they would bring in were just guest players. So, as such, you didn't have anybody with a whole vision of the story. You know, Wes did a lot of writing of some of the scarier elements, but you were still left with a sort of—goofy is probably too harsh—but sort of a tone with the movie-within-a-movie and the sort of Hollywood angle and stuff like that."

Konrad, on the hand, feels that the film might have been set up to fail due to the expectation fans had for the conclusion. Being that it wasn't written by Williamson allowed those vocal critics a scapegoat to place their blame.

"I think that traditionally and historically through time, be it this franchise or any others, there's always going to be, you can't ever make a fan happy 100% of the time. They're always going to find something, because what I've experienced when we used to do previews and sit there in audiences and hear them speak, all of which is their feedback is genuinely appreciated, to a certain degree. But you have to take it with this idea at hand that everybody likes to perceive themselves as an expert because that's how they see their value as an interactive member of what you're giving them. So, they want to be able to say, 'you know, I liked that cake, but it needed more vanilla.' 'Yeah, that was an interesting dish that you served me, but the chef that used to make it isn't here anymore. So, I don't like it.' Even if the only thing that's missing is a quarter teaspoon of pepper," the producer explained. "They're basically asking for the same thing and, I can't guarantee it, but I've seen it enough times that even if it had been a pure thing that Kevin had done, they probably would have had an issue with it because it's the third one. There's always one, be it *Alien*, be it any of them, be it *Star Wars*. People will look at it and go, what happened there?"

Scream 3's release also marked an end of an era for horror films. By 2000, tastes had started to shift again for the horror genre, favoring supernatural tinged films. Found footage ghost story *The Blair Witch Project* (1999) had come out the year prior and cleaned up at the box office, while *Final Destination* (2000) offered a nice transition from slasher films to ghost stories; *The Others* (2001) and *The Ring* (2002) would be released in consecutive years to big box office receipts. Standard slasher films still trying to ride the glossy, self-aware coattails of the *Scream* franchise began to struggle at the box office; both *Valentine* (2001) and *Urban Legends: Final Cut* (2000) had a hard time finding audiences in theaters.

"It's not so much *Scream 3*, but everything that came between *Scream 2* and *Scream 3* because so many similar self-aware horror films came out within that span of a couple of years," explained McKittrick. "You had like *I Know What You Did Last Summer* and that sequel. Ninety-eight you had *Urban Legend*. Then you had the revival of other slasher franchises that said, 'Whoa, wait a second. *Scream* kind of brought us back.'"

Many of the filmmakers believed their time visiting Woodsboro and the *Scream* universe was finished with this film after nearly a half decade. As a result, their feelings about wrapping the franchise were much more somber. "Definitely, [it] was so sad," said Maddalena.

SECTION 4

DON'T FUCK WITH THE ORIGINAL!

Composer Marco Beltrami, Editor Patrick Lussier, and Craven during the making of *Dracula 2000*. (Photo courtesy of Patrick Lussier)

19

CURSED IS WELL... CURSED

WITH THE RELEASE OF *SCREAM* 3, the planned *Scream* trilogy was complete. As such, the filmmakers moved on to other projects. Williamson had left *Dawson's Creek* by then and was in development for a new WB network show called *Glory Days* (2002). Craven turned his attention to developing new material and projects of his own, including an adaptation of the Japanese horror film, *Kairo* (2001), alongside his team of Maddalena, Mastandrea, and Besser. In 2002, Craven and Williamson were brought back together to work on *Cursed* (2005), a film that would go down in horror circles as a thing of legend due to its problem-plagued production.

A *SCREAM* RE-TEAMING

Mastandrea recalls working on *Pulse* (2006), which was their name for the *Kairo* adaptation (the Japanese title roughly translates to "circuit"). The film was about ghosts attempting to invade the human world through the internet. Development on the American version of the film began prior to the release of *The Ring*, which helped launch a wave of Asian horror remakes in the United States. "I thought it was a really good movie, and it would have been fun to do," Mastandrea explained. "We were really into *Pulse*. I know me and Wes really dug that idea. It wasn't a straight horror movie. I guess it was a horror movie, but it was a little psychological thriller there. It had a little more guts to it."

165

"Wes had written it, and Bob said he loved it. Then four weeks from shooting he said, 'I hate it.' Took us to the shed," Maddalena recalled about the project getting shut down. "He was really being mafioso at that time."

Weinstein pulled the plug on *Pulse* because he got excited about another project he wanted Craven to direct for the company instead. That movie, *Cursed,* would re-team him with Williamson. Right from the start there were disagreements about the direction of the project as Weinstein didn't like Williamson's idea for the movie because it was a werewolf movie that didn't have werewolves in it.

"His original idea was fucking awesome. It was brilliant," said Lussier. "Way better and they didn't want that."

That idea involved a college student studying to be a dancer. She possessed the gene of the werewolf, and although the gene wasn't active in her, she could jump a little higher, dance a little better. The main character used AA meetings and the recovery program to help fend off her cravings. She ends up getting attacked by a serial killer and while fighting back she scratches him, turning him into a werewolf. With enhanced powers, he stalks the streets of New York City for victims and goes back to find her to learn more about what is happening to him. While that concept was more of a slasher film than the finished product ended up being, it was also intended to be grittier than the *Scream* films had been.

"It was never written. I don't think the script ever existed, but somehow the notes from that company turned it into what it became," Plec explained.

One of the first changes to the script was to transport the action from the streets of New York City to sunny Los Angeles, a requirement that Craven requested if he was going to direct the film. The plot centered on three strangers meeting during a traffic accident where they are attacked by a werewolf and end up acquiring enhanced abilities. Somewhere along the way, the gritty tone was also scrapped.

Along with already being invested in directing *Pulse* as his next project, Craven wasn't sold on the idea of the movie due to his previous experience on *Vampire in Brooklyn.* "[Wes said], don't make me do this. I've made this movie; it was called *Vampire in Brooklyn* and it didn't work. You don't want to make this movie," Lussier recalled about Craven's hesitation to make the film.

Despite his instincts, one of the reasons the director signed on was because Weinstein again made him an offer he couldn't refuse. The producer offered to keep Craven's entire staff from *Pulse* on the payroll while they waited for the *Cursed* script to be completed.

Nevertheless, Weinstein was undeterred about bringing the film to fruition. He saw the re-teaming of the *Scream* filmmakers along with key cast members from the franchise—Skeet Ulrich, Omar Epps, Scott Foley, Portia DeRossi, and the voice of Ghostface, Roger L. Jackson, were all attached to *Cursed* at various points of its production—as a recipe for success. He was so sure about the project that he released a press release for the film before the cameras even began rolling.

"He is a gambler. Wes alone totals no good. Kevin alone, not good. Wes and Kevin together, good," Maddalena explained about Weinstein's thinking. "You really have to think of Bobby as a gambler. He put his money down on the combo, no matter what shape the script was in."

The press release had its intended effect.

"It was definitely hyped, and they were all excited about it. But they forget to have a script," Mastandrea said. "I honestly don't know how much Kevin was into it, or anybody was into it."

Production Shutdowns

Lussier offered his own perspective about why it's hard to successfully make a werewolf movie, though he acknowledges *An American Werewolf in London* (1981) and *The Howling* (1981) as examples of good werewolf movies. "I think werewolf movies are hard because you lose your actor. You don't in vampire movies. You don't in the slasher movie. Even if they're masked, right, once the reveal has happened, they can still be monstrous," Lussier said. "You see them become more horrific, not less. Whereas for a werewolf movie they actually had to become a werewolf and you lose the performance."

Rick Baker worked on the werewolf effects in both of Lussier's examples. In fact, he received an Academy Award for his work on *An American Werewolf in London*. Naturally, he was the one Weinstein turned to when it came time to design the werewolf in *Cursed*. He got the special effects wizard onboard by doing something that Weinstein was known to do—he threw money at him.

"Bob had these certain ideas. He wanted to work with Rick Baker, and Rick Baker didn't particularly want to do it. So, there was a lot of financial benefits thrown at everybody in order to have them on board," Besser said. "But nobody, they weren't invested."

While the script was being finalized, Beach and Katzman, who had initially been working on *Pulse*, were pulled over to cast *Cursed*. Along with several *Scream* alumni, they assembled a cast that included Corey Feldman, Mandy Moore, Christina Ricci, Milo Ventimiglia, Jesse Eisenberg, Scott Baio, Craig Kilborn, Robert Forster, Judy Greer, and fellow Craven alum, Heather Langenkamp.

Even with a cast in place and cameras ready to roll, the script was never locked in place. It was a problem that the team had experienced previously on *Scream 3*, but not to this level.

"Talk about a script changing. I don't know what was going on. The script was constantly changing. Whether that was Kevin being indecisive, or Wes," Miller recalled, adding, "I don't think Wes was ever indecisive. I think Wes was 'you tell me what you want me to film, and I'll film it' kind of thing. I'll make it work."

When production got underway, it was shut down prior to filming the ending, which was to take place at the grand opening of a wax museum. There were less than two weeks left at the time of the shutdown; they had filmed for almost two months at that point.

"We saw a cut of the first two-thirds of the movie and it just didn't feel like it was working yet and the idea of shooting the whole ending, which was never good to begin with and sort of ridiculous, seemed stupid," Plec recalled. "We stopped shooting to rewrite the ending, but in needing to rewrite the ending, we sort of realized that most of the movie didn't work. So, then we rewrote, like, most of the movie."

"I don't remember if it was they didn't like Skeet, or the chemistry, or what it was," Mastandrea said about the initial shutdown. "But again, in defense of everybody, if the script's not good, the story is not going to work, and I think they just kept trying to salvage it."

The re-writes called for major changes to the story, which also led many of the actors to leave the project, some of their own choosing and others not so much. Among the actors cut was actor John C. McGinley, who played one character's bullying father in the original iteration of the script; in the new iteration McGinley's character was dead.

"When they shot again, suddenly Jesse Eisenberg and Christina Ricci were brother and sister, there was no parents. The parents were dead, but the sequence—the Zipper sequence—from the original was still there. The wrestling sequence from the original was still there. Josh Jackson had come in to replace Skeet, then he was opening a nightclub called Tinsel as opposed to the wax museum," Lussier said, describing the changes that occurred between the original and final versions of the film. Lussier joined the production late, intending for it to be a six-week assignment; he ended up working on the film for 19 months.

With many of the actors exiting the film, a new round of casting had to begin. However, Beach and Katzman had moved on to other projects and weren't hired to do the second round.

"We did the first one, and I think that they didn't want to keep paying us our rate," said Katzman. "So, they went to someone with a lesser rate."

The new cast added some *Scream* alumni, such as Jackson, and singer Mya was added as a replacement for Moore, even though Moore had already completed all of her scenes. Ricci, Eisenberg, Baio, and Greer remained with the film.

Some of the creative team also left after the first shut down, including both Miller and Besser. "We did the first beginnings. Then it just wasn't working, there was this dead time. So, I took another project," Besser said about his exit. "It kept starting and shutting down. It was kind of obvious it wasn't on the paper. It wasn't coming together."

Filming eventually resumed and they shot for another month and a half before production came to a halt again. With multiple stops and starts, some would have considered scrapping the movie or just finishing and hoping to recoup some of the money spent. However, the producers kept running with it because an initial test screening yielded decent test scores.

"It scored in like the 60s…low 60s, but it was just high enough that, okay, the movie's not a disaster. Maybe if we keep spending more money, we can get it up to the 80s, you know where *Scream* was. *Scream* and *Scream 2* previewed high, 83-88, stuff like that," Lussier explained, adding that he thinks that score was an anomaly. "It's a bit of a fool's errand because you're chasing something and every other preview we had with every new version only always scored worse."

Interesting, Maddalena said that her and Craven's deal with Miramax included a clause for their films that Craven would receive final cut approval on the films if the test scores were high enough.

"We had a deal where at a test screening, if we hit 72 good and very good, we had final cut," Maddalena explained. However, that came with the concern that the Weinstein brothers might have been playing with the numbers to keep them from achieving the goal on their previous films. "We were always worried that Harvey was paying off the research company and [making] the numbers lower, but we can't prove it."

CHANGES UNTIL FINALLY BEING RELEASED

In an attempt to fix the issues, one area of the film that was continually being changed was the ending for the film. Jackson's character had originally filmed a more tragic ending. In the initial conclusion he is a more sympathetic character, having accidentally turned Greer's character into a werewolf, who has Ricci kill him. In the actual ending, he turns out to be the film's ultimate villain in a climatic fight with Ricci and Eisenberg.

"We went back and decided that ending didn't work, so we reshot [it]. Then we decided that ending didn't work, so we reshot it again," Plec recalled.

A last-minute decision was also made to trim the film from an R-rating to a more teen-friendly PG-13. This news only further fueled discord among fans, who had already gotten a chance to see gory pictures of Mya's death scene accompanying an article in a horror magazine. When the film was released—even the unrated DVD version—her actual death happens offscreen. In a further attempt to achieve the lower rating, Dimension brought in another director to shoot additional footage for the commercial. Some of that footage ended up in the final product as well.

When all was said and done, the final product of *Cursed* had a running time of 97 minutes, including opening and closing credits, and uses just 12 minutes of footage from the first attempt at filming the movie. After more than two years since that initial press release was sent out, the film finally made it into theaters in February 2005. With years of bad press from the problems on set, the film was basically D.O.A. at the box office. Critics weren't kind to it either, with the film scoring negative reviews. They weren't the only ones who disliked the film.

"It didn't make any sense to me, honestly," Mastandrea said. "As a whole, I wasn't a fan of it."

Lussier was a tad more kind in his review, saying, "There's good stuff in *Cursed*. I mean, there's [also] terrible stuff in *Cursed*, don't get me wrong." He still has archived in his possession assembled work prints of all of the discarded versions of the film, which the filmmakers all lovingly refer to as *Cursed 1*, *Cursed 2*, and *Cursed 3*, to differentiate the multiple times the production shut down and restarted.

Plec offers her own explanation about what went wrong with the film, "It just never knew what it was. It never knew, was it a spoof? Was it a comedy? Was it meant to be taken seriously? Was it meant to be scary?"

Its opening weekend gross was $9.6 million, coincidentally landing it in fourth place, the same position that *Scream* had opened to nearly a decade ago. Fate wouldn't deal them a surprise this time around, though. It would just barely double that opening frame's gross before it left theaters. Globally, it didn't even make back its reported $38 million dollar budget (though according to some of the filmmakers, the actual number is closer to $100 million).

The experience of filming *Cursed* was so negative that the normally quiet and mild-mannered Craven hung up a calendar at his house, counting down the days until he wouldn't have to deal with the Weinstein brothers any longer. Looking back, Maddalena doesn't mince words about their experience either.

"*Cursed* was the horrible experience. I think it was a bad idea to begin with," the producer explained. "Because [Weinstein] kept pulling the plug; what we should have done is just quit. He didn't like our vision, we can't... you can't tell me what my vision is. We should quit. He did that three times."

"I love everybody deeply and I was thrilled to be in that mix," Plec said, "but I'm not really sure creatively that it was something that needed to get made."

Pulse did eventually get made and was released the year after *Cursed*, but it was met with a similar fate. The film, starring Kristen Bell, Ian Somerhalder, and singer Christina Milian, was directed by Jim Sonzero, though Craven received a co-writing credit. Unlike *Cursed*, the indifference that fans showed the film couldn't be blamed on years of bad press or infighting. In the end, it grossed $20 million at the box office, with an opening of $8.2 million.

20

NEW DECADE, OLD PROBLEMS

As *Cursed* was being released, the Weinstein brothers were in the middle of a breakup with The Walt Disney Company, who had purchased the studio in 1993. That same year, the brothers left Miramax after a fight with the parent company over the release of Michael Moore's *Fahrenheit 9/11* (2004). As part of the exit, they launched their own independent studio, the self-named The Weinstein Company, and took Dimension Films with them. Despite producing some hit movies, its financials quickly became shaky, leading to layoffs beginning within five years.

Like the old saying goes, you can't keep a good man down. In Hollywood, that saying also refers to any franchise that is still seen as financially viable. Even though the series was always billed as being a trilogy, Dimension—specifically, Weinstein—was in need of a hit and decided to go back to the well for a fourth entry. It didn't hurt that in the ensuing years since *Scream 3*, almost every seminal horror movie had been rebooted, revived, or remade in some way, shape, or form. In fact, Dimension had a hand in many of them.

"I wasn't surprised. By the time you have a franchise, and at that point, it had been so long, so there was legit hunger for it. It didn't feel like it was over saturating the market. It didn't feel like it was being gratuitous," said Plec. "It felt like it was time. I think it was what, the 10-year anniversary, or 15-year anniversary? So, it felt time, and I was glad that they were coming back together."

Adds Ziembicki, "They released them, and then there was the pause and then rebooting, that's what a lot of the business now is about. It's the franchising. They made wise decisions, how to keep this without it going stale."

Almost a decade had passed when development started on the new film, and just enough time had gone by that bad feelings subsided from the train wreck that had been *Cursed*. Since that film's release, Craven had spread his wings and worked with other studios for his follow-ups, including the well-received thriller *Red Eye* (2005) and a segment in the anthology film *Paris, je t'aime* (2006). He returned to horror with *My Soul to Take* (2010), which was the first film he had both written and directed since *Wes Craven's New Nightmare*.

Despite the bullying and problems that Craven endured during his tenure with the Weinstein brothers, no one seemed surprised that he was willing to come back into the fold to make another *Scream* film; especially considering that *My Soul to Take* was another tough experience for the director.

"If you look at Wes's career, and it's not direct one to one; but he makes *Deadly Friend* and then makes *Serpent and the Rainbow*, right? He makes *Cursed*, then he makes *Red Eye*. He makes *Vampire in Brooklyn*; he makes *Scream*," Lussier offered as an explanation. He adds that after *My Soul to Take* was changed greatly from Craven's original vision, "a chance to go back into the *Scream* universe and make something that he had great success with makes total sense."

Mastandrea agrees with Lussier's assessment, adding that Craven was better equipped this time around because of his previous experience with Miramax and Dimension. Plus, the director was offered a chance to do what he loved to do. "He loved making movies. That's what he did, and this was an opportunity to make a movie," said Craven's longtime friend and colleague. "He'd done battle with them before."

Lussier explains that the large amounts of money that Weinstein was throwing around helped to soften the blow from their previous fights, or at least the memories from the disagreements. "As a friend of mine used to say, they never paid you for what they did. They only paid you for what they did to you."

It wasn't just about the money; Weinstein was also a great salesman, especially when it came to getting something done that he really wanted. "Bob, to his credit, is just a very convincing person," Plec said. "He has a lot of passion and he gets very passionate about wanting to make something. It's catching and it's contagious."

One Movie, Three Scripts

When *Scream 4* was released, Williamson explained that he came up with the idea for the film by partly recycling the idea he and Plec had originally come up with for *Scream 3*. He had always planned to return to Woodsboro; he just needed to find out where the surviving characters were today to really come up with the plot. Once he had that figured out, the writer pitched the idea to Weinstein. He was sold immediately.

Even so, Weinstein hadn't changed, and things quickly got off to a rocky start. Along with Williamson, he enlisted Craven and Kruger to write drafts for the film, but he didn't tell any of the men that the others were working on competing scripts.

"Bob was gambling. He was throwing a million dollars here, a million dollars here, a million dollars here to get the script out of those three. Maybe somebody else," Maddalena recalled. "Bob had a lot of writers at the same time, that didn't know about each other, working on it. There was a lot of fighting and it was bloody. I think Wes wrote a draft. Ehren Kruger wrote a draft. Kevin wrote a draft. And they didn't know about each other."

After all of the fights and issues that had ensued on the previous projects, there was one person who was more than happy to jump off of the Weinstein merry-go-round. Plec, now busy with *The Vampire Diaries* over at the CW, wasn't involved in the making of *Scream 4*.

"It's so funny because I read Kevin's first draft, I think. Then he's, like, Bob has so many notes. Bob wants to change this; Bob wants to change that. Bob wants to do that different," Plec said. "I was like, Oh, I'm not going down this road again. So, I just let him suffer with it while I kept the doors open at *Vampire Diaries*."

Officially, Williamson was the one who would get credit for writing the script. Kruger, however, received a producing credit on the film. As with *Scream 3* the filmmakers were plagued with the script constantly being in flux throughout *Scream 4*'s production. In fact, some who worked on the film say the script issues were even worse this time around.

"I remember more script problems in [*Scream 4*] than I do in any of them. I don't remember massive rewrites during the filming of [*Scream 3*]," Mastandrea said about the experience. He adds, "When you don't have a script or a story, it's hard for a movie to be successful. I didn't have great hopes for it because of that. But, obviously, I want everything I do to succeed."

At the time of the film's release, Williamson said in interviews that along with writing *Scream 4* he had mapped out the idea for a whole new trilogy if the new film successful. Those additional two films were never made. The fifth film in the series was conceived as an original idea by writers Guy Busick and James Vanderbilt. While developing the concept, the filmmakers reached out to Williamson, who is a producer on the film. He liked the idea and direction they had and didn't feel it necessary to bring up the remnants of his previously unmade second trilogy.

As work on the scripts for *Scream 4* was underway, Craven's team began to re-assemble for production. Many of them agreed to do the film based on their relationship with the director; however, the lack of a script made the cast and crew take pause.

"They said, 'We're gonna do four,' which I said, 'Okay let's do it.' And it was going to be in Michigan," Mastandrea said. "I remember getting there and talking to Courteney and none of us really had, we didn't have the script, and we're saying is this going to be okay? Is this going to be cool?"

DYSFUNCTION

"Everything was kind of falling apart then. The dysfunction was big with The Weinstein Company. Bob really made a lot of enemies when he had three scripts going on at once," Maddalena said. "So, I think it just needed a break."

Moreover, a key member of the previous films was being cut out of the new sequel. As development began, Konrad, who had been instrumental in getting the franchise off the ground, was having discussions with both Weinstein and Williamson about returning. But something happened along the way that led to the production moving on without her.

"I can't really speak to it because none of it made any sense. I mean we were very actively in conversation," said the producer. "I was obviously making another film, but nothing had happened on *Scream 4* yet, nor was it going to for a while. I think that what happens is, as tradition with the way Miramax used to roll, is if there's any opportunity to try to translate fine print into a language that services their benefit, especially if it has to do with money... Obviously, as the success of the franchise grew, so did the ambition level for all the players involved. Be it actors, be it Kevin, be it Wes, and you know the above the line continues to expand and if there's an opportunity to cut something off the vine, then you know, Bob and Harvey, are notorious for that."

That fine print referred to Konrad's availability to produce the film. "As was their custom and tradition, especially at Miramax, was to find a potential gray area in the language of exclusive availability, which was their interpretation of the language that I had to be exclusively available. Then they kept changing the start date to make sure that it fell in line, after knowing what my schedule was on a previous film, that I wouldn't be exclusively available," Konrad explained.

She filed a $3 million lawsuit against The Weinstein Company in December 2010 claiming that she was entitled to have the first opportunity to produce any of the sequels in the series. Instead, she found out about *Scream 4* through media reports. Part of the claim was that she was left out of the producing team so that Craven's wife, Iya Labunka, could be brought in as a producer, thus lowering the budget for the project. The lawsuit was settled prior to the film's release in April 2011 with undisclosed terms giving Konrad a cash payment and a small percentage of the film's back-end grosses. She is also listed as an executive producer on *Scream 4*.

"I think they believed they had a way semantically of not having me be involved to the level that my contract provided me, based on availability, which was proven to be not accurate," Konrad said about the lawsuit.

Additionally, actor Nico Tortorella, who uses the pronouns they and them, noted that Williamson was never on set during production. In fact, the two didn't meet until Tortorella booked a role in Williamson's television show, *The Following*. "He was detached by the time that I got attached," Tortorella said, referring to *Scream 4*. "He was never there. He had no hands in the pot. I know there was like a major rewrite and Wes kind of just took it all over with some new writers. There was some energy there. I'm not exactly sure what it was. But it was nice going into *The Following* knowing that I had some sort of relation to Kevin."

"I think Bob and Kevin weren't speaking, as I recall," Maddalena said. "It was just very dysfunctional, let's just put it that way. It could not have been more dysfunctional."

Mastandrea adds that Williamson's absence wasn't necessarily a new thing. The first A.D. said that after the first film, Williamson had been busy with his own career. "He wasn't around. I didn't really see Kevin much after [*Scream*] one, to be honest with you. He just, he was doing his thing and hugely successful. I love Kevin. Kevin always had a great attitude."

Because rumors of strife leaked to the press about Williamson possibly leaving the project, the writer was asked about it during the press circuit for the film's release. He shot down rumors of any ill will, saying his absence was due to contractual obligations to be on set for *The Vampire Diaries.*

Despite the trepidation that everyone had from the shaky start, the idea of Craven and Williamson teaming up again with the surviving legacy cast members created an instant buzz about the film.

"I don't know if I would be that interested if Wes and Neve weren't attached," actor Rory Culkin said. "That was probably the biggest draw for me."

TACKLING A CHANGED WORLD HEAD ON

The world had changed in the decade since the original trilogy was released, meaning the franchise had to pivot as well. Horror as a genre had gone through, and mostly come out the other side from, a torture porn phase that saw a return to the gruesome and graphic violence that people associated with films from the 1970s exploitation period. This resulted in a film that was darker than its predecessors and dealt with a more cynical generation impacted by social media and a yearning to be famous for the sake of being famous.

The idea of becoming famous for no discernible reason is actually a theme that might have been ahead of its time. At the time of *Scream 4*'s release, people weren't living their lives out for millions of people to watch on social media. Influencers were barely a thing, and definitely hadn't been fully realized in the way that they are a decade later. Social media has a dark side; people often feel emboldened to say anything anonymously without fear of real-world repercussions.

Culkin commented, "That's interesting because it was sort of, I mean social media was a thing, but it wasn't what it is today, right? Influencer wasn't a word that we used often."

"That's part of the whole theme too, the darkness is emerging from the society on social media," Jackson said. "I really like that idea that social media is the mask and people hide behind it. They say all kind of things online that they wouldn't say in person or they behave in ways that are just, you know, you can see it very much these days that people can really be monstrous."

It made sense that the franchise would incorporate technological advances. The first film was one of the first horror movies that had characters using cell phones. One of the ways that *Scream 4* played around with social media was to have the character of Robbie Mercer recording and live streaming his high school experience. It wasn't something that was as popular when the film was made as it is now, which meant the props department had to figure out the best way to have the headset work for the film.

"I don't think it was ever specified in the script as to how he is wearing it. It's kind of strange, because this was just before Twitch and all of these live streamers now. We do it on our phone, or our GoPro attached to us now. So, we never knew what, how they were going to live stream. The prop makers tried a few things with me, and then he came to that; the whole web cam attached to the headphones. I was fine with that, I thought that was a great idea because we can kind of flip it around and do the tricks that way," actor Erik Knudsen said. He adds that by the end of production he was happy to see it go away. "I couldn't really move my head really fast or else the camera would flop around everywhere. So, my acting was slightly limited. But no, I mean, I had no problems with it. At the end I was probably a little annoyed with it. It was a clunky object that's lopsided on your head, kind of limiting your range."

Still, these heady themes needed to be worked into a cohesive script, which the film didn't have by the time filming started.

"What else do you need other than script issues? If you have a bad script, Bob is lying to everybody; it just doesn't make for a good set. Let's put it like that," Maddalena warned.

21

ASSEMBLING A
CAST TO DIE FOR

THE ANNOUNCEMENT OF a new *Scream* movie was met with excitement by fans and actors alike. Many of the actors jumped at the chance to be a part of the next installment because of their affinity for the franchise. Another big draw was having Craven, Williamson, and the surviving legacy actors returning to play their beloved characters.

Since it came out 15 years after the original film's release, *Scream 4* marked the first time that many of the cast members had grown up with Ghostface as part of their lives. As millennials born in the late 80s to early 90s, the original *Scream* films were released while many of the new crop of victims were still too young to watch it; however, that didn't stop some of them from being traumatized by the character at an early age.

"My grandmother loved to scare us when we were kids. She constantly tried to scare us. The Ghostface mask was one of the tools she would use. She would put it on the vacuum, turn the lights off while we were downstairs, then push the vacuum down the stairs," remembers Knudsen about some of his first encounters with Ghostface. "It stuck with me; it was one of the things that scared me the most. When *Scream* came out, I was a huge fan."

Fittingly, Culkin was the one who used the mask to scare his siblings during their formative years. "I was Ghostface for Halloween when I was six, I think first grade, second grade. I scared the shit out of my sister once in the bathroom mirror," Culkin remembers. He adds that the original movie may have traumatized him as well, though, "I remember watching when I was way too young, like renting from Blockbuster, and that opening scene just brutalizing my mind as a kid."

Along with being fans of the original trilogy, the actors were just as aware of *Scary Movie*. Tortorella admits that they may have called David Arquette by his *Scary Movie* counterpart's name, Deputy Doofy, while filming *Scream 4*.

"I think a lot of people, the younger generation at least, grew up also watching *Scary Movie*, the comedy version of it, and they would confuse the two because *Scream* is a bit of a comedy as well," Knudsen said. "People wouldn't know. They don't want to watch a silly horror movie, when in fact it's actually pretty scary."

FINDING THE RIGHT ENSEMBLE

Casting director Nancy Nayor took over the reins from Beach and Katzman to cast the fourth film, along with Avy Kaufman. They began their work while the script was still being written. Prior to working on *Scream 4*, Nayor worked with Craven on the remake of his horror classic *The Last House on the Left* (2009), on which he served as a producer. She would also work with Williamson again after the sequel, for the television show *The Secret Circle* (2011).

"Usually, I read the script and then I have ideas. I find out if anyone is already set, or if anyone is returning from a prior story. Then I kind of usually come up with ideas of who I think, maybe a top dozen suggestions, of who I think might be interesting for each of the different characters and talk to the filmmaker and see if we are on the same page. We might have identical lists, or we might have slightly different lists, but we just need to be sure that philosophically, creatively, we are in the same ballpark," Nayor said about her process when starting a project. "I was really happy when we, I think, first talked about ideas we were definitely on the same page."

She said working on the film without the finished script didn't hinder anything. Things were locked into place enough that she could do her work.

"I don't remember it really altering the casting process that much. I mean, I think we kind of knew the basics of who the characters were," Nayor explained. "We knew the script was always evolving and anything could happen. So, you kind of had to have actors that not only could read those lines well but could completely adapt if suddenly the script took a left turn. They need to be the kind of actors that could pivot on a dime and improvise and be malleable and just be able to go with any changes that came up in the eleventh hour. Some can do that, and others are just not able to."

To help the cast during production, the filmmakers also hired an acting coach. The actors could utilize him if they had any issues with receiving the last-minute script revisions.

"There was a coach on set, an acting coach on set named John Kirby. He was actually [actor] Bruno Kirby's brother and he was there if you just wanted to, like, throw some ideas at him," Culkin recalled. "It didn't affect the actors in any way because if there was new dialogue, we had a guy to run lines with available."

Much like how *Scream 2*'s cast was larger than its predecessor, *Scream 4*'s cast included an even bigger cast than the previous films. With such a big ensemble, Nayor had to look for specific characteristics. Among those was finding actors who could work as part of a team both on camera and off-camera.

"I think it is a combination of who's sort of popular at the moment, who's very talented, who's okay in an ensemble, because sometimes you can overcast and choose people that just stick out. This is such an ensemble piece," the casting director said. She adds, "You want ones who play well with others, so you don't have obnoxious people on set off-screen and ones just nice when the cameras roll. Wes was so kind and so lovely that I would never want to put anyone with him that had a bad attitude on any level."

FINDING THE RIGHT KILLERS

Being able to blend in with the rest of the cast was crucial when it came to casting the characters who would be the killers. Sometimes having an uneven balance between known and unknown actors can give viewers a hint as to what is going to happen to the actor's character, which is what happened with the character of Olivia in *Scream 4*. As one of Jill's best friends, Olivia—played by a then-unknown actress named Marielle Jaffe—ends up being the first of the film's victims after the opening bloodbath.

"It does kind of tip the hand if someone is either more famous or less famous to sort of have a sense of what the ending is going to be," Nayor said. "You would think when you go into a movie you want to be surprised, and yet people are always trying to predict the ending."

As with previous films, there was great secrecy surrounding the project. Those auditioning had to sign non-disclosure agreements (NDAs) and auditioned using scenes from previous films.

That secrecy was taken to another level for actress Emma Roberts. Her manager told casting directors that the actress was no longer auditioning for roles and was instead "offer only." However, because she had yet to do a role like this, Craven wanted to meet with her prior to making an offer to ensure she was up to the task. Her work with Ryan Murphy, which she has arguably become most associated with, wouldn't start until two years after *Scream 4* was released.

"Sometimes that happens. They make it special. Instead of it being offer only, then well, if they could make it a meeting/reading, this actor or actress would like to feel special," Beach explains about the practice. "Sometimes its ego, but sometimes it's the agent."

With that in mind, a secret meeting was set up at Craven's house for Roberts to read for the role. But it had to be kept confidential. "We were really sworn to secrecy. She didn't come to my office. She needed to read; she hadn't really done a role quite like that with such a twist at the end. Even though she normally didn't read, for this project she read. But we kept it very much under wraps," Nayor recalled about the top-secret meeting. "It was very exciting that we scheduled a reading for her. I couldn't even tell my cameraman where we were going."

Craven was already in Michigan doing pre-production work on the film, so his daughter let them into the house. A camera and monitor were set up that fed live to Craven halfway across the country. He would then watch and offer direction from his location while she was recorded from Los Angeles.

"It was [a] very secretive, cool, stealth, sort of underground process," Nayor said.

After going through the audition process for Nayor, Culkin was brought in to meet with Bob Weinstein. It was during that meeting that he found out that he would be playing one of the killers in the film. But he almost missed out on getting the part because he skipped his initial audition.

"I think I was working, focusing on another project that I wanted, and my manager called me. She was, like, did you miss your audition? I was like oh yeah, I think so, because I'm like 20, I'm an idiot," Culkin said. "She goes, 'Well, this is a pretty good one, don't let the four dissuade you. This is a really cool project; I think you should be part of it.'"

With that, he went into a newly scheduled audition and was subsequently called to the producer's office to read the script. They weren't releasing the script, so the only way to read it was inside The Weinstein Company offices. Even then, the opening and closing of the script had been removed.

"Bob Weinstein came in and he pretty much just revealed how it's going to start, and the big reveal. He was describing the project to me and he said 'and the best part of all this,' and he went quiet. I leaned forward, like eyes wide and he was like, 'I love the look in your eyes. You're the killer.' Suddenly, like, it really spiced up the whole idea for me," the actor said, although his excitement about the meeting got slightly deflated after talking to his manager. "When I spoke to my manager after that meeting, I was like, 'Well, you know, I spoke to Bob Weinstein.' She goes, 'Did he have a dramatic pause at some point?' Yeah, that was kind of his thing. I thought that was unique for me."

While Culkin was informed about the twist prior to the start of filming, he wasn't sure who else was privy to the information. This meant he had to be careful while hanging out off the set with the cast members to not spill any details.

"Like the question, I think they all know that I'm the killer, but I'm not sure. I don't want to get drunk and start talking to these people too much," Culkin recalled. "It was funny because I didn't know who else knew that going on set. So, I didn't like, you know, I wasn't flaunting it. I kind of kept quiet and some hints like, 'Oh, he knows what's up.'"

Tortorella said that they recently heard that their character, Trevor, was also originally considered to be one of the killers. They guessed that the change was made because it would have been too much like the first film.

MAKING SURE TO HAVE BACK UP ACTORS

Actresses Lake Bell and Lauren Graham were originally cast in the film as Deputy Judy Hicks and Jill's mother, Kate Roberts, respectively. However, both ended up leaving the project prior to the start due to conflicts that came up. Another cast member dropped out, giving Knudsen his chance to join the franchise as Robbie Mercer, one of the founders of Woodsboro's Stab-a-thon. Nayor took the shifting cast list in stride, though.

"You always have to have levels of options if somebody suddenly becomes unavailable for any personal or professional reason. That can happen right down to the wire, and you have to know you have back up choices, too," the casting director said. She adds that shifts can also change based on other casting decisions. "Someone will get an idea, you suddenly cast one part and realize, oh now we have a red-haired, freckled person and then we want something different somewhere else. The lists are always changing and evolving during the process. You don't just pull the trigger on everyone at once. As you make your first choice and your second choice, it affects your third and fourth choices for other roles."

Instead of flying to audition in person for Nayor in Los Angeles, Knudsen recorded his audition just weeks before filming began in his parents' basement. Since he loved the series so much, just getting the chance to audition made him excited. He says it was one of the auditions in his career that he made sure to give his all in an attempt to gain the role.

"I was in Toronto at the time. A lot of kids, if you go to L.A., you just audition there. But I am more of a homebody, so I stay home. They just asked me to do a self-tape. I believe I self-taped in my parents' basement. I just set up a curtain, a tripod, filmed it with my girlfriend and sent that in," the actor recalled. He was given feedback and redid the audition tape another way that sealed the deal. "Tried it the second way, was told I got it. I think two weeks after that I flew out to Michigan to shoot."

With his casting coming so close to the start of production, he arrived in Michigan slightly later than the other cast members. His presence at the table read caught some of the actors off guard. "I think it was the read-through that we finally met everyone. They were a little surprised to see me. I think they were casting someone else, then they pick me last minute," Knudsen explained. "So, it was a little surprise."

Bell's exit from the film made way for actress Marley Shelton to take over the role. Shelton's audition is one that still sticks out to Nayor all these years later. About Shelton, Nayor said, "She was a lot of fun. We read a lot of people for that, but she's just so funny. I think people didn't realize how funny she was, so I think that was one that was really definitely pleasurable."

Another role that attracted a lot of attention was that of Rebecca Walters, Sidney's publicist and a fan favorite in the film. Alison Brie would eventually be cast in the role.

"I saw [Gabrielle] Union. We saw so many great actresses for that and they each made it so funny and unique, but [Brie] was just like the funniest and she's got a wicked sense of humor. She really won a role that I thought so many great actresses auditioned for," Nayor said.

However, the roles of Deputy Perkins and Deputy Hoss were slightly difficult to cast because they had to appear as a duo and have a certain kind of chemistry since almost all of their scenes were together. "That was really kind of challenging because sometimes you would find [an actor you] love but then you'd think they aren't quite going with this other actor I love. That doesn't work as well," Nayor explained. "There was a lot of mixing and matching."

Almost Losing A Role

For many of the actors, the audition process was an extensive one. Tortorella says the process was one of the longest they have gone through for a role. The film was one that, like the other sequels, everyone in Hollywood was trying to be a part of, which is what made them audition. "Every single person my age and their cousin wanted that job. It was a career-making, game-changing role. It was a no-brainer. I mean, I had done a handful of things, but I hadn't like properly broken yet, I would say," Tortorella said, who admits to not having watched any of the previous films in the series prior to their audition.

Nayor seconds Tortorella's statement about the excitement around the project, saying "Sometimes sequels get a lot of attention and other times they get less attention. I think because Wes was directing, this was an event, made it an event. I think people really were excited, for sure."

To secure the role of Trevor Sheldon, Jill's cheating ex-boyfriend, Tortorella went through multiple rounds of auditions on both coasts, including a meeting with Weinstein. After being offered the role, they almost lost it just as quickly due to an unscheduled announcement.

"I was in L.A.; I did a bunch with casting. Then I flew to New York and I met with the Weinsteins, did more casting, and went back to L.A. I think I did one more meeting in L.A. I can't remember who with, but it was literally 17 times. I don't think I've ever auditioned for something more in my life than that movie," Tortorella explained. "Then ultimately, I wound up getting the job and stupid, stupid me, I went on Twitter immediately. I was like, guess what, I'm in the new *Scream*, yeah, before there was a press release, and I was almost fired. So, I learned that the hard way."

22

ACTORS WERE HARMED IN MAKING THIS FILM

EVER SINCE THE FIRST FILM, Craven had been open to the actors ad-libbing lines. Many of them appreciated his willingness to let them explore the moment with their characters. Sometimes, he would even offer lines to improve moments in the films. It was the director himself who came up with one of Kenny's most quoted lines from the first film.

"'I'm not Jesus' is often quoted. It is an improv-ed line, but it was Wes's suggestion. [Gale says], 'Jesus, Kenny, the camera' and Wes goes, let's fill it up," Brown recalled about one his character's trademark lines came to be. "There were different things done, but I don't know, at one point, he goes, 'Hey, my name isn't Jesus, say that.' So, it was his idea."

The returning cast members for *Scream 4* were aware of the way that Craven worked, but the new cast wasn't sure how far to veer from the script's dialogue. Before doing so, they wanted to check with the director.

"He sort of let you go on your own direction and then will just nurture that idea if he approved," Culkin recalled. "I remember I talked to him early on over the phone about the first *Scream*. I was like, it's so amazing, that moment between Skeet Ulrich and Matthew Lillard when they're losing control of the situation near the end and Matthew Lillard has that line like my mom's gonna kill me, man, and Skeet Ulrich throws the phone off his head. Wes told me that wasn't scripted or anything. Skeet just bounced the phone off his head, and he liked that. So, when I heard that I was like, oh, in telling me that story he's giving me permission to play around and he'll probably keep it, if it's entertaining."

"I was kind of surprised with such a big movie. We would change dialogue on the day. There were a lot of lines there, a lot with Courteney, where we would do one take, then for the punchline she would say something else. Then we would do another take, a different punchline. It was hard because they were hysterical most of the time and we couldn't laugh," adds Knudsen. "When you are tied down so much, you're nervous about it and you don't want to screw it up. But if you know that you can just have fun with the character, you get a lot more personality out of your actor."

Jackson was known to ad-lib some of his lines to get more of a reaction out of the actors on the other end of the line. Similar to what he did with Jamie Kennedy, he got a strong reaction with one of his lines to Campbell. "I just sort of thought with number four there was a certain expectation, and by this point the darkness was appropriate, not so much charm," he explains. "One of the lines I improvised in that film that was used, sort of indicative of that, when I said to Neve Campbell, 'I'm going to slit your eyelids in half so you can't blink when I stab you in the face.' When Wes called cut, Neve said into the phone, 'You sick fucker.'"

As open to changing the dialogue as Craven was, the actors also knew that there were certain times that you couldn't add your own spin to the script. One of those times is when you are in charge of reciting the most famous line from the entire franchise: *"What's your favorite scary movie?"* In *Scream 4*, the honor fell on Knudsen's Robbie Mercer. The line comes early in the film when the teenager asks his classmates the questions live on his web stream. Similar to how Randy answered the question in *Scream 2* with *Showgirls*, Kirby offers a Disney movie as a joke answer. Still, the gravity of having that line wasn't lost on the actor.

"It's definitely big shoes to fill by saying that line because you know when you say it, it most likely will be in the trailer; it most likely will be a tagline somewhere. So, when you're filming it, you're like don't screw this up, don't screw this up," he said. "That was intimidating because that is the line of the movie. I have a bunch of pins, too, from *Scream* that says, 'What's your favorite scary movie?' I wasn't sure if, like, am I supposed to do it like they have in the past, or am I supposed to bring something new to it? So, I just did what I would do with the line, and just say it the way I would."

SCRIPT ISSUES

Even though they previously completed a successful trilogy, the filmmakers weren't prepared for the production issues this time around. Maddalena was working on another project and wasn't on set as much, which she says is evident in the way that Sidney is dressed in the film.

"I felt like she, Sidney, was a tough chick and she was selling her book. She wouldn't be wearing a dress and high heels. She would be wearing jeans, a leather coat, boots. She was tough, you know, she had survived. I wish I had been there," the producer said. "That's probably my biggest regret, is Neve's wardrobe...Sidney's wardrobe in *Scream 4*."

Worse than that, Mastandrea noted that he was never able to create a long-term shooting schedule due to the script delays and re-writes. "The script was never there. Emma was nice and Hayden was really nice. We still had our fun. But the problem with [*Scream 4*] is we just didn't have a script and it all starts there," he said. "We'd get new pages every day and try it this way, do this. I never did a schedule for more than two weeks because I never had the pages. But again, we were all together and it was fun."

Despite the chaotic process, Craven tried to shield the actors from the politics that were going on behind-the-scenes. According to Mastandrea, "I don't know how much they knew about it. In most cases, most actors are trying to stay away from all that stuff and just do their thing. I know Wes didn't dump a lot of that stuff on them. He's a classy guy; he's not going to go dime out people. He doesn't do that."

At one point during production Weinstein visited the set and frustrations came to a head. A dinner had been organized for the executive with the cast the same day that Tortorella's girlfriend was flying into town. They arrived late for the reservation and Weinstein wasn't amused.

"I walk into dinner late and I can't remember what exactly Bob said; he said something along the lines of, oh you finally showed up. And I was like, oh yeah, kind of like that script did too, huh? Something along those lines. Like I have always seen myself as an equal in any situation I'm in. I'm not like [the type to] fucking bow down to whoever the boss is in charge. But it was one of those things where everyone was like, holy shit, Nico just said that to Bob. I was like, no, where's our script? Like, where is our script? We're shooting a movie right now. We don't even know what we're doing," Tortorella recalled. He jokingly adds, "I'm surprised I didn't get hired for *Scream 5*. Let's be real. I'm a dream, a dream to work with. A dream. No, I mean everyone loved, first of all, everyone loved that I called fucking Bob out."

STAB-A-THON

After the leak inducing opening sequence in *Scream 2*, the franchise didn't film many other large crowd scenes. That changed in *Scream 4* with the introduction of the Stab-a-thon sequence. It's an annual event that the characters host to celebrate and screen all of the *Stab* movies. By this point in the franchise mythology, there are actually more *Stab* movies than *Scream* movies. The weakest of the movie-within-a-movie series introduces the concept of time travel. Still, filming the party scene offered the cast a chance to hang out in a relaxed group setting.

"It just felt like I was having fun. All the cast was there. There was no pressure. I got to have fun and relax a little bit," Knudsen said about filming the Stab-a-thon scenes. "I know the more fun I had, the more it would look like I was having fun on camera. You're getting up to stand up in front of a bunch of extras and perform your dialogue, but I was just having a good time."

It is during the Stab-a-thon that viewers are finally let in on a joke from the filmmakers. Using footage that was created for *Scream 2* with Heather Graham, the opening credits are shown this time around and it is revealed that *Stab* was directed by Robert Rodriguez. Contrary to rumors, he didn't actually direct any of the footage. Rodriguez, however, was a favorite of the Weinstein brothers. It was especially fitting because the Weinsteins courted him multiple times to take the reins of the franchise, including when Craven was almost fired from *Scream 2*. However, because Rodriguez and Craven were friendly, Rodriguez called the director to ask why he wasn't directing the film. When he found out the circumstances behind the offer, Rodriguez declined the job. Giving Rodriguez the credit for the *Stab* film was a slight nod to the director and provided another hidden Easter egg. In fact, if you know where to look, the series has been filled with little jokes, nods, and winks to the audience, and homages to the cast and crew's careers.

The Stab-a-thon is one of the largest set pieces in the film, involving many of the remaining characters, lots of extras, and tons of coordination for the crew. It was also a learning experience for some of the actors. For

Knudsen, he learned how to drive a car with a manual transmission. "There was a scene, that I think got cut, which was us arriving to the Stab-a-thon barn. They put me in the car to drive up and it was a stick shift, which I have never driven before in my life. So, I got my first stick shift lesson in a matter of three minutes and had to drive Rory up there and drive pretty fast and stop in front of the camera, like an inch away from the camera," Knudsen explained. "My skills were put to the test. It was amazing."

This wasn't the first adventure that the two actors had in a car during production, though. In fact, they went out one night with the plans to attend a party in Grand Rapids, but things started to go awry right from the start.

"[Knudsen] sort of dragged me out. We were going to Grand Rapids, Michigan, for some party and I was reluctant. I'm not a big party guy," Culkin recalled. "He clearly wanted a companion to travel with, so I went with him."

However, while en route to the party Knudsen developed a pain in his stomach, a pain that continually got worse during the trip. As they pulled up to their destination, he was in so much pain that he told Culkin he was going to hang back in the car. Eventually, it got so bad that the pair thought they should go to the emergency room, though Knudsen was initially hesitant.

"I didn't want to go to the hospital because I'm Canadian. I don't know how that worked with insurance and everything. I didn't want production to know and get angry at me for going to the hospital, but it just got to that point," Knudsen said. "Rory accompanied me to the hospital. We got pulled over while I was driving there because I was driving a little too fast."

"I remember Erik kind of trying to play the *Scream* card with the local cop, trying to say, 'Hey, we're just shooting a movie out here,' hoping he'd be like 'Oh, what are you shooting?' The cop just shook his head and was like not impressed with the fact that we were in *Scream* at all," Culkin adds. "It was a rough night for young Erik Knudsen."

When they got to the hospital, they learned why Knudsen was in so much pain—he was in the process of passing a large kidney stone.

"I remember standing next to his bed as he's in so much pain. They hooked him up and they gave him some kind of drug and I remember the look on his face totally shifting and he was like, hey man, I love you," Culkin said, quickly realizing, "Oh, oh, he's flying right now. Good for him. But that was a trip."

"Rory sat beside me in the hospital the entire night while I got my CT scan or whatever and got my medication," Knudsen explained, adding that the whole experience ended up bonding them. "Once he saw me in a hospital gown not caring about who sees what anymore, that's how you know we were good." He also clarified that he made sure to pay the ticket he received that night.

Knudsen wasn't the only one who hid an injury from the producers. Tortorella had thrown their back out the night before filming the Stab-a-thon scenes and was in excruciating pain. If you watch closely, Trevor doesn't move during the shots with Tortorella in them.

"Honestly, I threw out my back. It was underneath my shoulder blade. I, still to this day, have never been in more pain in my life on set than I was at that moment," Tortorella said. "That is the only thing that I remember about that Stab-a-thon scene. I had a hard time walking. I like fell in the trailer. I was down and out. But no, I didn't tell anybody about it. No one knew how bad of shape I was in. I was trying as hard as I could to hide it."

When asked why the actors didn't let anyone know about their ailments, Tortorella said they were worried because they had already been scolded for having too much fun during production. "Honestly, probably because we had gotten in trouble for partying too much. I wonder why Erik got fucking kidney stones. Let's be honest. Wonder why I threw my back out. I probably fell the night before. We were afraid. We were having way too good of a time to let anyone know," Tortorella said. They added that Craven's wife, Labunka, ruled the set. "I was definitely more nervous of her than I was of Wes. She was making big decisions."

Tortorella remembers that Labunka had an issue with their hair. "My hair's always been my thing. It's been very specific in everything I've been in and she wanted it to be classic and not trendy. Like she was the one making all of those decisions."

Still, the cast enjoyed having the additional people on set for the scene. It has been rumored that Matthew Lillard is hiding in the background among the extras, similar to his cameo in *Scream 2*, but the actor denies being in the scene.

As much fun as the cast had while filming that scene, the crew remembers it a little bit differently. Culkin, who met his wife, Sarah Scrivener, during the production, recalled her saying that the crew wasn't having a field day with the location.

"The actors had a lot of fun out there, but I think the crew hated it because we were off in a barn and they had to drag everything through mud, you know. I think it was a really rough day, actually there for the crew," Culkin said. "I remember asking [Scrivener] about that day after we shot. She was like, ugh, that, or those few days, she was like that barn stuff was the roughest for the crew. I had no idea."

23

A SUMMERLONG
FAMILY PARTY

IF THE FIRST FILM was like summer camp, by the time *Scream 4* came around, the atmosphere could have been described as its raucous frat party sibling.

"The first three movies, right, between Neve, Courteney, and David, there is like a hierarchy to the fraternity, or sorority, for that matter. They had basically been in this summer camp for years with other people circling in and out. So, they were like the head honchos. I don't want to use the word hazing, but it was like there was an initiation process to get into the family," Tortorella recalled. "During *Scream 4*, I mean, those are some of the wildest times of my life, looking back."

Tortorella adds, "There was just a lot of young energy on set. We had these older, wiser, successful actors who were keeping up and it was just like, back and forth. We were in the middle of Ann Arbor, which is a party town, just in general, in Michigan. College kids were still there, and I think we wrapped sometime late fall. So, college came back in full swing before we left. Yeah, the party was real. I am since sober. I've been sober for six years. That was like an intense time and I wouldn't trade it for anything."

It helped that along with the returning members of the cast and crew, some of the new cast had a built-in familiarity as well. Roberts, Culkin, and Tortorella had recently starred in the movie *Twelve* (2010) for director Joel Schumacher. Roberts and Culkin had also appeared together in *Lymelife* (2008).

197

"We did three films in three years together. So, every year I was working with Emma Roberts once. It was a joke where I would tell my friend I'm working on a new project. She's like, 'Oh cool, who does Emma Roberts play?'" Culkin said. "The first one we did was so like innocent, took place in 1979 in Long Island suburbs, and we're like kissing for the first time. Then the next one we did was called *Twelve*, we're like drug addict teenagers in New York City. It's just this progression of becoming worse and worse people with each film."

Since Knudsen didn't have that built-in camaraderie established with the other younger actors, and was such a big fan of the series, he admits it was daunting being on set initially. "It was more intimidating for me, the fact that I was going to be in a *Scream* movie, because it's historic. It's one of the biggest horror movie franchises. I was nervous about meeting the cast and crew. Wes Craven was the director. My nightmares were shaped by him. I was actually getting to meet my nightmare maker," the actor explained. He adds that his perceptions were quickly dashed, "I couldn't be any more wrong by being intimidated. Wes was the sweetest man alive. Neve, everyone, was amazing. No [one was] intimidating as soon as I met them. There was no, you know, sometimes you get actors that like to be by themselves. It wasn't like that whatsoever. We would hang out at Courteney's. We would hang out at Neve's. We would hang out everywhere. There was no seniority with them. They wanted us to feel part of the team as well."

He also remembers being nervous about the new cast members as well. Their resumes didn't help calm his nerves. "A lot of them worked on big projects. I'm just a Canadian kid, they probably never heard of me, and I've heard of all of them. They are all fantastic actors that have done some of the best projects. It's just intimidating as an actor to work with someone who has worked on a lot of big projects, and that I respect so much because they are great actors," continued Knudsen. "I wouldn't know how they were going to take me, if I was just the Canadian that came in there that they didn't really know and they all kind of have their clique."

HOTEL BONDING

Much like the first film, many of the cast and crew were staying in close proximity to each other. However, this time around instead of just one hotel, they were split among multiple neighboring hotels. Plus, Cox, Campbell, Arquette, and Roberts lived separately from their co-stars in houses rented during production. Unlike the situation during *Scream*, there weren't any problems with the cast creating too much noise for other hotel guests.

"We were behaved. If we were going to get into any debauchery, we would go to a bar or something like that," Knudsen said. "We were pretty well-behaved. Actually, we were very good. No complaints from the hotel. They liked having us there. We would switch rooms occasionally because we were there for so long. We wanted to upgrade, or just change a bit. But, no, we saved all the troublemaking for when we were away from the hotel."

Tortorella adds, "Hayden moved a couple of different times. I was in the same room the whole time."

"We all stayed at the same hotel together. All the cast was on the same floor. It was kind of like being in college again," Knudsen said. "You open your door, you see Hayden, Nico, Rory. As soon as we were done shooting, we would all go hang out. We would go to each other's hotel rooms, go to restaurants."

Knudsen, who says he was known for supplying the hookah, adds that by everyone living so close together, he got to hang out with some of the cast members that he didn't share any scenes with. He remembers that there was no delineation between cast and crew; everyone hung out together. "There were a few people that I never got to work with, but I would still hang out with them all the time just because they were in the hotel and nobody was not invited. They were welcoming everyone to hang out, and the people who didn't want to go out that night and go drinking and have some fun, they would stay in and that was fine. We would still catch up with them for another dinner. You got to meet everyone that way," the actor explained. "The cast would hang out with the rest of the crew too, because a lot of the crew wasn't from Michigan, so they were staying at the hotel as well. Every day, pretty much every day, because you couldn't escape them. You would be finished work, you go back and be next door neighbors to them, and everyone was kind of just bored."

Since everyone was from out of town, that also meant that when they had time off, they were left to amuse themselves. While much of their fun was innocent, Tortorella is glad that social media wasn't as widely used then as it is now.

"It was fun. I mean, honestly, there's a lot of glory moments for that time. There was a lot of partying, but I made some lifelong friends on that project," Tortorella said. Though they note how times have changed since then. "I think a lot about what that experience would have looked like, and what legacy we would have left behind, if we had social media. How much we would have been able to get away with that we did. I'm sure older actors talk about that a lot. But we, for the most part, no one knew who actors were outside of the characters that they play before Instagram, and that was kind of like the last generation. Really, that movie, for me, was like the last moment before people knew who we really were."

"We had some of the best times," agrees Knudsen. "Like at Neve's cottage, it was amazing. We would hang out all day, fish. Cut up the fish, fry it in the pan, hang on the lake. It was amazing. We'd go to Courteney's. They were so welcoming that everyone wanted to have fun with each other. We all were in a new environment, all in a hotel, and just needed each other to feel normal again."

Unfortunately for Culkin, the finale was scheduled to be filmed at the end of production. This meant that while he was having fun with the other cast members, he always had something hanging over his head. "I always had that lingering over me, like I'm going to have to deliver at the end of this. I'm going to have to have all of my shit sorted out," the actor explained. "I hung out with the cast a lot early on, and then I sort of broke away and separated myself leading up to the end. Yeah, it was task at hand, was definitely more important to me."

Along with worrying about being able to deliver his big scenes when the time came, he admits that he was conflicted about how close to get with his castmates. "I was 20, so I was still trying to figure out what kind of actor I wanted to be and how deep to go for certain roles. So, hanging out with all these people, like, I understand we're all doing a job, but in the back of my mind, I'm like I'm going to have to kill these people and like maybe I shouldn't be getting close," Culkin recalls. "I was in a weird head space trying to figure out what I was going to do at the end of this."

TURMOIL ON SET

While Craven has always kept his sets peaceful and calm as much as possible, some added drama was happening behind-the-scenes. The marriage of Cox and Arquette had become strained. After being married for 10 years, having wed prior to production on *Scream 3*, the couple decided to begin a trial separation right before production on *Scream 4* was set to begin. It's something that the other actors said they were aware of during the production.

During an interview with Howard Stern, Arquette said that it came about because Cox had tired of having to act like the parent in the relationship. The couple would go on to finalize their divorce three years later. In spite of any issues that might have been going on between the couple during production, they have infamously remained close. "They're so cute," said Maddalena. "I know they are really good friends, so it's very nice."

Despite the state of his marriage and any personal issues going on, Knudsen remembers that Arquette was the life of the party during production, just like he had been during the other film shoots. "David would be, obviously, the wild card, you never know what he was up to. He would be hanging out with us, then one minute he would be having a massive party at one of the bars with all of his friends from L.A.," the actor recalled.

He wasn't the only one who could be found partying. Tortorella recalled a time during production when they hit their lowest point. During production, they became close with one of the crew members, Gavin McGuire, and went to a house party. Gavin was the son of the film's costume designer, Debra McGuire, who had also worked with Cox on *Friends* during the show's run.

"We were partying at this house and somehow in a bathroom, the massive mirror fell off the wall and shattered everywhere. I swear I don't remember ever being part of it, but somehow the blame got put on me," Tortorella said, remembering that they received a warning call about their behavior. "Whether [the call was from] Wes or the Weinsteins, or whatever, that's like, 'Hey you need to get your shit together, or else it's not going to be good moving forward.'"

That wasn't the only incident that Tortorella remembers from production. The filmmakers have a long running tradition of dressing up prop master J.P. Jones in the Ghostface costume and having him try to scare the actors on set. They picked the wrong actor when Tortorella was selected because the actor's reflex was to punch Jones. "One night, he just popped out and I just clocked him straight in the head. I'm Italian, what do you want from me? You can't just jump out and expect me not to defend myself," Tortorella said about the incident. They said there were no hard feelings though. "J.P. ripped the mask off like it was a celebration."

Tortorella and Gavin got into the act as well, getting Ghostface masks of their own, and tried to scare the cast themselves. "We would go and scare the girls on a regular basis. We would just put the masks on, and creep through the neighborhood and show up at Emma's house at like two o'clock in the morning, and just start banging on the windows. It was fun," Tortorella said, before adding with a laugh, "I should have been fired."

CREATING A FAMILY

All these years later, the bond remains strong for the young cast.

"I ran into Rory on the train a few years ago. New York is actually pretty small, people don't really realize that, right? But yeah, it was. We just hugged; we didn't even say anything to each other. We just hugged. He was getting off and I was getting on," Tortorella recalled. "This was a nice moment."

Knudsen admits that he doesn't keep in touch with the cast members as much but says there is a good reason for it. "I have gone through about 30 phones by now, so I've lost contact, a lot of contacts, and the technology of the phones has changed quite a bit too," the actor said, though he adds, "You run into actors that know each other, so you say your hi's."

Tortorella says their favorite memory from the film was meeting their co-stars and the relationships that came from it.

"The family that we built. You know, it wasn't always perfect. There was tension. We took care of each other and held each other accountable and demanded that we look at ourselves. That's what family does," Tortorella said, admitting, "Family's messy, right? Blood is thicker than water. But it's hard to clean up. That's what I remember most about that experience, was how close we all got."

24
ANSWERING QUESTIONS ABOUT THE *SCREAM 4* FINALE

WITH ANTICIPATION HIGH for another *Scream* sequel, security was again of the highest importance during filming. The filmmakers employed similar tactics that had been used for the previous films, but by this point none of them was considered extraordinary by the cast.

"Just the usual at that time, which I think was every time we got a script revision, we would have to send it back in and they would shred it for us. I think they had a chart too to make sure that the draft we had was submitted back to make sure we weren't hanging on to any old drafts," Knudsen explained, adding, "That and not telling us [who Ghostface was]. Even Rory and Emma, none of them told us.

Tortorella, who has gone on to join *The Walking Dead* spin-off, *The Walking Dead: World Beyond,* said the security measures on the show are much more stringent than anything employed on the film. There also weren't concerns during the Stab-a-thon scenes in the barn because, while Gale does get attacked in the attic, no one is killed, and no major plot points are revealed that could have been spoiled by having so many extras on set.

WHO IS BEHIND THE GHOSTFACE MASK?

While it was important to keep the fate of the characters a secret, the biggest secret of all was the behind-the-mask identity of Ghostface. Only the cast involved in those scenes were given those pages. Unlike *Scream 3*, the cast were told before the film wrapped that the ones carving up their friends were Jill and Charlie. In fact, Knudsen had an inkling before he was officially told because he noticed something on set.

"We all had our suspicions because Rory was working out a lot. He had a trainer when he was there. So, we're thinking, like, they are getting him buffed up for something," Knudsen recalled.

Nayor laughs at the astute observation, saying, "There's always clues. That's so funny. It's really hard to keep things a secret these days, especially. But it's just really, really hard."

For his part, Culkin didn't consider that working with the trainer would be a clue to the others that he would end up as one of the villains. Nevertheless, he enjoyed the experience even though he wasn't sure how much the training would come in handy for the film.

"They had a personal trainer and they were teaching me like there's weightlifting and stuff, but they're also teaching me martial arts and things. It's like, it's great that I'm learning how to box for this, but I don't think I'm throwing a punch ever. I don't know, but I ran with it and I've been boxing for years because of it," Culkin explained. "I think that was Wes Craven's idea. I think he was like, yeah, teach him how to box while you're at it."

Perhaps his training paid off a little too well while filming the end fight scene with Campbell. It's a moment that he still feels bad about all these years later. "There's a moment where I ram Neve Campbell against the wall. I still think about this pretty often and cringe because I was clotheslining her and I didn't even realize it. It was a couple of takes. She asked me, 'Sorry, could you just sort of bring it down a little bit,' and I didn't even consider I was like hurting her, and of course I am. I was clotheslining her neck take after take and she was so nice. She didn't want to say anything, she just had to," Culkin recalls. "That's one of those moments laying down in bed at night like, oh, God, I can't believe it, clotheslining Neve Campbell like four times hard and didn't notice because we were rolling."

When it came to finding his motivation for that scene, Culkin wanted to have a talk with his director. He set up a meeting to talk with

Craven about Charlie's motive for taking part in the murderous rampage. The way he saw Charlie Walker was different from the other killers in the franchise.

"I was sort of coming at it like from a place of regret. I thought that would be interesting for Charlie Walker, because you watch all the other *Scream* movies and whenever there's the reveal, they seem almost all knowing, or they're almost godly. I was like, what would I want to see? What would be interesting, maybe, sort of a weaker version of that. A regretful, remorseful killer, I thought would be really interesting, and uncertain about himself," Culkin said about the character.

The actor said that when he pictured the character after he committed a murder, he saw Charlie going home and crying over what he did. So, the director helped to frame that characterization in another way to make sense for the actor.

"Wes said, 'When a soldier puts on a uniform, he's not a killer. He's not a murderer. He's a soldier, right? Just put on your uniform and then it's not as big of a deal. Do your job.' And he didn't mean do your job as an actor, saying your lines; he meant do your job and kill people when you put your mask on," Culkin recalled. "It clicked and that made so much sense and was amazing. That's all I needed, was just a few minutes of Wes's time, and he would have given it to me at any point. But I requested it and tried to make it special. But yeah, he's incredible, just he said it like it was nothing. But it was brilliant. It just meant so much to me."

The art department even loaned the actor a Ghostface costume to wear in his hotel room, as well as some prop knives, to help him feel comfortable in the role. Craven's analogy became even more apparent when it was revealed that Jill, Sidney's cousin, is the mastermind behind all of the carnage and Charlie is merely her soldier carrying out the battle plan. Her motivation is to gain fame from the tragic events and not live in the shadow of her famous cousin any longer. She was able to get Charlie to help her by manipulating the teen due to his unrequited love for Kirby, a crush that only starts to come to fruition while everyone is hunkered down at her house in the final act of the film.

"I assumed he was just really into Kirby and it never happened. Maybe Jill took advantage of this sort of lost guy and obviously she became his obsession," Culkin explained. "I think Jill just sort of picked up the pieces that Kirby didn't even know was there."

Having worked with Roberts before helped Culkin with that aspect of the role. "It was really cool because there's already that built-in chemistry and, you know, Charlie Walker's deeply in love with Jill," Culkin said. "We've done a lot of scenes together as different characters, so I already knew she was great and I didn't have any questions about her going in. It was nice, too, because it's like this road that we've taken working all these projects together sort of leads to us killing people together."

Tortorella alluded that there might have been some art imitating life with the trio. "Emma and Rory were super close at one point. Me and Emma were really close. There was this situation triangle, if you may. I'm just going to leave it at that," the actor said. "I'm a very hands-on actor, I would say. I was treating them as the relationships that we had off-screen in a lot of ways. It definitely influenced a lot [of] what was happening on camera."

When it came to on camera tricks, the filmmakers didn't want to give the audience any clues as to who might be Ghostface based on their height. Just as many of the characters in *Scream* had to wear black boots to avoid tipping off the audience, many of the actors in *Scream 4* had to stand on apple boxes.

"I'm pretty short, Emma's pretty short. There were a few of us shorties on that, and whenever they would shoot us, they would put us on apple boxes to kind of make our height sort of normal so you couldn't tell who it was in the costume," Knudsen explained. "It would be pretty obvious, because I'm pretty short next to Nico."

SOLVING LINGERING QUESTIONS ABOUT CHARACTER DEATHS

There isn't much ambiguity with many of the character deaths in the *Scream* series. However, *Scream 4* has a few characters that perished and left behind some questions that have been debated since its release. One of those characters is Robbie Mercer. Robbie, breaking one of the main rules from the original film, is wandering around the grounds of Kirby's house drunk when he stumbles upon Ghostface. Coming face-to-face with the killer, Robbie utters a line that has left some fans curious.

To fully understand what he utters, you have to look back to an earlier scene in the film. During a meeting with cinema club, Robbie states that the old rules no longer apply when trying to survive a horror movie and to successfully survive nowadays "that you pretty much have to be gay." When the time comes, Robbie blurts out to a confused Ghostface, "I'm gay…if it helps" before being stabbed.

This single line has left many fans wondering if Robbie was actually coming out as he was literally staring death in the face, or if he was just saying it in an attempt to save his own life. The actor said that while he doesn't know for sure what Williamson intended, he sees it as Robbie just trying to save himself.

"The way I saw it was that he was just trying to save himself from dying. But you never know. Maybe that's why he was so confident because he thought he was not going to make the cut. Maybe he's gay and he's going to survive this film," Knudsen said. "I think he was just trying to survive. He knew the formula. It was his last-ditch effort to try to stay alive."

The actor adds, however, "That would destroy his whole formula, too, that anyone gay survives in the end of a horror movie. And that is *Scream*. They like to switch things up. I was never told how to play it, gay or anything. But it could be."

Alas, it didn't work for poor Robbie. But if his death has created questions among fans, they are even more divisive about another character's ending. For over a decade, Kirby's attack has been one of the rallying cries among fans.

Near the climax of the film, Kirby and Sidney are attempting to hide from Ghostface in the basement. Charlie, covered in blood, stumbles to the door before the outside lights go out and the phone rings. Ghostface duct tapes Charlie to a lawn chair on the patio and quizzes Kirby in a scene reminiscent to the opening of *Scream*. Before Ghostface can even finish the question about remakes, Kirby impressively rattles off every possible horror remake and the phone goes dead. While helping to untape Charlie, he stabs her in the stomach. Charlie walks away with his unrequited crush still writhing in agony and bleeding out on the patio. The general rule in horror movies is that if you don't see a character actually die, then they aren't dead. This has led to the is-she-or-isn't-she question, with many hoping that the fan favorite character somehow survived the attack. You can add Culkin to the list of people who's on Team Kirby.

"Well, I never saw the life leave her body and I feel like Charlie stabbed her to just hurt her, you know, not to take her life. To hurt her, because she's hurt him, and I think Charlie Walker was really remorseful and maybe he didn't show it. But when he would go home, he would cry and think about the lives that he took," Culkin explained. "I think maybe he gave her a chance. He didn't go in for another stab because if you survive, then you've earned it. So, I'd like to think Kirby lives, but I don't know."

On the other end of the spectrum, one person who doesn't have any ambiguity in their death is Trevor. Along with getting shot in the head, Jill first shoots her cheating ex-boyfriend in a more delicate place. It's a stunt that Tortorella's castmates were surprised they were doing themselves.

"I get shot in the nuts, right? There's a squib that is an explosive unit for when you get shot that actually explodes, and they go and they put it basically on my underwear next to everything. Neve comes up to me before the scene and was like, 'I've done, this is my fourth one. I'd never do what you're about to do right now. Can't they use a stunt double for this? Why are you doing this?'" Tortorella recalled. "And I was like, 'You're scaring the shit out of me right now. Let me just get this done.' I did. We did one take and that was it."

Years later, Tortorella found out that their bloodied costume from that scene was sold online with a special surprise for the buyer. There was a draft of a letter, drenched in fake blood, that Tortorella had written to Craven and Labunka to thank them.

Another thing the actor remembers about the scene is how intense it was and how different each of the actors behaved between takes. "It was intense. It was late. It was probably early in the morning," Tortorella recalled. "Rory had this thing where he was chugging Red Bulls. He would go through six to eight Red Bulls like it was nothing. So, he was just fucking pacing around the house all over the place. Emma always had a book in between. This is what I remember working with Emma more than anything else, she always was reading. She always had a book in between every take. She was reading, she didn't like to interact with other people in between takes. She would just go straight to her book."

ALL ABOUT THE JUMP SCARES

When it came time to film the hallmark opening sequence for *Scream 4*, the filmmakers took a different approach. The opening itself is unique; it includes two fake openings that turn out to be the start of the fictional *Stab* movies, before getting to the "real" opening featuring actresses Britt Robertson (then credited as Brittany Robertson) and Aimee Teegarden as characters related to the events in the remainder of the film. Nayor said they held off on filming this sequence until the end because they wanted to see how the rest of the movie came together first.

"They didn't shoot that at the same time as the rest of the film because they wanted to see how they were going to change. They were going to sort of tailor the beginning once they saw the film. I think they were going to have multiple people, but I don't think that they had it completely written at the time we shot the rest of the movie," Nayor explained. She added, "Some of those girls had come and read for other roles, I don't remember exactly who, but other roles in the movie. Then we realized we wanted them as the cameos at the beginning, like the Aimee Teegarden and Britt's. I think that we kind of added on later."

Despite trying to tailor the opening to the rest of the film and waiting to film it, much of the footage from the original sequence was scrapped and re-shot in January 2011. The changes included shifting the focus from Robertson's Marnie Cooper to Teegarden's Jenny Randall. The original version is included on the DVD among the deleted scenes.

That wasn't the only scene that was re-shot. Allison Brie's death scene in the parking garage also had additional footage filmed. At the time, the official word regarding the re-shoots was to make the scenes scarier, something that, a decade later, Maddalena agrees with. "I think it was. It's always about the jumps," said the producer.

It was the middle of winter in Michigan, and temperatures were around zero degrees. Jackson, who was called back for the re-shoots to perform the phone calls with the actresses, said that he was taken care of and kept warm during the re-shoots. "The parking garage ones. Where was I? I think I was in a van with the sound equipment," the actor recalls. His wife came with him for the re-shoots, which led to an interesting dichotomy while he was filming. "My wife came with me and was sitting in the room with me while I'm threatening the actress over the phone. I'm threatening to kill somebody, and she's doing her knitting."

With the re-shoots completed, *Scream 4* wrapped production and was ready to be unleashed on the world.

25

SCREAM 4 FINDS ITS AUDIENCE EVENTUALLY

THROUGHOUT PRODUCTION, *Scream 4* was being hyped by the media and fans. However, the film was met with a shrug from audiences. Upon its debut on April 15, 2011, critics were kinder to the film than its predecessor. While many enjoyed the film, some described it as stale and claimed it hadn't evolved enough in the decade that passed between the series entries.

Horror writer Amie Simon was among those skeptical about how the franchise—which had been groundbreaking 15 years prior—would be able to re-invent itself for a new generation. "I read the description, it was like, I don't know how this is going to translate to a world where it's like at the beginning of vloggers and, you know, YouTube peeps and younger people. Like I don't know how I feel about this," Simon recalled.

Ultimately, the film did win her over. "*Scream 4*, I think, works, in part, because it's like how scary is it to think that there are these shitty teenagers that, like the first one, are just disgruntled and bored and they're just like, 'well, we need something for our YouTube channel, so we're just going to kill people.' Which was also an amazing sort of misdirect away from the real mastermind of the whole thing."

She said that it was through a partnership with the Halloween Horror Nights at Universal Studios theme park in Los Angeles that initially helped her get excited. "You got on the tram and then it acted like you were going to a release party for *Scream 4*. It was like this giant warehouse-like party situation and then Ghostface would kind of pop out at you or run around chasing people," Simon explained. "But the scariest part was to get out of that party; you had to walk in between two trams that were filled with Ghostfaces. Some of them were real, and some were mannequins. But you couldn't tell because they were all very still. Then they would send you one at a time between the two trams. Even though I knew it wasn't real, I knew it was all pretend, it was terrifying to me to have to look at these eight or 10 Ghostfaces on each tram and try to figure out which one was going to move and slash at you if you ran."

For some, the behind-the-scenes drama—which was widely covered in the press and internet blogs leading up to the release of the film—dampened their enthusiasm for the film.

"I 100% believe the behind-the-scenes drama impacted the final film. Kevin Williamson had a very specific vision for how [the film and the potential new trilogy] would play out. Apparently, the Weinsteins didn't feel the same way," said Meece, adding, "I really got the sense that Kevin Williamson was back in his groove [with *Scream 4*], dialed-in to the pulse of pop culture once more. It was fresh, fun, and completely bonkers."

A Disappointing Debut

The film opened in second place with more than $18 million in grosses, behind the animated parrot movie, *Rio* (2011). During its second weekend, the film slipped to fifth place with a 62% decrease in revenue. Domestically, it made just $38 million versus its $40 million budget by the end of its run. Fortunately, the film fared better overseas, which helped to bring the film's worldwide gross to just under $100 million.

In the years between, many horror movie franchises had seen reboots, remakes, and sequels made, along with new franchises like *Paranormal Activity* (2007) and *Insidious* (2010). Whereas Dimension Films and New Line Cinema had previously been the leader in the genre, Blumhouse Productions was churning out horror movies regularly to keep fans jumping in the aisles. Could a saturation of the marketplace be to blame for the lukewarm reception at the box office? Knudsen, who also appeared in the *Saw* franchise, seems to think so.

"People were sick of horror movies being done a million times, the same thing over and over again and losing the charm of the original, which I don't think any *Scream* has ever done. *Scream* has always had that certain charm that isn't in any other horror movies. I think maybe a lot of people didn't go to the theater because they thought, oh here we go, another horror movie that needs to have 10 different versions," the actor said. "Nothing will beat the first one. At that point, a lot of people were just not ready for it. Halloweens come around over the years and people do actually watch it because it's a scary movie to watch and they realize it was worth watching."

Culkin admits that he didn't know what to expect from the film, but it was a life changing experience. "I didn't think I would be talking about it 10 years later at all. It's a journey. It's a trip that it's been that long even. I didn't really know what to expect because when you have a 'four' after a title, it's like, I'm not sure about, you know, *four* what? But it's almost like a reboot. It was like a reboot and a sequel," Culkin explained. "I grow fonder of it as time goes on, I think. I believe it was Wes Craven's last film, so that's just a great honor to be able to work with him. Yeah, and it's where I met my wife. I have a lot to be thankful for the *Scream* franchise."

Tortorella, on the other hand, knew that joining the franchise would be a part of their career forever, and was also aware that it would have a long shelf life. "I knew that it was going to be something that affected my life forever, if not more in the future than it did in the immediate. I knew that for sure. Yeah, it was one of those things that was just like, 'okay, this is going to be part of my life until I die.'"

The Walking Dead: World Beyond actor doesn't shy away from the spotlight that *Scream* brought to their resume, either. In fact, their role in the television show has led them to talk more about the film. "It's funny, now that I'm on *Walking Dead* I find myself talking about *Scream* a lot more than I have, maybe even ever, because one of the questions that I always get is how was it stepping into such a large franchise on the *Dead*. I'm like, I'm used to it. This isn't something new for me," Tortorella said. "I've been here before and I hope to continue to do it as I step into Marvel or DC or whatever my future looks like. There's legacy in that and *Scream* was my first step into a much larger universe, right? Because the *Scream* franchise, it's a universe that was built out of make believe."

With the chilly reception from audiences, plans to complete a second trilogy were put on hold. The idea of releasing another film in the series wouldn't be revisited for almost a decade. Over time, however, the film received a better reception from audiences. "Because of Williamson's plot for *Scream 4*, it actually helps the film age quite well," says Meece.

"The tech being used in 2011 is practically the same stuff being used now, and the tech that may have been viewed as a reach in 2011, Robbie's live stream, is actually an everyday occurrence now."

ADAPTING *SCREAM* FOR THE SMALL SCREEN

While the franchise might have seemed dead after *Scream 4*, it turned out it was just waiting for a new incarnation to come along. In 2015, it was revived as a television series that premiered on MTV. The show, while trying to keep the tone and feel of the *Scream* movies, wasn't well-received by the franchise's fans. Following the blueprint of the movies, there was an initial opening death from a well-known actress, Disney Channel alum Bella Thorne. The subsequent characters fit into the archetypal footprints of their cinematic predecessors, though they were updated to fit how times had changed. Instead of having a tabloid reporter like Gale, the character of Piper hosted a podcast that was investigating the mystery of Brandon James. In the show's universe, James was an infamous murderer who the killers were using to copycat.

It was that Brandon James connection that led to the biggest point of contention during the first two seasons. The killer in the television show was using a mask that James had previously worn instead of the infamous Ghostface mask. Moreover, Roger L. Jackson wasn't involved as the voice of Ghostface on the phone either.

Regarding the lack of the Ghostface mask, Maddalena thought it was a mistake. "What were they thinking? I guess Bob couldn't make a deal. I don't know the details, but that was so silly," she opined.

Despite the Ghostface mask being so closely tied to the franchise, Weinstein told *The Hollywood Reporter* that the decision was made because the show's mask was part of the overall story and that the costume from the films had no significant connection to the characters who wore it. In fact, while investigating the murders in the original film, the police note that the costume is sold in every "five and dime in the state."

"You probably had people watching that show and saying, it's *Scream*, but where's the elements of *Scream* that I recognize?" said McKittrick. "It would be like making a *Halloween* movie and not having Michael Myers in it, as we saw with *Halloween 3*. It's people going, what is this? This is not what I remember."

Maddalena and Craven lent their names to the series as executive producers, but they were never intimately involved in the show's development or daily production. The TV series did have one connection to the film series, though—Patrick Lussier directed the second season's finale. They had originally approached him to direct the pilot, but he wasn't able to at the time due to commitments to other projects. When the opportunity came back around, he was more than game.

"Richard [Register] and Michael [Gans], they were the E.P.'s on the second season. They had, I think, done *Scream: The Musical* several years for Halloween. They had made a musical version of it and they were awesome. I really love working with these guys. I think that was a huge component, because they were such big fans of the original series and fans of Wes," Lussier said about the experience. "They were all very much fans and very excited to be part of it and the cast was great fun. They all really enjoyed the legacy that they had come to be part of."

When the shortened third and final season was ordered, the producers did a complete creative reboot with a whole new cast and creatives behind-the-scenes. This time around they brought back the Ghostface mask as well as Jackson to voice the role. But the series' fate was already sealed. After sitting on the shelf for years, it was shipped to sister station VH1 and the six-episode season was burned off over the course of three nights in the summer of 2019.

26

AN ENDURING LEGACY

IT HAS BEEN A QUARTER of a century since the first film was initially released, and many of those involved in the early films have children coming of age who are now discovering the movies. It's something that all those involved are proud to see living on for future generations.

"My kids, when they watched them for the first time and all, they really liked them. But, you know, you don't expect this stuff. It's just sort of the way it works out. It's definitely cool. It's a blessing," Beltrami remarked.

Adds Besser, "I smile when one of our godchildren or friend's children gets to that age where they are watching it on DirectTV or something and will call, or my kids when they got old enough to watch it."

Konrad said that when her sons were younger, they would run around wearing the masks. Now they are old enough to watch the movies, and she recently watched it with them. Brown also admits that his daughter's friend was such a fan of the movie that he gave him the robe that he received as a production gift when the first film wrapped.

YOUR FAVORITE HUMANITIES PROFESSOR

So much of the legacy of the *Scream* films is tied to Wes Craven. Even though Kevin Williamson wrote the film, Dimension made it known who they thought the creator of the franchise was when they sued Columbia

Pictures. The latter was promoting *I Know What You Did Last Summer* and the tagline on top of the posters said, "From The Creator Of *Scream*." Dimension declared that people would think it was referring to the director and filed a lawsuit. Rather than deal with a court battle, Columbia released a new round of posters with a more specific tag, touting "From The Writer Of *Scream*." The lawsuit was also a way for Miramax to exact revenge. Sony, the company that owns Columbia Pictures, sued them the previous year claiming that the title of *Scream* was too much like their own film, *Screamers* (1996), starring Peter Weller and Jennifer Rubin. Regardless of the motive, they publicly made a case that Craven deserved credit as creator of the franchise.

As the franchise went on and Williamson started to move away from it, Craven was the one maintaining the creative vision. This was especially true since he contributed to the scripts for *Scream 3* and *Scream 4*. Plus, it was more than just his work behind the camera; it was him as a person that brought many of the cast and crew returning film after film.

"I remember when I got to know him better, by being in all those, and I thought, how is this man the director of the slasher films because he's so quiet and gentle and sweet and kind. You're like, this makes zero sense," O'Dell said. "I thought, well, maybe that's why it does work, because he is quiet about it. He creates the unexpected and that's what he would do in such a talented way."

It's true that when you think of a horror director, Wes Craven might not be the idea that pops into your head. Stereotypically, someone more like Tim Burton or Rob Zombie might fit the mold of what someone would expect a horror director to look like. That said, Craven never set out to be a horror director. In fact, many close to him viewed him more as a college professor, perhaps due to his work teaching at Clarkson College.

"Your favorite college humanities professor, both in his demeanor and his bearing. When I went in [for] the Wes Craven Project, I expected this dark, little macabre man, like most horror auteurs are, and that wasn't the case at all," described Brown about his expectation when first auditioning for *Wes Craven's New Nightmare*. "I spent a lot of one-on-one time with him. We would go to lunch, and I consider him one of my life's great teachers."

Schreiber agrees, "He was exactly that. He was like your favorite humanities professor. But I wouldn't be here had it not been for my favorite humanities professor, so that's actually a very special description."

Even though he left teaching behind professionally, many remember times he made a profound impact on them with a comment that other people might have brushed off. Beach remembers a time during a casting session when an actor had gotten on her nerves during an audition. After he exited, she made a comment that men were pigs. Craven heard her and corrected her. "Wes turned to me and said, 'I don't ever want to hear you saying that again because men aren't pigs. This guy just happened to be. Just because he is a man doesn't mean all men are pigs,'" Beach recalled. "I will never forget that because I was kind of dressed down by Wes Craven. But I realized how fair he was. If he wasn't going to hear that about a man, imagine how he would not take that well if somebody said that about a woman, or another disparaging comment."

McRee had a similar interaction with the director. The normally mild-mannered and relaxed Craven had appeared agitated. When the actress asked what was wrong, he told her, "It's a Miramax kind of day." When she saw him later, despite committing a faux pas of sitting in the director's chair, Craven's mood had changed. "I am sitting in his chair, unbeknownst to me, he walks over and he just kind of smiles at me and says nothing. He sits in one of the producers' chairs next to me. We chat and I said, 'You seem much calmer now. Except for this morning, you always seem so calm. What's the secret of calm?' He stood up and started to walk away," recalls the actress. "I went, *what*? That's not his attitude. He took about three steps, he looks at me over his right shoulder, and he says, 'Perspective, Lynn, perspective.' I'm going to take that to the grave with me. The secret to calm is perspective, and it's true."

LOYALTY AND CREATING A FAMILY

Craven was also well remembered for having parties at his house. Showing how beloved he was, the guest list always included those from many of his films who simply wanted to get together.

"He always made you feel welcome and it just shows you how it is if you got to know him. He would have dinner parties and it would be like Robert Englund will be there and Angela Bassett would be there. Neve and Courteney would be there, all the different worlds that he touched," Kennedy explained. "He had all these amazing collectibles from each movie at his house. I'll never forget, he had the arm from the one Freddy wore, that really long one. It went from his living room, I swear like 30 feet, all the way through his kitchen. It was so cool."

Adds Beach, "There was always this great group of people who wanted to come together for a party. There wasn't this feeling like, oh my God, I have to go to this party tonight because you know I have to go to this party tonight. It was never like that. It was like, oh my God, Wes is having a party, great, fantastic."

More than that, Craven remembered the important times for his colleagues, like when Kennedy turned 30 and Craven showed up. "He came to my 30th birthday party, too," the actor recalled. "But he was that kind of guy that if I had something, if he was available, he came. He was very, very, very cool."

Lussier also remembers the support that Craven showed for his directing career after seeing the remake of *My Bloody Valentine* (2009), which Lussier directed. "He came to see the premiere of *My Bloody Valentine*, and they had these testimonials afterwards—you know, 'I just saw this movie. It was awesome.' He went up to record one right away. I didn't know he was going to do that. I didn't know until I saw it the next day. I just remember thinking, wow, that's really lovely that he did that, that he was that supportive and kind."

That kind of kinship meant Craven had created a second family for himself among his film collaborators. It was a family he started cultivating over 30 years ago. The group of actors, producers, filmmakers, and creatives were, and are, fiercely loyal and protective of the director, and he was the same in return.

"Everybody would come back. I could only do three weeks on *My Soul to Take*. I definitely went back to do it," explained Lussier.

"We just had a film family that we loved working together and having fun together, hanging out together. We respected each other and everybody wanted to do it. I mean, it started with Wes, obviously. We all adored him, and we all wanted to work together," Mastandrea said. "But when I think back, I just think of all the fun times, and how many beautiful people I've met and the friendships that have maintained. That's kind of really a special thing for me because when you work in the movie business you give up so much of your life, your personal life, and when your personal life actually becomes part it, it makes it really special."

Even if the projects might not have always been a box office success, or turned out the way they had hoped, Plec adds that there is good that can come from the bad. "I believe that the process of making art doesn't have to be an insufferable process. I believe that you can make something good and build a family and a community of artists around you, or you can make something bad and still enjoy your community, a family, and artists around you, and both things can be okay," said Craven's former assistant, who's since gone on to a highly successful producing career creating multiple television series.

For many of the young actors that Craven worked with, he took on a surrogate paternal role. As Maddalena states, many of the cast had never worked with a director of Craven's caliber prior to joining the *Scream* franchise. "A lot of these actors never worked with a good director. They're kind of on TV. I'm not saying they aren't good, but they come in and out. They get to work with this master, who they can trust because he was intelligent and there was a reason he taught behind his direction," his partner said. "It's underestimated how many actors don't have that, and they don't feel safe, and they don't feel like someone is even listening to them or [trust] when someone says, we got it, cut, we got it. A lot of actors think you didn't really get it, I don't trust you. But you don't have the time. But they trusted Wes that when he said, 'You got it,' you got it. They could trust they did a good job, and he was happy with it, they would be happy with it."

Knudsen adds, "He was like the grandfather I never had. He was just the sweetest man. I thought there'd be some dark, twisted side to him maybe. But I couldn't be any more wrong. He was just always sweet, especially when we were shooting long hours, a lot of night shoots. Usually you kind of get to see people's personalities change in that time, especially with a lot of stress."

McGowan also referred to the director as a paternal figure, saying, "In our world, in the movie world, it was like he was the perfect parent. That was something I hadn't really had either. He used to babysit my dog, Bug, on the weekend. I had a puppy, my Boston Terrier puppy, on the set. I would go back to L.A. and he would take care of her for the weekends. He was just obsessed with her."

The last time Jackson saw the director was following re-shoots of the parking garage scene in *Scream 4*. They rode back to the hotel early in the morning after wrapping for the night in the middle of winter. "We were riding back from the set in the snow, in the middle of the night, about three or four in the morning, back to the hotel. We're driving up, there's a blanket of snow everywhere. The trees are covered with snow," explained Jackson. "We're driving up the driveway to the hotel, and I look out the window and there's Wes with a camera in the middle of the night, taking pictures of the night birds because he loved birds, and he looked over, gave us a little wave, and I thought, God, after all this whole night's work, he's out doing this."

After Craven died in 2015, following a private battle with brain cancer, many of the cast and crew attended the director's memorial and funeral. Afterward, his film family—including Maddalena, Miller, Mastandrea, Beach, Williamson, Plec, and more—gathered at the Chateau Marmont.

The bonds have remained strong for the cast and crew of the *Scream* franchise. Many of the cast and crew have come back together to work on other projects. McGowan and Arquette re-teamed for the wrestling comedy *Ready to Rumble* (2000) while Lussier directed both Kennedy and Omar Epps in *Trick* (2019). Craven and Maddalena served as producers on Lussier and Mastandrea's directorial debuts, *Dracula 2000* and *The Breed* (2006), respectively. Elise Neal and Duane Martin also appeared on the television show *All of Us* (2003) a half decade after co-starring in *Scream 2*.

CREATING A NEW TYPE OF FINAL GIRL

The final girl trope has long been a horror staple—she's the one who outlasts all of her other friends either by wit or dumb luck, and then goes on to vanquish the killer. *Scream* provided a new take on the final girls as characters who were smart and fought back throughout the film. Not a single one of the female characters in the original film, nor most of the sequels, went down without a valiant effort.

It was through *Scream* and this added feminism that filmmakers really began to take notice of the large contingent of young females who were coming out in droves to see horror films. It wasn't just an audience of teenage boys looking for blood and guts anymore. Women, specifically teenage girls, were shelling out their hard-earned money as well.

The characters of Sidney, Gale, Tatum, and Casey weren't weak and helpless. It was something revelatory and celebrated. Even though Tatum and Casey are eventually killed, they don't make it easy for Ghostface and fight back right up until the end. They try to outsmart the killer and fight when need be.

"Sydney is pretty smart. I mean, I do love the whole concept of her being like, I don't watch that shit because they're always running up the front stairs, instead of going out the door and that's exactly what she does.

But it's like at some point something clicks in for her and she's like, wait, I can use my closet door to brace my door. I can maybe crawl out the window. I can type 911," said Simon. "Even Laurie Strode, who makes some smart decisions in *Halloween* doesn't make the best ones all the time. Like hiding in a closet is probably not the best idea, you know, or after you stab the guy with a knitting needle maybe don't drop the butcher knife. Laurie Strode's final girl-ness was almost an accident. She did some shit that was really dumb, and then she did some smart stuff, and then by the end she did some shit that was really dumb again."

Simon likens Sidney more to another one of Craven's muses, Nancy Thompson, played by Heather Langenkamp in the *Nightmare on Elm Street* series. Moreover, having Sidney survive through so many films has also given the character a chance to grow as well as show the toll that continual trauma can have on a person. It began in *Scream 2* when she was always questioning her boyfriend's motives and continued in *Scream 3* when she hid away so that no masked killers could find her.

"By the time we get to 'four' and she is being terrorized, she's just like, again? So, she's just kind of resigned to it. She's like well, this is what we do. We fight back. We don't freak out. We fight back. And by the time it's revealed that it's her [cousin], she's just like fuck, whatever, I'm just going to kill you. I don't care," explains Simon. "She learned something from every attack, and she's gone through all the emotions. She's gone through the grief; she's gone through the fear. She's gone through the trauma, and she's come out on the other side of it."

It's a notion that Ziembicki agrees with, giving Campbell credit for helping give the character her depth. "Neve Campbell is a good actor, but that role's kind of limiting. It's like, you know, it is what it is. You just kind of react and get chased around and scream, sometimes. But the whole idea of fighting back and a different kind of heroine, which we now see and those kinds of movies are being promoted," said the *Scream 2* set designer. "That kind of says quite a bit for her. That was kind of trailblazing."

AN ENDURING LEGACY

Twenty-five years after its release, *Scream* has an enduring appeal, making annual lists of the "Scariest Movies." It has withstood the test of time, continuing to be referenced in pop culture outside of the horror genre. The question becomes, is Ghostface here to stay forever?

"The most important factor is going to be how long the Ghostface icon exists in culture. You know, as long as that's still a Halloween costume that people will go to, those kinds of elements are what stand the test of time," McKittrick said. "People who even know the name Boris Karloff, think of that when they think of Frankenstein. Same thing with Dracula. You know, we've had a ton of Dracula vampire stuff come and go, and much better-looking vampires on stuff like *True Blood,* but Bela Lugosi *is* Dracula. That is the image that is so pervasive throughout our culture. Ghostface is not quite Boris Karloff, but that character look is still so dominant in our culture and you'll still see that costume for sale at every Halloween pop-up store that you visit."

All these years later, many of the actors say they still see a noticeable uptick in fans reaching out to them on social media every October as they seek out the films and television stations that begin running them more frequently.

Jamie Kennedy theorizes that this has something to do with how technology has evolved, making it easier for things to continue to stay in public consciousness. "Time is different now than it was. If you were a star in the 70s, only a few people transferred to the 90s and on," the actor explained. "But the 90s was this kind of thing where a lot of things haven't gone away. I think *Clueless* is as relevant as it ever was, multiple generations love it. *Romeo + Juliet*, as relevant as it ever was. I think *Titanic* is as relevant as it ever was. So, there was something about the 90s that just kept things around that people liked."

He also remembers that while working on the television show *The Ghost Whisperer* (2005), actor Barry Bostwick, who also starred in the cult classic *The Rocky Horror Picture Show* (1975), appeared in an episode. The two got to talking about the longevity of certain projects, and how they can follow actors throughout their careers. "Now I don't know if that movie [*Rocky Horror*] is as relevant as *Scream*, but it's impactful as hell. I feel like we're much different than *Rocky Horror Picture Show*, but I remember seeing that with him [Bostwick] and he's like, yeah man, sometimes you can get a movie and it can just last your career. When he said that to me, *Scream* was about 12 or 13 years old. I'm like, I think *Scream* is going to be like that," Kennedy recalled. "He's like, oh yeah. That's not ever going to go away."

In fact, Nancy O'Dell said that sometimes she learns about sequels and franchise news from social media when people ask if she's involved. "When they announced *Scream 5*, it just didn't stop. Oh my gosh, the social media between Twitter, Instagram, and Facebook, it was mostly Twitter. People will be like are you in *Scream 5*? Are you in *Scream 5*? It was before I even saw it and I'm an entertainment reporter. Before I even knew there was a *Scream 5*," she explains. "They just become very attached to it and love the movies and can't wait for the next one and ask for a sequel. I think that's why maybe it will keep going and going and going."

Phil Pavel agrees about the fans being enthusiastic about the films. Some have even sent him artwork that they created. "Someone sent me [information about] someone who did painted figures that they did of each of the characters. The fan base is so rabid. There's like a picture of me as Officer Andrews and then this very disturbing looking art piece that somebody did of Officer Andrews," Pavel said. "There's a blog of just every character that's died and ranked the deaths. People just love slicing and dicing it in so many different ways."

Knudsen should know a thing or two about the legacy that can be carried by certain horror movies. Along with *Scream 4*, he also battled Jigsaw's torture devices in *Saw 2* (2005). "I knew as soon as I got the part, it goes down in history. It's not just one of these movies that I'll do and maybe a few people will see it and never talk about it again," Knudsen explains. "Almost every Halloween, it's such a big movie that no matter what, people will talk about it. It's an honor. I know that I am part of horror movie franchise history because of getting cast in [*Scream*]."

Julie Plec adds that she thinks it's the fact that the right movie came along at the right time. The film took familiar elements from many beloved archetypes and turned them on their head. "I think it, humbly speaking, took a genre that was struggling to hold on to its identity and its voice, and just shook it up in the right blender to re-invigorate a part of the genre that nobody had been able to do well for a really long time," Plec said. "Who knows, but it was, you know, it's the teen movie, whatever form it comes in. People love that and people aren't always willing to make that. So, it reminded Hollywood that you can put John Hughes and Wes Craven in a blender and make a hit movie, and that was good."

All these years later, Nicholas Mastandrea still marvels at the lasting impact of the films. Even beyond the *Scream* movies, he sees it with the films he made with zombie maestro George Romero. "Those horror film people are just a whole fan base on their own. I still marvel; I never go to any of those conventions, but I know guys that I did *Dawn of the Dead* with and all that. Obscure zombies sell autographs for $25 bucks," Mastandrea said. "It's just mind boggling to me. But it's great and when you look back and you think of something like that, that just really touched people in a certain way. I mean, that's why you make movies, to entertain people and scare them, make them laugh, make them cry. When something holds up for 25-30 years, I think that's magnificent and it's kudos to Wes."

And to think, it all began with a single *Scream.*

The cast and crew of *Scream* gathered for dinner at Ca'Bianca in Santa Rosa. (Photo courtesy of Nick Mastandrea)

BIBLIOGRAPHY

Austerlitz, Saul. *Generation Friends*. Dutton, 2020, p. 36.

"Matthew Lillard on How He Was Supposed to Return as the 'Scream 3' Villain (Exclusive) | Entertainment Tonight." *Entertainment Tonight*, Entertainment Tonight, 14 May 2020, https://www.etonline.com/media/videos/matthew-lillard-on-how-he-was-supposed-to-return-as-the-scream-3-villain-exclusive.

Belloni, Matthew. "Weinsteins Pay to Settle Producer Cathy Konrad's 'Scream 4' Lawsuit (Exclusive) | Hollywood Reporter." *The Hollywood Reporter*, 5 Apr. 2011, https://www.hollywoodreporter.com/thr-esq/weinsteins-pay-settle-producer-cathy-175058.

"Biggest February Weekend at the Domestic Box Office." *The Numbers*, https://www.the-numbers.com/box-office-records/domestic/all-movies/biggest-weekend-by-month/february. Accessed 23 Mar. 2021.

Biskind, Peter. *Down and Dirty Pictures*. Simon and Schuster, 2013.

Boucher, Ashley. "Skeet Ulrich's Look Inside Open Heart Surgery on Operation Anniversary | PEOPLE.Com." *PEOPLE.Com*, PEOPLE.com, 7 Aug. 2019, https://people.com/tv/skeet-ulrich-look-inside-open-heart-surgery-operation-anniversary-graphic-photo/.

Bueno, Antoinette. "David Arquette Talks Courteney Cox Joining 'Scream 5' (Exclusive) | Entertainment Tonight." *Entertainment*

Tonight, Entertainment Tonight, 13 Aug. 2020, https://www.etonline.com/david-arquette-talks-courteney-cox-joining-scream-5-exclusive-151301.

"CNN - Kevin Williamson Enjoying Reign as King of Horror Flicks - August 7, 1998." *CNN International - Breaking News, US News, World News and Video*, http://edition.cnn.com/SHOWBIZ/Movies/9808/07/kevin.williamson/. Accessed 23 Mar. 2021.

Harmata, Claudia. "David Arquette Says He and Ex Courteney Cox 'Never Battled' Through Divorce or Co-Parenting." *People.Com*, 24 Aug. 2020, https://people.com/movies/david-arquette-says-he-and-ex-courteney-cox-never-battled-through-divorce-or-co-parenting/.

Hochman, David. "'Scream 2' Is Giving Nothing Away | EW.Com." *EW.Com*, EW.com, 28 Nov. 1997, https://ew.com/article/1997/11/28/scream-2-giving-nothing-away/.

Hoffmann, Bill. "BLOODY 'SCREAM 3' GRO$$ AT BOX OFFICE, TOO." *New York Post*, New York Post, 7 Feb. 2000, https://nypost.com/2000/02/07/bloody-scream-3-gro-at-box-office-too/.

Kennedy, Michael. "Wes Craven's Vampire in Brooklyn: How a Stunt Went Fatally Wrong on Set." *ScreenRant*, Screen Rant, 8 Nov. 2020, https://screenrant.com/vampire-brooklyn-movie-wes-craven-stunt-fatally-wrong-how/.

Kilday, Gregg. "Hollywood Lawsuits from 1997 | EW.Com." *EW.Com*, EW.com, 26 Dec. 1997, https://ew.com/article/1997/12/26/hollywood-lawsuits-1997/.

McDermott, Emmet. "Wes Craven's Last Interview: Horror Maestro Explains Why Original Ghostface Mask Is Too 'Perfect' to Scrap | Hollywood Reporter." *The Hollywood Reporter*, 17 Apr. 2015, https://www.hollywoodreporter.com/news/wes-cravens-last-interview-horror-788393.

Orwall, Bruce. "Miramax Concedes It Overstated for Its 'Scream 2' Movie - WSJ." *WSJ*, The Wall Street Journal, 22 Dec. 1997, https://www.wsj.com/articles/SB88274533053451500.

"'Scream 2' Is a Real Howl at Box Office - Los Angeles Times." *Los Angeles Times*, Los Angeles Times, 15 Dec. 1997, https://www.latimes.com/archives/la-xpm-1997-dec-15-ca-64218-story.html.

"Scream Franchise Box Office History - The Numbers." *The Numbers*, https:// www.the-numbers.com/movies/franchise/Scream#tab=summary. Accessed 23 Mar. 2021.

"'Scream' Led to Tripling of Caller ID Use and 4 More Fun Facts About Horror Classic." *The Wrap*, https://facebook.com/thewrap, 26 Oct. 2020, https://www.thewrap.com/scream-trivia-slasher-film-led-to-caller-id-use-tripling-and-4-more-fun-facts/.

Shepard, Dax. "Matthew Lillard — Armchair Expert Podcast." *Armchair Expert*, Armchair Expert, 3 Sept. 2018, https://armchairexpertpod. com/pods/matthew-lillard?rq=matthew%20lillard.

"Shock Waves: Episode 191: Having a SCREAM with Kevin Williamson on Apple Podcasts." *Apple Podcasts*, https://podcasts.apple.com/ us/podcast/episode-191-having-a-scream-with-kevin-williamson/ id1109880594?i=1000475391039. Accessed 23 Mar. 2021.

Stack, Tim. "'Scream 4' Writer Kevin Williamson Discusses His 'Massive Fight' with Bob Weinstein—EXCLUSIVE | EW.Com." *EW.Com*, EW.com, 7 Apr. 2011, https://ew.com/article/2011/04/07/scream-4-kevin-williamson/.

Staff, Toofab. "Scream 2 Star Would 'Be So Down' to Return for Scream 5." *Toofab*, Toofab, 15 June 2020, https://toofab.com/2020/06/15/elise-neal-into-the-dark-scream/.

"Scream 3 Turns 20: Interview with Parker Posey." *Toofab*, Toofab, 3 Feb. 2020, https://toofab.com/2020/02/03/celebrating-the-20th-anniversary-of-scream-3-with-parker-posey/.

Weiss, Shari. "David Arquette Opens up about Courteney Cox Split, Admits to Sleeping with Jasmine Waltz - New York Daily News." *Nydailynews. Com*, New York Daily News, 12 Oct. 2010, https://www.nydailynews. com/entertainment/gossip/david-arquette-opens-courteney-split-admits-sleeping-jasmine-waltz-article-1.191938.

INDEX

Padraic Maroney

PADRAIC saw *Scream* on opening night in theaters and it helped him decide to become a writer. He began professionally writing while still in high school, before becoming a freelance entertainment journalist and marketing professional based in Philadelphia. He has won awards in both fields for his work.

In between work and writing, Padraic is an avid runner—having completed multiple half marathons, a marathon, triathlon—and recently took up drumming as a hobby.